"This is an exceptional book that _____ public administration from a wide _____ housing. Each chapter is well-writ _____ _____ relate to every facet of public administration, the book should be required reading for all students in the field as well as for practitioners."

*Norma Riccucci, Rutgers Newark University, USA*

"Rutherford and Meier have collected an exceptional group of established and emerging scholars to tackle a thorny but often ignored issue that is vital to our politics and governance. Each chapter speaks to scholars and practitioners by relying on theory and empirical evidence to explore governance issues around race, representation, and inequality. The volume should be used as a core text for Public Administration courses and would be a nice addition to race and politics courses."

*Don Haider-Markel, University of Kansas, USA*

"Rutherford and Meier have assembled a superb cast of scholars to reflect on the importance of race and racism in public administration. The volume offers an accessible introduction to the main currents of research in this area and marks a significant step forward in efforts to understand and address racial injustices in the administrative state. Highly recommended for students as well as advanced scholars."

*Joe Soss, University of Minnesota, USA*

# Race and Public Administration

Issues of race permeate virtually every corner of policy creation and implementation in the United States, yet theoretically driven research on interactions of policy, race, and ethnicity rarely offers practical tools that can be readily applied by current and future civil servants, private contractors, or nonprofit boards. Arguing that scholarship can and should inform practice to address issues of equity in public affairs, rather than overlook, ignore, or deny them, *Race and Public Administration* offers a much-needed and accessible exploration of current and cutting-edge research on race and policy.

This book evaluates what contradictions, unanswered questions, and best (or worst) practices exist in conducting and understanding research that can provide evidence-based policy and management guidance to practitioners in the field. Individual chapters are written by established and emerging scholars and explore a wide range of policy areas, including public education, policing, health and access to health care, digital governance, nonprofit diversity, and international contexts. Together, the chapters serve as a link between theoretically informed research in public administration and those students and professionals trained to work in the trenches of public administration. This book is ideally suited as a text for courses in schools of public administration, public policy, or nonprofit management, and is required reading for those actively involved in policy analysis, creation, or evaluation.

**Amanda Rutherford** is an Assistant Professor in the O'Neill School of Public and Environmental Affairs at Indiana University, USA. Her research focuses on organizational accountability and performance, inequality between majority and minority groups, and executive careers and decision-making processes and is often situated in the context of U.S. education. Her work has appeared in leading journals in the fields of political science, public administration, and higher education policy. In her spare time, Amanda swaps stories with her husband, Jeff (an administrator), plays in the park with her daughter, Kendall, and generally tries to keep Ken Meier sane.

**Kenneth J. Meier** is a Distinguished Scholar in Residence in the Department of Public Administration and Policy in the School of Public Affairs at American University, Washington, DC, USA. His research considers institutional theories of organizations and politics and spans areas of representation and equity, comparative public administration, education, health care, and local government. Ken has published over 20 books and over 250 articles and has served as the editor of four journals in the fields of political science and public administration. Ken enjoys a good Cajun dish, watching NCAA track and field championships, and, above all, time with his wonderful wife, Diane.

# Race and Public Administration

Edited by
Amanda Rutherford and
Kenneth J. Meier

Routledge
Taylor & Francis Group

NEW YORK AND LONDON

First published 2020
by Routledge
52 Vanderbilt Avenue, New York, NY 10017

and by Routledge
2 Park Square, Milton Park, Abingdon, Oxon OX14 4RN

*Routledge is an imprint of the Taylor & Francis Group, an informa business*

*Library of Congress Cataloging-in-Publication Data*
A catalog record for this title has been requested

ISBN: 978-0-367-89671-3 (hbk)
ISBN: 978-0-367-86199-5 (pbk)
ISBN: 978-1-003-01763-9 (ebk)

Typeset in Bembo
by Taylor & Francis Books

To Kendall—may you encourage your generation to love all, regardless of race, ethnicity, or nationality.

# Contents

# Tables

# Contributors

**Adrian Brown** is an Instructor in the School of Public Affairs in the Watts College of Public Service and Community Solutions at Arizona State University. Brown's research interests include e-government, information and communication technologies, broadband access, digital literacy, program evaluation, and public administration and policy education.

**Andre Dantas Cabral** is a PhD candidate in the State, Government and Public Institutions at FGV/EBAPE, Brazil. His main research interests focus on representative bureaucracy as related to policing and education.

**Seong K. Cho** is a doctoral student in the School of Public Affairs at Arizona State University. Her research focuses on housing policy, social equity, and public policy processes.

**Jason A. Grissom** is an Associate Professor of Public Policy and Education in the Department of Leadership, Policy, and Organizations at Peabody College at Vanderbilt University, where he also serves as faculty director of the Tennessee Education Research Alliance. His research uses large data sets and draws on the perspectives of political science, public administration, and economics to study the governance of K-12 education, including both its leadership/management and political dimensions.

**Ashley Jones** is a doctoral student in the department of Leadership, Policy, and Organizations in the Peabody College at Vanderbilt University. She is interested in researching academic achievement gap closure for students of color and low SES students, specifically how implementing comprehensive social services within schools can impact racial disparities in academic achievement.

**Eunji Lee** is a master's student in organizational theory at Hankuk University of Foreign Studies, the Republic of Korea, and a former student at FGV/EBAPE, Brazil. Her research interests currently focus on organizational diversity.

**Kelly LeRoux** is a Professor of Public Administration in the College of Urban Planning and Public Affairs at the University of Illinois in Chicago. She conducts research on nonprofits' voter mobilization and political advocacy activities and also studies issues of nonprofit performance, accountability, and networks.

**Kenneth J. Meier** is a Distinguished Scholar in Residence in the Department of Public Administration and Policy in the School of Public Affairs at American University, Washington, DC. His research considers institutional theories of organizations and politics and spans areas of representation and equity, comparative public administration, education, health care, and local government. Ken has published over 20 books and over 250 articles and has served as the editor of four journals in the fields of political science and public administration.

**Karen Mossberger** is a Professor and the Frank and June Sackton Chair in the School of Public Affairs at the Watts College at Arizona State University. Her research interests include local governance, urban policy, digital inequality, the evaluation of broadband programs, and digital government.

**Jill Nicholson-Crotty** is an Associate Professor in the O'Neill School of Public and Environmental Affairs at Indiana University. Her research focuses on both public and nonprofit management and the role of those sectors in the policy process. She is one of a limited number of scholars who examine the policy role of traditional charitable organizations.

**Sean Nicholson-Crotty** is a Professor and Director of the Ph.D. Programs in Public Affairs and Public Policy in the O'Neill School of Public and Environmental Affairs at Indiana University. His primary areas of research include intergovernmental relations and the diffusion of public policies among subnational governments.

**Alketa Peci** is a Professor in the Brazilian School of Public and Business Administration, Getulio Vargas Foundation, Rio de Janeiro, Brazil. Her research focuses on the transformations of public bureaucracies, organizational reputation and symbolic representation, media reputation and bureaucratic strategies, and independent bureaucratic institutions.

**Amanda Rutherford** is an Assistant Professor in the O'Neill School of Public and Environmental Affairs at Indiana University. Her research focuses on organizational accountability and performance, inequality between majority and minority groups, and executive careers and decision-making processes and is often situated in the context of U.S. education. Her work has appeared in leading journals in the fields of political science, public administration, and higher education policy.

**Vanessa Brulon Soares** is a Professor of Organizational Theories at Rio de Janeiro's Federal University (UFRJ). She has a PhD in Administration, from Getulio Vargas Foundation (EBAPE/FGV), Rio de Janeiro, Brazil. Her main research interest focuses on policing in stateless territories.

**Kenicia Wright** is an Assistant Professor in the School of Politics, Security, and International Affairs at the University of Central Florida. Her research interests include the interactive effects of race, gender, and other social identities on the policy-making process, policy preferences, and policy outcomes across groups.

**Ling Zhu** is an Associate Professor in the Department of Political Science at the University of Houston. Her research interests include public management, health disparities, social equity in health care access, as well as the implementation of public health policies at the state and local level.

# Preface

This book project stems from a conversation in the summer of 2016 related to what the field of public administration should be talking about. Further, we wanted to consider how to connect knowledge generated by our research to those who might be best suited to actually use it—students in our own class-rooms who would enter the workforce in the public sector (as well as the nonprofit and private sectors). While a line of research has developed that focuses on representative bureaucracy and, to a lesser extent, managing diversity, individuals who study bureaucracy—and those who work within it—do not explicitly talk nearly enough about differences in access and outcomes along racial lines. We continue to observe gaps in health and well-being, gaps in educational attainment and educational disciplines, gaps in the affordability of housing, and gaps in employment in managerial roles for people of color in the United States. And while the contours of majority groups and dominant races or ethnicities shift by country, race generally presents a common denominator in determining who gets what and how when it comes to the creation and implementation of public policy. It's time we talk about why. Further, this conversation will not get old and should only continue until either gaps in opportunity and outcomes are narrowed and/or such gaps are explained by factors that do not circle back to race (as inequities related to issues of income, education, etc. often do).

We circulated a call for papers about race and public administration through a variety of list serves and personal networks in the fall of 2016. Proposals were encouraged to consider race and public administration in a substantive policy, how public administrators deal with racial disparities, or how racial disparities are or are not changing when it comes to the receipt of public goods and services. Several individuals received an invitation to present their papers at a conference at Texas A&M University in College Station, Texas, in May of 2017. Importantly, smart people who care about racial inequities gathered in a room to talk about race and public administration for two days. While this in and of itself solved no problems, the fruitful con-versations further encouraged us to publish a book that was accessible to both scholars interested in understanding racial inequities or finding solutions to alleviate such inequities as well as students as future practitioners who will be required to face inequity along racial lines in some manner in their professional careers.

The chapters in this book are written by individual scholars who are experts in their particular policy area. Not all chapters were proposed and presented at the 2017 conference, and not all of the papers presented at the conference are included in this text. Given the process of self-selection present among the group of collaborators in this book and issues of timing to get multiple individuals in the same place at the same time, there are certainly chapters missing here. Areas lacking include, but are not limited to, those related to the environment, housing, and employment. Nevertheless, the grouping of chapters that are represented here can be read together or separately, and all explicitly acknowledge issues of race that permeate the creation and implementation of public policy.

Some discussions that stem from this book, and perhaps most particularly those in the classroom, may be uncomfortable for some for a variety of reasons. We do not see that as problematic at all. Rather, this text can be used as a tool to educate, discuss, and debate the status of current and future problems as well as offer viable solutions that can work to alleviate racial inequities. The chapters here simply try to grapple with the reality that race has been used time and time again to divide groups and privilege some while marginalizing others.

# Acknowledgments

We must also pause here to thank several individuals who help facilitate this book and the original conference associated with the text. This includes Kristen Carroll, Apolonia Calderon, Miyeon Song, and Seung Ho An. We also thank Routledge for their support and continued assistance in publishing this text. Laura Stearns and Katie Horsfall were particularly delightful to work with on this text.

# 1 The Common Denominator

## Persistent Racial Gaps in the Administration of Policy

*Amanda Rutherford and Kenneth J. Meier*

## Introduction

Issues of race, race relations, and representation have become increasingly present in the United States and in several other countries around the world. Demographically, the U.S. is expected to have no single majority race or ethnicity by the year 2055; although attention is often directed at Latin America, Asia has replaced Latin America and Mexico as the biggest source of immigrants entering the U.S. (Cohn and Caumont, 2016; Pew Research Center, 2015). The proportion of multiracial Americans is growing at a rate that is three times larger than the population rate increase overall (Parker et al., 2015). Recent Census estimates include an adult population consisting of over 2 percent (now close to 10 million) individuals who identify as multiracial; Pew Research estimates this number may rise to nearly 7 percent of the U.S. adult population even though many individuals do not self-identify themselves in this way (ibid.). Yet recent maps informed by NASA mapmaking techniques show that while the U.S. is more diverse, many cities are still defined by racial segregation (University of Cincinnati, 2017). Stories of racial divides continue to fill political news headlines at the local, state, and federal levels. Issues of race are not confined to the U.S. context either, though the majority of this text is U.S.-centric given that race and ethnic issues range over geographic locations and are, thus, affected by local contexts. This includes the ethnic profiling of Roma throughout the European continent, hate speech targeting Koreans in Japan, and positive connotations of whiteness in Latin American countries.

Despite the salience of race as an identifier, one that is accompanied by a multitude of presumptions, theoretically driven research seeking to understand attitudes, biases, and experiences that differ by race and ethnicity in a way that can offer tools to practitioners tasked with public policy and management issues has casually ebbed and flowed within public administration scholarship. This text argues that there is a clear need to provide timely information on what we do and do not know about issues of race and equity to current and future civil servants, private contractors, and nonprofit governing boards. That scholarship can and should inform practice that can be used to address issues of race and equity rather than overlook, ignore, or deny them.

The aim of this book is not to argue for or against scientific research related to distinctions across racial categories. We agree with scientists working across fields from biology to sociology that race is a social construct with little biological or genetic meaning. Indeed, scientific research has consistently failed to identify a clear and objective logic for racial distinctions. That said, the social constructions of race have been and continue to prove powerful bases for how policies are formed and implemented throughout the world. These differences are observed across more policy arenas than can be counted—health, education, environment, social welfare, housing, the labor market, energy, public safety, and more. As such, the primary goal of this book is to synthesize what various bodies of research have discovered about race in a set of policy areas as well as to identify what contradictions, unanswered questions, and best (or worst) practices exist in understanding how to move forward in conducting theoretically informed research that can provide evidence-based policy and management guidance to practitioners in the field of public administration.

It is also not the intention of this book or its contributors to ignore other areas in which conversations on equity or discrimination should occur and, at times, overlap with race. Instead, we would argue that these groups merit a separate study that cannot be easily incorporated in the current text in order to be discussed adequately and to provide more than a passing nod to decades of history, policy development, and other changes that affect the lived experiences of millions of people.

This chapter sets the stage for this discussion in four sections. First, a small set of key terms are defined as a reference that can be used when reading each of the substantive chapters in the volume. Second, we discuss changes in the role and representation of racial minorities—most often those who are Black—in the U.S. bureaucracy. While we do not intend to emphasize one race more than others, necessarily, most research until the 1980s has focused on the status of Black individuals in the bureaucracy rather than Hispanics, Asian Americans, or Native Americans, among other groups. Third, a brief history of research on race, including the normative desire to achieve social equity, in the field of public administration will be reviewed. For the practitioner reading this text, this should provide some framework for considering the development of a fairly new field as it overlapped with policy changes and politically salient events. For the scholar, such a history should provide a window into considering the continuous need for understanding the role of race in politics and administration rather than simply controlling for racial groups as additional variables. Finally, an overview of the book, including a summary of each chapter in this volume, is detailed prior to jumping into the rest of the text.

## Important Terms

Before discussing race in public service and how public administration scholars have studied issues related to race, it is important to define a few terms that are woven throughout the rest of the text. These serve as a reference guide to the reader and a starting point for gaining knowledge of other concepts.

*Racialization* can be defined as the process of constructing racial meaning, whether in the policy process or through interpersonal interactions. This includes the process of defining racial categories and how these categories relate to other ideas. In other words, this helps us to understand race as a social construction rather than as some constant that does not change over time. Racialization includes decisions of who might be counted as part of a particular race, which often leads to different assumptions and types of treatment for each of these constructed groups.

Next, *racism* can be broadly defined as a system of advantage or disadvantage based on race (Tatum, 2001; Wellman, 1993). This definition has been broken down into multiple types of racism, though here we will highlight two. First, we often consider overt or discreet acts of individual or *interpersonal racism* involved in direct, face-to face interactions between two or more people. It is this type of racism that includes name calling, the use of slurs, and other forms of aggression. While debated, many groups argue that this type of racism is, in some places, less prevalent today than in prior decades. A second form of racism, however, is just as important and is often less well recognized. *Institutional racism* involves instances of racial discrimination or inequality in organizational or institutional contexts. This type of racism may or may not have an overt intent but can be tied to inequality across racial lines. Examples might include how state appropriations are allocated to local school districts, where nuclear waste sites are located, or how accessible voting sites are for minority communities. In many cases, misperceptions of groups can be formalized more permanently through institutions and public policy.

Aside from racism, policies may often be formed or implemented in a way that is identified as *race-conscious* or *race-neutral*. The former type is typically aimed at closing a particular gap between or among racial groups. For example, the recent *Fisher v. University of Texas* (2016) case revolved around the constitutional use of race as one component of review for admission to postsecondary education. In this case, the University of Texas considered race as one of many factors in determining which students would gain admission. On the other hand, race-neutral policies do not explicitly take race into account. In the case mentioned here for admission to universities, this might look like a policy that places weight on socioeconomic status or geographic location, while not taking account of race of the applicant. Other common examples include not hiring someone with a felony conviction or not renting to individuals with felony convictions. It should be noted, of course, that while these policies do not explicitly touch on race, they are likely to have adverse effects that further racial inequities. For example, racial minorities are much more likely to experience some level of contact with police. This overrepresentation in the criminal justice system will likely lead to housing or hiring policies that have a disproportionate effect on people of color.

Finally, two particular types of policies beyond those that are generally race-conscious and race-neutral should be highlighted when considering race in public administration. First, *equal employment opportunity* is defined by the United States Equal Employment Opportunity Commission (EEOC) as "freedom from discrimination on the basis of protected classes such as race, color, sex, national origin, religion, age, disability or genetic information." Such protected classes—often those defined via Title VII of the Civil Rights Act of 1964—fall under federal (and often state) laws, which are enforced by the EEOC. This generally includes hiring, firing, promotion, training, and a variety of other organizational level policies and processes. Second, *affirmative action policies* are defined as, "those actions appropriate to overcome the effects of past or present practices, policies, or other barriers to equal employment opportunity" (EEOC, 1979). Affirmative action policies and plans may be voluntary (particularly in the private and nonprofit sectors), part of compliance with federal regulations, or part of a court mandate following evidence of discrimination, and are generally seen as a more proactive step than equal employment which only prohibits discrimination. Importantly, following the *Regents of University of California v. Bakke* (1973) case, the judicial system in the United States has ruled that quotas are illegal and do not constitute affirmative action, though many misperceptions related to affirmative action policies involve the equating of affirmative action to quota systems. In the same case, the court also determined that affirmative action policies should pursue a "compelling government interest" and that they must be "narrowly tailored to pursue that interest" (*Regents of University of California v. Bakke* 1973). This means such policies are held to the most stringent standard—strict scrutiny—of judicial review when issues of constitutionality are raised.

## Race and the Development of the Civil Service in the United States

With these terms in mind, we next provide a condensed history of the role of racial minorities in the U.S. bureaucracy. As mentioned above, much of the early history revolves around the Black-White divide, as this was most salient to prior scholars until the late 1900s. Nevertheless, the story is telling of what progress has been made as well as what gains have yet to be achieved.

As the American colonies developed into an independent nation, and a system bureaucracy was established to aid in governance processes, employment in the federal service was understood to be limited to White citizens. Voting, of course, would provide additional limitations for political participation for people of color until at least the post-Civil War years, if not longer, in many jurisdictions. In terms of civil service, though there was often a shortage of troops during the Revolutionary War, few were eager to enlist Black soldiers. As additional systems of bureaucracy were statutorily cemented in the early 1800s, non-White individuals (and more specifically Black individuals) were explicitly barred from carrying mail for the post office (Krislov, 1967); this statute was strictly enforced through the 1820s and was not dropped until the 1860s.

After the passing of the 15th Amendment, electoral and appointed positions were highly desirable commodities among many communities of color as a way to gain influence and status that might not otherwise be attainable. Though a multitude of barriers to representation were still faced in many areas of the country (this included but was not limited to the South), minor civil service appointments were encouraged and praised. In 1869, the first Black person was selected to hold a federally appointed position as Ebenezer Bassett became the minister to Haiti. Later, under President Rutherford B. Hayes, additional positions were filled by racial minority groups; this was perhaps in an attempt to appease groups of color when federal troops were withdrawn from the South after Reconstruction. Perhaps unsurprisingly, gains in minor administrative roles in the federal civil service were at times more accessible than both appointed and elected positions in states and local municipalities, where Jim Crow laws and segregation presented formidable forces. Even in the Northern states, increasing rates of immigration brought to the surface various forms of explicit stereotypes and biases toward many racial and ethnic minority groups. Additional gains and losses for people of color would depend on the party and executive in office. By the end of the 1800s and following the adoption of a merit system for many civil service positions, estimates, though imperfect, suggest there were nearly 3,000 Black employees in Washington, DC (ibid.). The 1900 Census estimated the total population of the United States to be 76,212,168. Of this total population, an estimated 8.8 million, or 11.6 percent of the population, were Black.

In the early 1900s, preferences were still made for White employees. For example, James Aswell of Louisiana introduced a bill in Congress that would require segregation among federal employees and would also prohibit the employment of a Black person as the superior of a White person (Commission on Reform in the Civil Service, 1914); the policy was not successfully passed but was quite revealing in illustrating the biases of many powerful individuals in government. Under President Woodrow Wilson, the federal government resegregated its workforce, resulting in the reassignment of many Black federal employees. In many cases, photographs were also required as part of an individual's job application and could be used to make distinctions among candidates in discriminatory ways.

World War II and the New Deal provided some prospects for additional employment for people of color in bureaucratic posts. Additionally, Executive Order 8802 under Franklin D. Roosevelt in 1942, prohibiting discrimination in the national defense industry was generally considered the first federal action to promote equal opportunity. Importantly, World War II created imbalances in labor supplies and demands that provided work for a number of minority groups, though many were employed in temporary or lower-level positions. In 1948 with Executive Order 9981, President Truman desegregated the armed forces and prohibited discrimination on the basis of race, color, religion, or national origin in the military services. In 1961, President Kennedy established a more expansive committee on equal employment. A few years later, the Equal Employment Opportunity Commission (EEOC), a bipartisan five-person commission and a general council, was established by the Civil Rights Act (CRA) of 1964 and was tasked with the enforcement of federal laws related to discrimination. The CRA included protections in federal employment not just for race but also for color, religion, sex, and national origin. While many implementation and enforcement issues remained, the EEOC and CRA provided a step forward for many racial and ethnic groups.

Since the early 1980s, wider availability of data on the federal workforce has enabled research documenting minority employment. Such work shows that racial minorities, including Blacks, Hispanics, Native Americans, and Asian Americans, tend to be overrepresented in lower-level positions (grades) and underrepresented in higher-level grades; this type of trend is often referred to as position segregation. The average grades of each of these groups has improved over time, but none have outgained or surpassed White bureaucrats. Between 1981 and 2000, the average grade in the executive branch went from approximately 8.6 to 10.1 for Whites, 8.4 to 9.8 for Asian Americans, 6.5 to 8.7 for Hispanics, 6.4 to 8.4 for Blacks, and 6.5 to 8.2 for Native Americans (Kim, 2005). Further, in 1980, White males accounted for 86 percent of the Senior Executive Service, the highest level of federal employees. In 2008, this share decreased to 65 percent, and discussions of diversity and representation at the top of the civil service continue (Pitts and Wise, 2010). Additional research using the Federal Human Capital Survey or the Federal Employee Viewpoint Survey shows that non-White bureaucrats tend to have more negative perceptions of the quality of work done by their agency and lower perceptions of job satisfaction (Pitts, 2009). There is also some evidence that job satisfaction rates improve for racial and ethnic minorities when higher levels of racial and ethnic diversity are observed at the managerial level in these federal agencies (Choi, 2013).

## Developing the Discussion of Race in the Study of Public Administration

As the participation of racial minorities in bureaucratic positions has evolved, a range of articles, books, and commentaries that mention racial discrimination (unequal treatment) or racial inequality (unequal outcomes) in some way in public administration scholarship have appeared. Most of these developments have occurred in the last 60 years, beginning around the time of the civil rights movement and continuing through today.

Prior to the 1960s, the job of the public administrator was largely focused on being efficient and economical (as it often is today), such that issues of inequity or injustice were not perceived as salient or central in a normative or descriptive way (Fredrickson, 1990). However, whether in conjunction with or in response to the civil rights movement of the late 1950s and early

1960s and the passage of landmark pieces of legislation, including the Civil Rights Act and the Voting Right Act, the term "social equity" was proposed as an additional pillar of public administration (the other three are efficiency, effectiveness, and economy). While this may often link to issues of race, such a term can also broadly refer to being responsive to the needs of citizens, which can include needed recognition of implicit or explicit racial biases. Social equity can also be described as fairness or as the understanding of different equalities of outcomes in the process of policy implementation. Interestingly, while social equity was proposed and debated as part of the responsibility of the public administrator, it would take some time before this pillar was more formally embraced by national associations. Many have since noted the dearth of scholarship in leading journals that directly speaks to issues of social equity. For example, Gooden (2015) recently found that less than 5 percent of the scholarship published in the highly regarded journal *Public Administration Review* between 1940 and 2013—a total of 208 articles—related to the term social equity.

Greater attention to equity, under which racial disparities can fall, continued through the 1970s as proponents of New Public Administration placed greater emphasis on normative questions and supported the idea that administrators should use public administration as a tool for social justice. Many scholars also joined in, calling on administrators to advocate for underrepresented groups and to ensure all groups were represented in government. Renewed work on the importance of a representative bureaucracy, or a bureaucracy that reflects the make-up of the population it represents, appeared during this period (e.g., Meier, 1975; Meier and Nigro, 1976). Nevertheless, some tensions remained, and few schools formally incorporated this type of training into their education of students who would enter government or related positions. Even at the doctoral level, Walter Broadnax (2010) recalls, "It was suggested that if you wanted to pursue a 'good academic job,' you would not write a dissertation exploring the impact of racial and ethnic minorities on municipal public organizations."

In 1981, the American Society for Public Administration, one of the largest professional associations for public administrators in the United States, included in its publications on professional ethics the importance of equality, or the idea that citizen A is equal to citizen B, and equity, or the adjusting of provisions such that citizen A is made equal to citizen B (Fredrickson, 1990). Acceptance of social equity as a pillar of public administration, though certainly contested, gradually became more widespread among scholars (whether this was also more accepted among practitioners is an open question). This came at a time when immigration rates in the United States were increasing. In 1980, the Census recorded that 6.2 percent of the U.S. population was foreign-born, and this share increased to 7.9 percent by 1990 (Gibson and Lennon, 1999). Yet, race was not often made a central discussion of either policy formation and implementation or organizational management in research within the public administration discipline.

The 1990s brought some shifts in research, as increasing technology and data availability allowed scholars to more carefully examine trends related to race and ethnicity in the workforce (e.g., Cornwell and Kellough, 1994; Kim and Lewis, 1994; Lewis and Nice, 1994; Riccucci and Saidel, 1997). The Organized Section on Race, Ethnicity, and Politics was established in the American Political Science Association in 1995, where scholars developed increasing interest in voting laws and patterns and the link between particular voting rules and the representation of racial minorities in locally elected positions. These advances also led to scholarly evaluation of how organizations were "managing diversity." The term diversity management spread via practitioner-based reports and academic scholarship and essentially focused on tactics that allowed organizations to foster work environments that welcomed people from a variety of backgrounds (Kellough and Naff, 2004). Yet whether diversity programs that fall under this umbrella term are meaningful or not is still debated (e.g., Dobbin and Kalev, 2016), and they can fail to bring the importance of race to the forefront of the practice of public administration.

Instead, two topics have held the focus of much discussion related to racial biases, equal treatment, and equal outcomes among those active in the field of public administration—the discretion afforded to front-line (or street-level) bureaucrats and the normative good found in the pillars of representative bureaucracy theory. Bureaucratic discretion has been at the forefront of public administration since the inception of public administration as a field of study. While discretion itself is inevitable—administrators have to answer new questions, address gaps in formal policies, and more—questions have revolved around how much control politicians can and should have over bureaucrats, the difficulty in monitoring full implementation of policy at the local level, and how to develop professional norms and expectations among front-line workers. Recent examples abound. Stivers (2007) considers discretion in the wake of Hurricane Katrina and finds that administrators stuck to policies, fraught with institutional discrimination, rather than creatively aiming to lessen harm. Similarly, Keiser, Mueser, and Choi (2004) find that non-Whites are sanctioned at lower rates than Whites overall in the context of Temporary Assistance for Needy Families (TANF) and that this occurs because non-Whites live in areas with lower overall sanction rates. The authors also find that non-Whites are sanctioned more compared to Whites in local areas, raise questions related to administrative discretion in the provision of sanctions, and argue that, regardless of the underlying explanation, welfare reform and policy implementation are not race-neutral.

Second, representative bureaucracy has attracted persistent attention in recent years, and many public administration scholars agree normatively that a bureaucracy that reflects the population it serves is likely to have benefits for policy implementation and public responsiveness (or in the words of Krislov [1974], "the many minds brought to bear may not guarantee the best decision but they clearly guard against the worst"). Like bureaucratic discretion, this concept extends back to at least the 1940s and received growing attention in the 1960s and 1970s. The theory argues that different social origins lead to variance in social experiences which, in turn, then shape attitudes and behaviors. Two forms of representation have been studied within this theory. Passive representation occurs when various demographic groups are proportionately staffed in an agency—this focuses primarily on what an organization looks like descriptively and does not require consideration of any actions, though there is recognition that the mere presence of groups may influence an individual's own actions, the actions of other bureaucrats, or the actions of clientele. Second, active representation encompasses what actions and behaviors link the presence of a group to policy outcomes or other benefits experienced by the group an individual represents. Within the field of public administration, research abounds, though passive representation is often admittedly easier to measure than active representation. A database hosted by the Project for Equity, Representation, and Governance (2019) lists 191 entries for recent research on representative bureaucracy, and the database is certainly not all-inclusive. Of course, while research continues to document the potential positive influence of representation on policy outcomes for racial minority groups, it does not consider the full scope of the role of race in the creation, implementation, and management of policy. Assumptions within the theory may also have limitations. For example, in comparing representative bureaucracy theory and the perceived advantage of representation for clientele to street-level bureaucracy theory and the constraints that may hamper discretion, Watkins-Hayes (2011) found that many Black and Latina clientele do not view same-race welfare administrators as sharing some distinct commonality, though opinions also varied according to specific experiences. In other words, organizational constraints and contexts can play a key part in shaping the role of race in administrator-clientele relationships.

While this research has certainly grown within academic circles, popular attention to racial disparities beyond the confines of representation or administrative discretion has also burgeoned in the last few years. In 2014, as the public watched news stories about Michael Brown and unrest in Ferguson, Missouri, one of dozens of jurisdictions where the actions of administrators were questioned, additional scholarship was circulated on the need to pay attention to race in public administration. In *Race and Social Equity: A Nervous Area of Government*, Gooden (2014) argues that racial inequity must be tackled head-on rather than feared or grouped in with managing diversity or a number of other discussions. Additionally, Foldy and Buckley (2014) in *The Color Bind: Talking (and Not Talking) About Race at Work* remind readers that color blindness can reinforce existing structures, including existing systematic racism, while a color-cognizant approach can provide more productive outcomes. Similar to Gooden, the authors recognize that openly addressing race can be uncomfortable for many; they also argue that color cognizance can be difficult to enact, which leaves organizations and its employees in a difficult bind. Finally, Alexander and Stivers (2010) speak directly to scholars in discussing the "ethic of race." Here, the authors state:

Remarkably little public administration scholarship has explored the dynamic of race as manifest in patterns of policy interpretation and discretionary judgments of individual administrators. We argue that scholarship in the field has failed to come to terms with how this neglect has contributed to maintaining long-standing policies and practices with racist interpretations.

They argue that failing to talk about race within the field serves as a hindrance to fundamental notions of democratic politics.

## The Role of This Book

This book serves as a link between theoretically informed research in public administration and those students and professionals trained to work in the trenches of public and nonprofit organizations. Recent calls have certainly been made to face racial inequality head-on and to have meaningful conversations about the formation and implementation of policy that can lessen (and eventually eradicate) the current institutional racism that perpetuates unequal treatment and outcomes across a range of policies. Interestingly, many students in public administration programs and public affairs schools may be likely to earn a degree without exposure to such discussions; those who do are in classes where adequate materials and meaningful texts can be hard to come by without being too broad or too narrow in scope. For example, thousands of students earn a Masters of Public Administration in the course of each academic year. However, the National Association of Schools of Public Affairs and Administration (NASPAA) does not require any specified diversity, equity, or race component to curriculum for schools seeking accreditation, and the majority offer very low levels of any type of curriculum related to the general topic of social equity (Perry, 2005).

We view race as a critical component in this learning process. While other types of diversity are of vital importance, individuals, particularly those in the United States, are often socialized in terms of some racial identity that stems from current social constructions. It remains a powerful force that penetrates virtually every aspect of an individual's lived experience, particularly in terms of direct or indirect interaction with government, including policymakers and bureaucrats. As such, we need a current guide—a roadmap of sorts—to better understand what we do and do not know about race in a variety of policy realms.

## Overview of the Book

In the following chapters, this volume seeks to identify the current state of affairs of race in public administration in five particular policy areas—education, health, digital access, criminal justice, and nonprofit governance. In addition to these policy areas, where most research is U.S.-centric, the volume includes a chapter commenting on race in public administration in contexts around the world. Each policy chapter provides a discussion of current knowledge, policies, and trends and also offers an assessment of which questions are still unanswered and which problems persist. Importantly, while these policy realms receive a great amount of attention in this text, many others—the labor market, housing, environment, social welfare, and local government, for example—do not. This should not be taken as an indicator of lack of importance but rather reflects natural limitations that exist in assembling a range of experts with limited time constraints to communicate about race in public administration and policy in a timely manner. In some cases, themes may arise across chapters that provide takeaways for areas of policy not covered in depth in this text; in other cases, themes and the ability to transfer tools from one area to another will be rather limited.

Chapter 2, by Jason A. Grissom and Ashley Jones, focuses on race among teachers and administrators in the K-12 education system. Teacher and principal racial and ethnic diversity has become an important subject of education policy conversations at the federal, state, and local levels, yet the K-12 workforce is not keeping pace with the changing racial and ethnic demographics of the student population enrolled in public schools. This chapter reviews the evidence on educator diversity on two fronts. The authors first synthesize research from multiple disciplines on the benefits of a diverse educator workforce for public school students. An accumulating body of rigorous evidence suggests that these benefits, particularly for students of color, are substantial and span multiple outcomes, including achievement, discipline, absenteeism, and assignment to gifted education. Second, the authors discuss what is known about the factors associated with recruiting and retaining educators of color; these factors are particularly important, given that pipeline strategies have many holes and often prove insufficient. The authors note that challenges in this area are substantial and require intentional, multifaceted strategies to be implemented to diversify the workforce and realize the benefits of educator diversity. Despite its focus on K-12 education, Chapter 2 has broad applicability to public organizations in general as it demonstrates the various ways that public employees can affect an organization's clientele and illustrates the generic problems of increasing the diversity of the public sector workforce. The concerns of K-12 education are often replicated in other service delivery organizations that interact with diverse populations.

In Chapter 3, Jill Nicholson-Crotty and Sean Nicholson-Crotty discuss race in the criminal justice system with a particular focus on the salient issue of policing in the United States. Given the large body of evidence that racial minority groups are disproportionately more likely to experience a variety of encounters with police—traffic stops, car searches, arrests, and more—the authors synthesize and critique existing research on the causes of and solutions to these inequalities. In considering both individual level and institutional or environmental level biases, the authors look for patterns among a mixed body of sometimes contradictory findings. After discussing some partial solutions that may be achievable through a number of local-level policy changes, the author discuss questions that remain—such as who Black police officers feel they should represent—and give needed attention to institutional factors that may accentuate or lessen the role of implicit bias in decision-making.

Ling Zhu and Kenicia Wright provide an in-depth review of the role of race in health care policies and services and highlight clear inequities in health along racial lines in Chapter 4. The authors offer a synopsis and critical assessment of existing research on the determinants of health and health care inequalities. The authors compare trends in racial and ethnic diversity in the U.S. population with the composition of health care bureaucrats and show that the increased diversity of the public has significantly exceeded the growth of minority health care workers, despite evidence and expectations that more racial and ethnic diversity among these administrators is likely to have some effect in reducing inequalities. The authors consider new frontiers in health inequality with a particular focus on research related to race, representative bureaucracy, and health inequality as well as intersectionality theory and health inequality across scholarly disciplines.

Digital governance, which generally aims to foster links between government and citizens through information sharing and interaction, is examined in Chapter 5 by Adrian Brown, Karen Mossberger, and Seong Cho. Through open data portals, social media, and mobile applications, the ways governments connect with citizens are growing ever more varied. Both scholars and practitioners acknowledge the democracy-enhancing potential of technology as a key benefit and goal of digital governance strategies. While technology can provide a pathway for access to government, for people of color, historical discrimination leading to exclusion from political engagement, as well as race and place-based differences in technology access and use can potentially preclude citizen engagement online. As such, the authors focus on communities of color, specifically addressing the role of race and ethnicity in internet access and use (devices, platforms, and activities online), how technology use is patterned across cities and neighborhoods, and the implications of these trends for inclusive governance. The authors consider mobile versus internet use, the promotion of affordable broadband, and the effectiveness of outreach programs.

Kelly LeRoux next turns attention to nonprofit organizations in Chapter 6 with original data and analysis. Nonprofit organizations play an essential role in the American safety net, providing for basic needs and essential social services in local communities throughout the United States. Despite shifting demographics in the American population, nonprofit human service organizations remain surprisingly unrepresentative of the communities they serve. As such, nonprofits are facing increased demands to diversify their governing boards according to the notion that the commitment to diversity begins at the top. At the same time, nonprofits are receiving additional pressure for performance from their funding entities as well as the public. Using a mixed-method explanatory sequential design, this chapter combines quantitative and qualitative data to first present an analysis demonstrating a statistical link between racial diversity on nonprofit boards and both objective (financial) and subjective (self-reported) measures of performance. The underlying mechanisms of the diversity-performance relationship are further studied through a multi-case comparison based on document analysis and interviews with nonprofit CEOs and board chairs.

In Chapter 7, Alketa Peci, Andre Dantas Cabral, Eunji Lee, and Vanessa Brulon Soares provide a glimpse of the larger role of race in multiple international contexts. The authors argue that public administration can play a role in institutionalizing racial categories, biases, and unequal outcomes but can also promote racial equity within and beyond the public sector, often creating contradictory effects. The authors discuss a range of social and historical contexts around the world that shape modern discussions of race in particular countries and argue that this same context should play a large role in understanding how public administrators can seek to achieve racial equity in their jurisdictions today. To support their arguments, the authors examine race in the United Kingdom, Brazil, and South Korea.

The book's conclusion in Chapter 8 by Kenneth J. Meier and Amanda Rutherford reviews common themes across chapters and identifies additional insights for recognizing the role of race in public administration, including in policy implementation, performance management, and policy feedback. They add discussion of other areas of public policy where race is an important concern, including employment, housing, environment policy, and welfare policy. These additional cases illustrate how the issues raised by other chapters often play out in similar manners across policy areas. Recommendations are provided for how to move the discussion of race forward by both current and future practitioners as well as scholars of public administration.

## References

Alexander, Jennifer, and Camilla Stivers. 2010. "An ethic of race for public administration." *Administrative Theory & Praxis* 32(4): 578–597.

Broadnax, Walter D. 2010. "Diversity in public organizations: A work in progress." *Public Administration Review* 70: S177–S179.

Choi, Sungjoo. 2013. "Demographic diversity of managers and employee job satisfaction: Empirical analysis of the federal case." *Review of Public Personnel Administration* 33(3): 275–298.

Cohn, D. Vera, and Andrea Caumont. 2016. "10 demographic trends shaping the U.S. and the world in 2016." Washington, DC: Pew Research Center. Available at: www.pewresearch.org/fact-tank/2016/03/31/10-demographic-trends-that-are-shaping-the-u-s-and-the-world/. (accessed July 1, 2019).

Commission on Reform in the Civil Service. 1914. "Segregation of clerks and employees in the civil service, hearings before the Commission on Reform in the Civil Service." Available at: en.wikipedia.org/wiki/United_States_Civil_Service_Commission

Cornwell, Christopher, and J. Edward Kellough. 1994. "Women and minorities in federal government agencies: Examining new evidence from panel data." *Public Administration Review* 54(3): 265–270.

Dobbin, Frank, and Alexandra Kalev. 2016. "Why diversity programs fail, and what works better." *Harvard Business Review* 94(7): 52–60.

EEOC (U.S. Equal Employment Opportunity Commission). 1979. *EEOC Guidelines on Affirmative Action*, 29 C.F.R. § 1608.1(c). Available at: www.law.cornell.edu/cfr/text/29/part-1608

Foldy, Erica Gabrielle, and Tamara R.Buckley. 2014. *The Color Blind: Talking (and Not Talking) About Race at Work*. New York, NY: Russell Sage Foundation.

Frederickson, H.George. 1990. "Public administration and social equity." *Public Administration Review* 50(2): 228–237.

Gibson, Campbell J., and Emily Lennon. 1999. "Historical Census statistics on the foreign-born population of the United States: 1850 to 1990." Working Paper no. 29. Washington, DC: U.S. Census Bureau.

Gooden, Susan T. 2014. *Race and social equity: A nervous area of government*. Armonk, NY: ME Sharpe.

Gooden, Susan T. 2015. "PAR's social equity footprint." *Public Administration Review* 75(3): 372–381.

Keiser, Lael R., Peter R. Mueser, and Seung-Whan Choi. 2004. "Race, bureaucratic discretion, and the implementation of welfare reform." *American Journal of Political Science* 48(2): 314–327.

Kellough, J. Edward, and Katherine C. Naff. 2004. "Responding to a wake-up call: An examination of federal agency diversity management programs." *Administration & Society* 36(1): 62–90.

Kim, Chon-Kyun. 2005. "Asian American employment in the federal civil service." *Public Administration Quarterly* 28(3/4): 430–459.

Kim, Pan Suk, and Gregory B. Lewis. 1994. "Asian Americans in the public service: Success, diversity, and discrimination." *Public Administration Review* 54(3): 285–290.

Krislov, Samuel. 1967. *The Negro in federal employment: The quest for equal opportunity*. Minneapolis, MN: University of Minnesota Press.

Krislov, Samuel. 1974. *Representative bureaucracy*. Englewood Cliffs, NJ: Prentice-Hall.

Lewis, Gregory B., and David Nice. 1994. "Race, sex, and occupational segregation in state and local governments." *The American Review of Public Administration* 24(4): 393–410.

Meier, Kenneth J. 1975. "Representative bureaucracy: An empirical analysis." *American Political Science Review* 69(2): 526–542.

Meier, Kenneth J., and Lloyd G. Nigro. 1976. "Representative bureaucracy and policy preferences: A study in attitudes of federal executives." *Public Administration Review* 36(4): 458–469.

Parker, Kim, Juliana Menasce Horowitz, Rich Morin, and Mark Hugo Lopez. 2015. "Multiracial in America." Washington, DC: Pew Research Center. Available at: www. pewsocialtrends.org/2015/06/11/multiracial-in-america/ (accessed July 1, 2019).

Perry, Susan White. 2005. "Social equity for the long haul: Preparing culturally competent public administrators." PhD dissertation, Virginia Polytechnic Institute and State University.

Pew Research Center. 2015. "Modern immigration wave brings 59 million to U.S., driving population growth and change through 2065: Views of immigration's impact on U.S. society mixed." Available at: www.pewresearch.org/hispanic/2015/09/28/modern-immigration-wave-brings-59-million-to-u-s-driving-population-growth-and-change-through-2065/

Pitts, David W. 2009. "Diversity management, job satisfaction, and performance: Evidence from US federal agencies." *Public Administration Review* 69(2): 328–338.

Pitts, David W., and Lois R. Wise. 2010. "Workforce diversity in the new millennium: Prospects for research." *Review of Public Personnel Administration* 30(1): 44–69.

Project for Equity, Representation, and Governance. 2019. "Representative bureaucracy DB." Available at: https://d2wldr9tsuuj1b.cloudfront.net/6327/documents/2019/4/RBdatabase.html (accessed March 15, 2018).

Riccucci, Norma M., and Judith R. Saidel. 1997. "The representativeness of state-level bureaucratic leaders: A missing piece of the representative bureaucracy puzzle." *Public Administration Review* 57(5): 423–430.

Stivers, Camilla. 2007. "'So poor and so black': Hurricane Katrina, public administration, and the issue of race." *Public Administration Review* 67(s1): 48–56.

Tatum, Beverley D. 2001. "Defining racism: Can we talk?" In P.S. Rothenberg (Ed.) *Race, class, and gender in the United States: An integrated study* (pp. 100–107). New York, NY: Worth Publishers.

University of Cincinnati. 2017. "New digital map shows changing racial diversity of America." Available at: www.sciencedaily.com/releases/2017/04/170421123301.htm (accessed July 1, 2019).

Watkins-Hayes, Celeste. 2011. "Race, respect, and red tape: Inside the black box of racially representative bureaucracies." *Journal of Public Administration Research and Theory* 21(suppl. 2): i233–i251.

Wellman, David T. 1993. *Portraits of white racism.* 2nd edn. New York, NY: Cambridge University Press.

## Cases Cited

*Fisher v. University of Texas,* 579 U.S. (*2016*).
*Regents of University of California v. Bakke,* 438 U.S. 265(1978).

# 2 Racial and Ethnic Diversity in the Public Sector Workforce

## Insights from Public Education

*Jason A. Grissom and Ashley Jones*

**Practitioner Points**

- Studies from the K-12 public education sector provide rigorous evidence of the benefits of teacher racial/ethnic diversity for student outcomes along numerous dimensions. These benefits are especially important for students of color, though a growing literature suggests that workforce diversity benefits students more generally.
- There are numerous potential mechanisms linking teacher diversity to outcomes for diverse students. Some of these—differences in teacher behaviors or attitudes that differentially impact students of color—echo representative bureaucracy literature. Yet studies increasingly emphasize student-centered (client-side) mechanisms, such as role modeling, alleviation of stereotype threat, and increased family engagement that have received less attention in public administration.
- Despite the importance of teacher diversity, K-12 workforce diversity is not keeping pace with the changing demographics of the public school student population.
- The pipeline of people of color into teaching has numerous holes, including insufficient numbers of people of color attending college or majoring in education, disparate impacts of licensure examinations, and hiring discrimination in local school districts. These holes demand a variety of strategies to increase the numbers of college-educated workers entering teaching.
- Recruitment or pipeline strategies are unlikely to be sufficient. Retention of teachers of color is a major challenge, particularly given the systematically more challenging working conditions of the schools into which such teachers sort.

The benefits of racial and ethnic diversity in the public sector workforce and the need for increased diversification have long been topics for public administration scholars (e.g., Choi and Rainey, 2010; Krislov and Rosenbloom, 1981; Pitts, 2005; Wise and Tschirhart, 2000). Workforce diversity discussions in both the academic and policy worlds have become especially salient in public education. Recent widely read reports commissioned by advocacy organizations and think tanks, including the report by the National Collaborative on Diversity in the Teaching Force—a collaborative of education and advocacy organizations—"Assessment of Diversity in America's Teaching Force: A Call to Action" (National Collaborative on Diversity in the Teaching Force, 2004); the Center for American Progress's "Teacher Diversity Matters," which is a state-by-state analysis of teacher diversity (Boser, 2011); and the Shanker Institute's "The State of Teacher Diversity in American Education" (Albert Shanker Institute, 2015), have all examined the underrepresentation of people of color in teaching and the attempts that states have made to address this underrepresentation. Former Secretaries of Education Arne Duncan and John B. King, Jr., both used their bully pulpit to call attention to the need to increase teacher diversity and launched initiatives at the U.S. Department of Education aimed at increasing the numbers of teachers of color.[1] In parallel, foundations have begun funding programs targeted at improving teacher diversity, such as the Bill and Melinda Gates Foundation's grant-making to teacher preparation programs that recruit teachers of color, the W.K. Kellogg Foundation's funding for improved pipelines for teachers of color in the District of Columbia Public Schools, and the Tom Joyner Foundation's partnership with the National Education Association to fund teacher certification programs at historically Black colleges and universities. Several states and school districts have enacted programs designed to recruit and retain teachers of color as well, including Illinois' Grow Your Own Teacher and Boston Public Schools' High School to Teacher Program, both of which provide mentorship, training, and pathways to certification for aspiring teachers of color. These relatively small-scale efforts reflect the growing urgency around the need to move from discussion to action in the area of teacher diversity and likely signal new efforts as states implement new plans under the most recent reauthorization of the Elementary and Secondary Education Act, known as the Every Student Succeeds Act, or ESSA.

In a sense, this heightened attention to educator diversity in education policy discourse has been a long time coming. A large body of research documents the importance of teacher and principal diversity for student outcomes—particularly for students of color, who lag behind their White peers on virtually every important schooling indicator. Unfortunately, as the composition of students in American schools becomes ever more diverse, diversity in the educator workforce is failing to keep pace. As Grissom, Kern, and Rodriguez (2015) show, the proportion of students of color in public schools increased by 10 percentage points from 2000 to 2012 (from 33 percent to 43 percent), while over this same time period, the fraction of teachers and principals of color each increased only 1 percentage point (16 percent to 17 percent for teachers and 18 percent to 19 percent for principals). The U.S. Department of Education (2016) projects that, by 2024, the proportion of students of color in the U.S. public education system will grow to 54 percent. These numbers suggest that policy discourse must translate into policy action to curb the trend of increased mismatch between the race/ethnicity of the educator workforce and that of the student population it serves.

The aim of this chapter is to summarize what we know about racial and ethnic diversity in the public education workforce and why it matters. In particular, we review evidence on the impact that educator diversity has on student outcomes, such as academic achievement, gifted identification, and high school graduation as well as the mechanisms that link them. We discuss research demonstrating the benefits of educator diversity for students of color as well as the small but growing body of research suggesting that this diversity benefits other students as well. A main takeaway of this review for public organizations more generally is just how important workforce diversity is for a wide range of outcomes. That is, a plethora of high-quality, large-scale studies using national, state, and local data sources is conclusive that workforce diversity has substantial benefits, particularly to students and families of color but to White students as well, and that these benefits show up in both short-term and long-term outcomes for students. We also review evidence on the recruitment and retention of teachers of color and find that the challenges here are immense, both in growing the pipeline of teachers of color and in keeping them in the profession. Overcoming those challenges is unlikely without comprehensive, multifaceted diversity strategies.

The intersection of public policy and diversity has received sustained rigorous research attention in public education, more so than in many other sectors of public service. An advantage of researching issues of diversity in public schools is the availability of high-quality data, including longitudinal administrative data at the individual level and in-depth data from federal survey programs. Data availability often has meant that researchers can apply quasi-experimental methods and can give attention to multiple outcomes. Education research has provided evidence on the importance of workforce diversity, why it matters, and theoretical and empirical evidence for mechanisms that promote or inhibit workforce diversity. We suggest that the lessons that we are learning regarding both the impacts of diversity at the street level and strategies for diversifying the workforce in education can inform diversity management and administration in other policy areas, an idea to which we return in the conclusion of this chapter.

## Benefits of Educator Diversity for Students of Color

We begin by summarizing the benefits of a diverse educator workforce for students of color. Quantitative research suggests that these positive impacts can be substantial across a variety of important outcomes. Payoffs from teacher diversity in particular to students of color have policy relevance because educational outcomes for Black, Hispanic, and other racial/ethnic groups historically have fallen far short of those for White students.

## Student Achievement

The strongest empirical evidence linking teacher diversity to improvements in student outcomes comes from studies of impacts on student test scores. Several early studies using organizational-level data link teacher diversity to student achievement (e.g., Meier, 1993; Meier and Stewart, 1992), though the aggregated nature of these data placed limits on the causal claims that could be made. In a seminal causal study of the effects of same-race teachers on student achievement, Dee (2004) re-analyzed data from the STAR experiment, a four-year randomized experiment in Tennessee designed to estimate the effects of smaller class studies in elementary school. Randomized experiments are the gold standard for empirical research because they generate clean estimates of effects that remove the confounding from other factors often present in non-experimental studies. Dee took advantage of the fact that the STAR experiment randomly assigned students to teachers within schools—which meant that Black and White students were randomly assigned to Black and White teachers—to estimate the effect of having a same-race teacher. He found that Black students randomly assigned to a Black teacher scored 3–6 percentile points higher on a standardized reading test and 4–5 percentile points higher on a standardized math test; both were statistically and substantively meaningful differences. White students also scored higher when assigned to a White teacher, though the effect size was smaller.

Other analyses of student-level data have reached similar conclusions. In a quasi-experimental study using large, student-level administrative data sets from North Carolina and Florida, respectively, Clotfelter, Ladd, and Vigdor (2010) and Egalite, Kisida, and Winters (2015) found similar patterns of higher test scores for students with same-race teachers. In both cases, the authors employed a statistical method that allowed them to compare the average achievement gains for a student in the years he or she was taught by a same-race teacher to gains for *the same student* in years he or she was taught by another-race teacher. Clotfelter et al. (2010) found that Black teachers had more positive effects on Black students' standardized test scores than White students. Egalite et al. (2015) estimated gains for assignment to a same-race teacher for both White and Black (but not Hispanic) students. Effects were especially large for Black students, particularly in math and in the elementary grades. They also found that the effects of same-race teachers were even greater for lower-achieving students, emphasizing the potential importance of teacher diversity for educational equity.

## Gifted Assignment

Studies also suggest that teacher diversity is associated with greater numbers of students of color in gifted programs. Students of color are significantly underrepresented in gifted programs in the United States relative to their proportion in the general student population (Donovan and Cross, 2002;

Grissom, Rodriguez, and Kern, 2017). This underrepresentation, which occurs even when comparing White students and students of color with the same math and reading achievement scores (Grissom and Redding, 2016), is important both from the perspective of basic fairness and because gifted identification gives students access to intellectually challenging environments with equally able peers that results in increased engagement with schooling and better student-teacher relationships, among other outcomes (Vogl and Preckel, 2014). Under-identification means that many students of color are deprived of important educational benefits.

Because the identification process typically starts with a teacher referral, teachers play a "gatekeeping" role in gifted assignment. Teacher diversity may affect gifted identification if teachers' own background and characteristics inform how they exercise this gatekeeping discretion for different groups of students (Grissom, Kern, and Rodriguez, 2015). Indeed, studies of nationally representative data collected by the federal government show that schools with higher proportions of teachers who are Black or Hispanic assign larger proportions of students from those racial/ethnic groups to gifted services (Grissom, Nicholson-Crotty, and Nicholson-Crotty, 2009; Grissom, Rodriguez, and Kern, 2017), especially in schools where students of color are very underrepresented in gifted programs (Nicholson-Crotty, Grissom, and Nicholson-Crotty, 2011). Schools led by Black principals also are more likely to assign Black students to gifted services (Grissom, Rodriguez, and Kern, 2017). Consistent with the gatekeeping hypothesis, analyses of student-level data show that Black students assigned to Black classroom teachers are assigned to gifted services at similar rates to observationally equivalent White students, whereas Black students assigned to White teachers lag substantially behind in assignment to gifted programs (Grissom and Redding, 2016; Nicholson-Crotty, et al., 2016).

### Discipline

Impacts of teacher diversity on exclusionary discipline may be important for reducing the academic achievement gap, given that such discipline results in lost instructional time (Morris and Perry, 2016). Studies find effects of teacher-student racial/ethnic match on discipline, which, like gifted assignment, is an outcome in which teacher discretion can factor heavily. In two analyses of North Carolina data, both Holt and Gershenson (2015) and Lindsay and Hart (2017) document that students with other-race teachers experience higher rates of discipline (see also Kinsler, 2011). Holt and Gershenson (2015) find that the statistically significant difference in rate of suspensions among students with different race teachers was driven almost entirely by non-White male students in classrooms with White teachers. They find a 15 percent increase in the baseline probability that an elementary school student in their sample will be suspended, given they have a different race teacher.

Lindsay and Hart (2017) use student fixed-effects to compare students' rate of discipline during years that students had same or different-race teachers, and they find that Black elementary and middle school students with same-race teachers are less likely to be suspended or expelled. The reduction is particularly apparent for offenses that require subjective interpretation, such as defiance, suggesting that teacher discretion is a driving factor. Unexpectedly, however, the authors find that Black high school students with greater exposure to same-race teachers are *more* likely to be expelled, which the authors note may be a result of principals matching students with a history of disciplinary problems with Black teachers more frequently and the greater rate of Black teachers in "hard-to-staff" schools that use exclusionary disciplinary practices more frequently.

### Absenteeism

Teacher racial diversity has been found to have an impact on other outcomes for students of color as well. Absenteeism is one. Using data from an urban southwestern school district, Farkas et al. (1990) found that Black students were absent less often when taught by Black teachers. In a more recent analysis of longitudinal student-level administrative data from across North Carolina that allows them to compare years a student had a same-race and other-race teacher, Holt and Gershenson (2015) similarly conclude that a racial match between teacher and student decreases absenteeism among elementary school students. They use student fixed-effects to control for years in which students had other-race teachers compared to years that they did not and classroom fixed-effects to compare different race students within the same classroom. They find that students with other-race teachers are significantly more likely to be chronically absent than students with a same-race teacher, and that the higher likelihood that a Black student has an other-race teacher is a significant reason why Black students average 1.2 more absences per year than White students.

### Other Outcomes

Emerging research links assignment to same-race teachers to improved longer-term outcomes. Using data from Miami-Dade County high schools, Grissom, Kabourek, and Kramer (2020) find that high school students taught math by same-race teachers progress further in the high school math curriculum and are more likely to take honors and advanced placement courses. Similarly, Gershenson et al. (2017) examine the high school trajectories of Black students assigned to same-race teachers in elementary school in North Carolina. They find that Black students who are taught by even one Black teacher in grades 3 through 5 have significantly lower probabilities of dropping out of high school, particularly among low-income male students, a finding they replicate using data from the Tennessee STAR class size experiment. They also find that having a same-race teacher significantly increases the likelihood that Black, low-income students will aspire to attend a four-year college. Findings that payoffs to exposure to teachers of color may show up later in a student's schooling career and then translate to post-schooling life impacts further underscore the importance of attention to increased teacher diversity.

## Mechanisms Linking Educator Diversity to Improved Outcomes for Students of Color

As detailed in the last section, a growing body of empirical research demonstrates that access to diverse educators improves outcomes for students of color. But what mechanisms underlie this connection? Research suggests that the mechanisms are varied. In this section, we survey research from multiple fields to describe the mechanisms that scholars suggest link educator diversity with these improved outcomes.

### Representative Bureaucracy

For scholars of public administration and political science, the primary lens for thinking about diversity in public education is through the body of research on bureaucratic representation, which is the idea that the makeup of the public sector bureaucracy (including teachers in public schools) helps determine whose interests are reflected in the implementation of public policy (Mosher, 1968; Selden, 1997). Traditionally, this research has focused on two types of representation: descriptive and active. Descriptive or passive representation describes whether the demographic characteristics of an organization, agency, or the bureaucracy as a whole are similar to those of the clients it serves (Meier, 1993). Descriptive representation is simply about the degree of demographic alignment between bureaucrat and client; it says nothing about whether that alignment affects government service delivery. In contrast, active representation means that clients realize substantive benefits from having public services delivered by bureaucrats with similar characteristics. Importantly, research in this area has investigated representation with respect to many characteristics, including gender, sexual orientation, and religion, though the largest portion of this research has focused—as we do here—on race and ethnicity.

Representative bureaucracy scholars have hypothesized a number of mechanisms linking descriptive with active representation. Early theorists suggested that the linkage arises through partiality: minority bureaucrats would exercise their authority to benefit minority clients, in part to counter discriminatory behavior by nonminority bureaucrats (Mosher, 1968). As this body of research has developed, however, researchers have identified numerous other mechanisms that may induce patterns of benefits to minority clients of government from a diverse bureaucratic workforce (Grissom, Kern, and Rodriguez, 2015). Some of these mechanisms relate to differential behaviors of diverse bureaucrats (in the spirit of traditional ideas of active representation).

For example, these bureaucrats may be better equipped to communicate with clients with shared background and language or may advocate for the interests of clients "like them" in setting or changing organization policy. Other mechanisms emphasize differential responses of clients to the presence of diverse government workers, even when those workers' behavior is no different from that of their White colleagues. For instance, clients may feel more comfortable advocating for themselves while interacting with a bureaucrat with whom they more easily identify, or they may increase their own efforts or otherwise change their behaviors in ways that improve their outcomes—a mechanism sometimes referred to as "coproduction inducement" (Lim, 2006).

This theme—that workforce diversity may impact clients by producing differences both in how bureaucrats approach their work and in how clients respond to diverse bureaucrats—continues in education researchers' discussion of the mechanisms linking educator diversity to outcomes as well. Education researchers investigate how diverse teachers approach the work of teaching differently, as well as how diverse students and families respond differently to diverse teachers. Thus, although the perspectives, language, and approaches of education researchers who study teacher diversity differ from public administration scholars and political scientists who study representation, they do overlap in many ways. Next we turn to what education research says about the contributions of teacher diversity through differences in teacher approaches and differences in student and family responses to diversity.

## Diverse Teachers Approach the Work of Teaching Differently

A major impetus for efforts to diversify teaching is the observation that teachers of color behave, communicate, and even think differently than their White colleagues (Putman et al., 2016). These differences inform their micro-level interactions with students, the classroom environment they create, and their broader impacts on the school in ways that can benefit students of color. The broad areas discussed below are not meant to be exhaustive in representing how teachers of color approach teaching differently; rather, they represent aspects of the work in which researchers have documented important differences.

First, we consider diverse educators' perceptions and expectations of students. Numerous studies find that teachers of color hold more positive views and express more positive expectations of students of color than do their White colleagues (e.g., Ferguson, 1998). When asked about the reasons for the achievement gap between White and Black students, White teachers are more likely to see determinants of the gap as misbehavior, lack of student effort, uncooperative parents, and problems in the home, whereas Black teachers believe that low teacher expectations are the main cause (Uhlenberg and Brown, 2002). In a study of teachers asked to describe the same student on a survey, Black students were described less favorably by White teachers who tended to rate the student as more inattentive, more disruptive, and less likely to complete homework (Dee, 2005). Similarly, Gershenson, Holt, and

Papageorge (2016) find that Black teachers are less likely to say a Black tenth-grader will drop out of high school and more likely to say he or she will complete college than is a White colleague describing expectations for the same student. These findings are similar to those from older studies of teachers' subjective ratings of students that also found that White teachers gave lower ratings of Black students' likelihood of attending college and of whether they would recommend them for academic honors, believe the student relates well to others, ever spoke to the student outside of class, and believed the student was a hard worker (Ehrenberg, Goldhaber, and Brewer, 1995; Oates, 2003). In a study of younger children, Ouazad (2014) also finds that White teachers give lower subjective ratings for students' academic ability. Using longitudinal, nationally representative data that follow students from kindergarten through fifth grade, he finds that same-race teachers assess the same student's performance 4 percent of a standard deviation higher in English and 7 percent of a standard deviation higher in mathematics.

These differential perceptions and expectations of White teachers and teachers of color matter. Inconsistencies in teacher expectations seem to at least partially explain why rates of assignment of Black students to gifted programs are substantially higher in classrooms led by Black teachers (Nicholson-Crotty et al., 2016). Experimental evidence shows that teachers' expectations of student performance—even when false—can predict student achievement gains (Rosenthal and Jacobson, 1968). Expectations can affect how school resources or teacher time are directed at different students. They can also create self-fulfilling prophecies through chain reactions. That is, once teachers determine their expectations of a student's achievements, these expectations influence their interactions with the student which then lead students to lower their aspirations, self-concept, and academic performance such that they are likely to fulfill the original expectations held by the teacher (Villegas and Irvine, 2010).

Next, in terms of cultural responsiveness, teachers of color can affect students by more easily engaging in "culturally responsive teaching," which research shows is effective in improving outcomes for students of color (Foster, 1993; Hollins, 1982). Villegas and Lucas (2002) define culturally responsive teachers as being aware of sociocultural differences, teaching based on culturally specific ways that students learn, and having affirming views of students' backgrounds. Black teachers bring culturally based pedagogical approaches to the classroom and are better able to understand same-race students' culture, including style of presentation and language (Irvine, 1989). Black teachers are also more likely than White teachers to serve as cultural translators for Black students whose culture at home and in the community is vastly different than school culture (ibid.).

Irvine (1988) uses the term "cultural synchronicity" to describe what allows teachers of color to advance academic outcomes and overall school experiences of students of color more so than White teachers often can facilitate. Teachers of color can more easily build connections between what is already familiar to students and the new content and skills that they are teaching (Villegas and

Irvine, 2010). They may be able to use language patterns with which students of color are familiar and possess knowledge of students' community norms that fosters a greater opportunity for success in reaching those students (Foster, 1993; Hollins, 1982). In culturally responsive classrooms, this success is largely attributed to the fact that teaching and learning are learner-centered and students' strengths are identified and utilized (Richards, Brown, and Forde, 2007).

Possibly due to more positive perceptions of Black students and in hopes of actualizing their high expectations, teachers of color are more likely to advocate on behalf of students of color. Teachers of color often advocate for students of color by serving as a voice for them when communicating with other teachers and administrators and by questioning school or district rules that are not in the students' best interests (Irvine, 1990). Teachers of color are especially equipped to advocate for the needs of students of color because they often have experienced similar inequalities and alienation in their own schooling, which allows them to relate to students (Nieto, 1999). As one example, Black teachers express heightened attention to the over-representation of Black students in special education programs and cite reversing that pattern and advocating for Black students with special needs as a primary motivation for going into special education (Belcher, 2001).

### Students and Parents of Color Respond Differently to Diverse Educators

An important observation about the effects of same-race educators is that those effects may occur even without differences in the approach to the work of teaching for educators from different demographic backgrounds. That is, the presence of diverse teachers may matter for student outcomes because of how students or their parents react to that presence.

Teacher diversity may positively impact outcomes for students of color via role model effects. Role model effects occur when an outstanding person seems relevant and has similarities to another individual so that they thus inspire to attain comparable success (Lockwood and Kunda, 1997). Black teachers can serve as role models for Black students by allowing Black students to see a successful professional adult from the same background (Stewart, Meier, and England, 1989). Their presence may raise Black students' academic motivation and expectations and disrupt implicit assumptions that White people are better suited to hold positions of authority (Fuller, 1992). Students of color from impoverished backgrounds may especially benefit from teacher role models in terms of development of self-esteem and identity (Cole, 1986). Black teachers often actively take on this role as they see themselves as "exemplars of possibility" for students of color (Johnson, 2008).

A specific psychological mechanism whereby the presence of role models of color may positively impact student academic performance is through the alleviation of stereotype threat. Stereotype threat refers to student apprehension about confirming a negative stereotype, which can in turn hinder their academic performance and subsequent achievement (Steele, 1997; Steele and

Aronson, 1995). Black students are particularly impacted by stereotype threat, as they worry about not confirming the negative societal stereotype regarding Black people's intellectual ability and competence (Steele and Aronson, 1995). This stress produces attentional deficits, reluctance to respond to teacher questions, excessive self-monitoring, and focus on suppressing negative thoughts and emotions rather than on the cognitive tasks at hand (Osborne, 2001; Schmader, Johns, and Forbes, 2008). In the presence of same-race role models, students of color may reduce their perception of negative stereotyping, which in turn should benefit their academic performance (Dee, 2015; Gershenson, Holt, and Papageorge, 2016; Grissom, Kern, and Rodriguez, 2015), though this hypothesis has not been tested directly.

Diverse educators may also increase parental engagement. Family involvement from students' parents or caregivers can include volunteering at or visiting school, attending school functions, participating in parent-teacher associations, and helping children with school work. Parents (or caregivers) who are more engaged with their child's teacher have a better understanding of their child's needs, have more positive attitudes toward teachers, and have higher educational aspirations for their child, which can positively impact student achievement (LaRocque, Kleiman, and Darling, 2011). Unfortunately, research finds that parents of color are less likely to be involved with their children's schools (Desimone, 1999).

To facilitate greater involvement, teachers can engage the broader community to gain a better understanding of barriers to access and learn to respond flexibly to families that make an effort to advocate for their children (Auerbach, 2007). Same-race teachers may have a greater understanding of family contexts and thus interpret parental involvement or attempts to be involved more positively, which can make parents more comfortable. They may also be more effective at communicating with diverse parents and otherwise responding to parents' needs.

Consistent with these expectations, several studies have found evidence of greater parental engagement with school when children are taught by a same-race teacher. In elementary schools, White teachers reported less parent-initiated contact with parents of non-White children and lower attendance of those parents at school meetings than White children in their classrooms (Vinopal, 2018). Similarly, Markowitz, Bassok, and Grissom (2017) found that within the same Head Start center, Black parents volunteer more and are more satisfied with the school when their children's teacher is Black. Increased parental engagement and advocacy for their students at school may be one mechanism driving more positive outcomes for students with same-race teachers (Grissom, Kern, and Rodriguez, 2015), though research on these impacts is in its nascent stages (e.g., Nicholson-Crotty et al., 2016).

## Benefits of Teacher Racial/Ethnic Diversity for All Students

Aside from the benefits of teachers of color on students of color, there may be positive impacts of educator diversity on all students. A smaller literature discusses these broader impacts. For example, the presence of teachers and administrators of color can teach White and non-White students to respect people of color in "roles of authority and see them as examples of competent professionals" (Cole, 1986, p. 334). Providing a multicultural education also transforms the curriculum in a way that helps prepare students to be effective citizens in a pluralistic and democratic society (Banks, 1994). More widely, students who have diverse classrooms are more prepared to navigate a global economy in which they must collaborate and work within multicultural environments (The Century Foundation, 2017). Many studies have shown that providing intentional opportunities for interracial interactions is associated with a reduction in racial biases and prejudices (e.g., Pettigrew and Tropp, 2000; Richeson and Nussbaum, 2004). These findings are consistent with intergroup contact theory, which suggests that creating specific kinds of productive opportunities for groups to interact with one another can reduce biases of group members (Pettigrew, 1998). White students may benefit more from diversity-related initiatives than students of color in developing positive attitudes toward members of other racial groups (Tropp and Pettigrew, 2005).

Along with being prepared to work in a global, diverse economy, having a diverse teacher workforce may also improve the classroom environment for all students. Using data from students in the sixth to the ninth grades, Cherng and Halpin (2016) find that, on average, all students have higher ratings of Black and Latinx teachers than White teachers across seven measures, including how well the teacher motivates students to high academic standards, manages the behavior of students in the classroom, and builds supportive relationships with students. These effects are found after controlling for student demographic and academic characteristics, other teacher characteristics, work conditions, and teacher efficacy. These results suggest that teachers of color may be better able to build rapport with students, regardless of their demographic background.

Researchers suggest that exposure to racial/ethnic diversity helps students because as they learn and collaborate with students from different backgrounds and with different perspectives, their problem-solving, critical thinking, and creativity skills are enhanced. Cross-race contact is an important means of curbing students' implicit biases and reducing racial prejudices (Paluck and Green, 2009; Pettigrew and Tropp, 2006). Aside from bias reduction, going to more diverse schools is associated with seeking out other integrated settings later in life and an improvement in intellectual self-confidence (Page, 2008; Pettigrew and Tropp, 2006 ; The Century Foundation, 2017).

## Recruiting and Retaining Teachers of Color

The previous sections established the importance of building a robust cadre of teachers of color for the American educational system. Here, we turn to what we know about the challenges of recruiting and retaining this diverse teacher workforce. These challenges are substantial.

Because teachers of color are more likely to persist in difficult-to-staff urban schools and are more committed to teaching students of color (Scafidi, Sjoquist, and Stinebrickner, 2007; Villegas and Irvine, 2010), it is important to investigate ways to successfully recruit and retain teachers of color to expand the overall supply of teachers for often understaffed schools and promote teacher stability—which comes with additional benefits (Ronfeldt, Loeb, and Wyckoff, 2013)—within those schools.

### The "Leaky" Pipeline for Teachers of Color

A recent report from the Brookings Institution describes the difficulties K–12 schools face in bringing a larger group of teachers of color into the profession (Putman et al., 2016). One foundational challenge, the authors note, is that young people from racial and ethnic minority groups are substantially less likely to pursue and complete college degrees, a prerequisite for obtaining a job in teaching.[2] Of the 18–24-year-olds enrolled in degree-granting postsecondary institutions in 2013, 58 percent were White, compared to only 15 percent Black and 17 percent Hispanic (National Center for Education Statistics, 2017). Moreover, even among the group of students pursuing or completing a college degree, interest in teaching is lower among those from non-White groups than among Whites. U.S. Department of Education data show that about 7 percent of White college students major in education, compared to just 4 percent (each) for Black and Hispanic students. Talented college students of color, especially those with aptitudes in math and physical sciences, often are attracted to careers in the private industry, where salaries and benefits are more lucrative (Torres, Santos, Peck, and Cortes, 2004).

Among those who pursue careers in education, however, the teacher certification exams required in most states constitute an additional barrier to teachers of color (Petchauer, 2012). Teaching candidates of color are substantially less likely than White candidates to achieve a passing score on the Praxis basic skills exam, a common test for teacher licensure (Nettles et al., 2011). The barrier these tests create is particularly troubling in the context of concerns about their validity as a predictor of job performance; in fact, evidence suggests that such exams may be less predictive of future performance for Black test-takers (Goldhaber and Hansen, 2010).[3]

These numbers suggest that diversifying teaching will mean focusing policy attention on the pipeline into teaching, long before principals and districts consider their hiring pool. Yet research also suggests that teachers of color are disadvantaged at the hiring stage. White education majors are more likely to work in teaching than Black and Hispanic education majors, though the specific reasons are unclear and could include, for example, poorer outreach and recruitment among non-White communities (Putman et al., 2016). One recent study documents a more insidious reason. In an analysis of multiple years of application and hiring data from a single large district in which approximately 27,000 applications were submitted for

2,400 positions, D'Amico et al. (2017) found that Black teaching applicants were less likely to be offered positions than White applicants. In fact, Black candidates made up 13 percent of the applicant pool but only 6 percent of offered positions; a Black applicant was 51 percent less likely than a White applicant to be offered a job. These differences were found even when controlling for other applicant qualifications, suggesting employment discrimination against Black teachers explains hiring differences. Notably, when they were offered employment, Black teachers were more likely to be placed at schools with high proportions of Black students.

The authors also found that Black applicants were more likely to be offered positions by Black principals. This pattern has been shown in other studies as well; for example, Bartanen and Grissom (2019) showed that principals of color in Missouri and Tennessee were much more likely to hire teachers of color than White principals in the same schools in different years. These results suggest that increasing diversity in the school leadership ranks is an important component of strategies to diversify the teacher workforce.

### Difficulties Retaining Teachers of Color

Getting teachers of color into the teaching workforce is only part of the educator diversity equation. The other is retaining them once they enter teaching. Ingersoll and May's (2011) look at national data shows that, in 2003–2004, 47,600 teachers of color entered the teacher workforce, but by the next year, 56,000 had left teaching. In fact, in recent years, teachers of color turn over at higher rates than their White colleagues (Ingersoll and May, 2011; Putman et al., 2016), a difference that was not present in national studies of teacher turnover prior to the 2000s (Achinstein et al., 2010). It appears the rate of turnover among teachers of color is escalating, with a more recent report by Ingersoll and May (2016) showing the overall turnover rate (both moves to other schools and exits) of Black teachers grew from 13 percent in 1988–1989 to 19 percent in 2012–2013.

A major reason for the gap in turnover rates between White teachers and teachers of color is that the latter disproportionately work in urban schools with larger numbers of low-income and low-achieving students and students of color, which often have less desirable working conditions (Grissom, Viano, and Selin, 2016; Simon and Johnson, 2015). These conditions include less able leadership, high rates of disciplinary incidents, inadequate instructional resources, lower quality facilities, and less teacher control over pedagogical decisions (Ladd, 2011; Loeb, Darling-Hammond, and Luczak, 2005; Torres et al., 2004). Among these factors, leadership may be particularly important (Grissom, 2011). One study using national survey data concluded that dissatisfaction with school conditions is the largest factor in explaining turnover for teachers of color (Ingersoll and Connor, 2009). Notably, teachers of color are less likely to leave hard-to-staff environments than White teachers (Achinstein et al., 2010; Scafidi, Sjoquist, and Stinebrickner, 2007), but their higher concentrations in hard-to-staff schools nonetheless make challenging working conditions a formidable factor in their higher turnover rates.

Teachers of color may also face feelings of racial and/or ethnic isolation often associated with serving on a mostly White faculty, which can lower job satisfaction and make it more likely they exit (Bristol, 2014). Racial mismatch with the school's principal may also contribute to turnover. In a study of national turnover data, Grissom and Keiser (2011) find that Black teachers report higher levels of administrative support, autonomy, and recognition when their principal is Black and that Black teacher turnover rates are substantially lower in cases of same-race teacher-principal matches. Using two-way teacher and principal fixed effects models in panel data spanning multiple decades from Missouri and Tennessee, Bartanen and Grissom (2019) show that Black teachers are substantially more likely to be retained in a school with a Black principal.

A key observation regarding the impact of working conditions on the turnover decisions of teachers of color is that the conditions themselves are policy-amenable (Ingersoll and May, 2011). Changing school decision-making processes, improving facilities, increasing instructional resources, and raising salaries all are strategies that can be employed to reduce teacher turnover, and—given the kinds of schools in which they often work—turnover among teachers of color in particular.

### Conclusion

The foregoing review of the evidence from studies of K-12 education demonstrates the policy importance of greater diversity in the teaching workforce. Increasing the share of teachers of color in public schools and, therefore, exposure of students of color to diverse teachers would yield substantial benefits to those students. Rigorous empirical evidence shows that being taught by a same-race teacher increases both achievement in math and reading and non-achievement outcomes for students of color. These latter outcomes include a higher probability of receiving gifted services, lower likelihood of receiving exclusionary discipline, and lower rates of absenteeism. There is also evidence that there can be longer-term benefits on outcomes such as high school graduation and college aspirations, suggesting economic impacts of teacher diversity that may extend beyond the schooling years. Evidence suggests that the mechanisms for these effects vary but include both differences in teachers' expectations and approaches as well as differences in students' and parents' responses to those teachers (e.g., role modeling effects). More research is needed to understand how these mechanisms work so that changes can be made to school processes to better serve students of color in particular.

Benefits of teacher diversity extend in several ways to White students as well, including potentially reducing implicit biases. In short, workforce diversity in public schools matters, and perhaps in a more far-reaching ways than researchers and policymakers previously have realized. The implications of this observation for other areas of the public sector, where data often are less available, are potentially large, and suggest the need for increased scrutiny of workforce diversity impacts in other kinds of public organizations.

Yet despite this evidence, the U.S. teaching workforce remains "over-whelmingly homogenous" (U.S. Department of Education, 2016, p. 31), and the student population is diversifying faster than the teacher population along racial and ethnic lines, suggesting that teachers are actually becoming less demographically representative of the students they serve over time. Moreover, sitting passively and simply waiting for those children of color to become adults who can teach is unlikely to solve the teacher-student diversity gap problem. The pipeline into teaching for people of color is a leaky one with too few people of color completing college degrees, let alone pursuing teaching, and schools' capacities to hire teachers of color undercut by biases in licensure examinations and hiring discrimination. We suspect that these pipeline issues are salient elsewhere in the public sector. Even when people of color do find their way into teaching, difficult working conditions make it less likely that they will stay. Without affirmative policy strategies consciously designed to improve both recruitment and retention efforts, mismatches between the teaching workforce and student population are unlikely to improve.

The complexity of the recruitment and retention problem means that states and districts must work together to implement many strategies in tandem to make meaningful changes in teacher diversity (Putman et al., 2016). Potential components of these strategies are numerous. Teachers of color might be targeted by early prospective teacher identification initiatives, including those in two-year college settings and the military, then offered financial aid or loan forgiveness options to go into teaching, and provided with tutoring to increase the passage rates on licensure exams (Bireda and Chait, 2011; National Education Association, 2015). Another recommendation for bringing higher numbers of qualified teachers of color into the profession is investment in student access to historically Black colleges and universities (HBCUs) and Hispanic-serving institutions (HSIs) as well as teacher preparation programs for students enrolled in those institutions (Albert Shanker Institute, 2015; U.S. Department of Education, 2016). HBCUs and HSIs can provide robust avenues to bachelor's degrees for people of color, and high-quality preparation programs on those campuses can help attract bachelor's degree-seekers into the education profession.

Other strategies can recognize that many Black teachers enter the profession through nontraditional pathways, often after changing careers later in life (Madkins, 2011). Scholars describe Black teachers as often deliberate in their path into teaching, seeing teaching as a calling and their role as "lifting as we climb" (Dixson and Dingus, 2008)—one potential reason why they are more likely to persist in high-needs schools. Investment in alternative pathways to teacher certification, such as teacher residency programs, may be an effective means to pull more teachers of color into the profession.

Alternatively, states can give teacher preparation programs and school districts incentives to increase diversity. In this vein, the Tennessee Department of Education recently announced plans to award $200,000 in grant funds to preparation programs to design innovative approaches for increasing teacher diversity and another $100,000 for districts to address acute diversity needs after the state's data showed that approximately 85 percent of districts employed not a single Hispanic teacher and nearly 20 percent employed no Black teachers (Tennessee Department of Education, 2017). This example points to the importance of state-level monitoring and accountability for teacher diversity—states must prioritize, measure, and report workforce diversity—as a foundational component of any diversification strategy (Albert Shanker Institute, 2015).

States and districts can also create initiatives aimed at reducing turnover among teachers of color. Addressing poor working conditions in schools that employ teachers of color is key (National Education Association, 2015). Strategies might include induction and mentoring programs to support teachers of color in the critical early years in the profession when the propensity for turnover is highest. Accountability for hiring and retaining teachers of color might also be made a part of evaluation systems for district and school leaders (Albert Shanker Institute, 2015).

Strategies to diversify school leadership through recruitment and preparation programs aimed at potential leaders of color also are important. Leaders of color are more successful at recruiting and retaining teachers of color (Bartanen and Grissom, 2019; Grissom and Keiser, 2011) and are more likely to hire teachers of color (D'Amico et al., 2017). Leadership diversity may also have positive impacts on outcomes for students of color, either indirectly through impacts on teachers or school policy or more directly by, for example, resulting in lower use of exclusionary discipline policies for those students (e.g., Bartanen and Grissom, 2019; Grissom, Rodriguez, and Kern, 2017; Kinsler, 2011). However, the empirical research base in this area is small, and the field needs further investigation of the impacts of leadership diversity on teachers and students.

## Discussion Questions

1   Are there implications of findings regarding teacher diversity in education for other domains of the public sector? Do these implications also apply to employees in various parts of the private or nonprofit sectors?
2   What are the primary benefits of teacher racial/ethnic diversity for students of color? For White students?
3   What mechanisms link increased teacher diversity to student outcomes? Are there mechanisms you think are relevant that are not discussed in the chapter?
4   How are barriers to recruiting and retaining teachers of color likely to be similar or different in other areas of public service? Why do you think current recruitment and retention strategies have not yet been successful in closing the gap between student and teacher diversity?

5    What strategies appear most promising for increasing the number of education majors in colleges and universities? Do these strategies differ for White students and students of color?

## Notes

1  See, for example, Duncan's Teach.gov initiative, which made teacher diversity a priority.
2  The authors' figures show that about 47 percent of White 22-year-olds have earned a bachelor's degree, compared to 28 percent and 20 percent for Black and Hispanic adults, respectively, of the same age.
3  Recent evidence suggests that standardized licensure exams for school principals suffer from similar problems with low predictive validity and disproportionate impacts on candidates of color (Grissom, Mitani, and Blissett, 2017).

## References

Achinstein, Betty, Rodney T. Ogawa, Dena Sexton, and Casia Freitas. 2010. "Retaining teachers of color: A pressing problem and a potential strategy for 'hard-to-staff' schools." *Review of Educational Research* 80(1): 71–107.

Albert Shanker Institute. 2015. "The state of teacher diversity in American education." Washington, DC: Albert Shanker Institute. Available at: www.shankerinstitute.org/sites/shanker/files/The%20State%20of%20Teacher%20Diversity%20in%20American%20Education_0.pdf

Auerbach, Susan. 2007. "From moral supporters to struggling advocates: Reconceptualizing parent roles in education through the experience of working-class families of color." *Urban Education* 42(3): 250–283.

Banks, James A. 1994. *An introduction to multicultural education.* Needham Heights, MA: Allyn & Bacon.

Bartanen, Brendan, and Jason A.Grissom. 2019. "School principal race and the hiring and retention of racially diverse teachers." EdWorkingPaper No. 19–59, Annenberg Institute at Brown University. Available at: http://edworkingpapers.com/ai19-59.

Belcher, Rebecca Newcom. 2001. "Predictive factors for the enrollment of African American students in special education preservice programs." Paper presented at the Meeting of Partnership for Rural Special Education, San Diego, CA, March 29–31.

Bireda, Saba and Robin Chait. 2011. *Increasing teacher diversity: Strategies to improve the teacher workforce.* Washington, DC: Center for American Progress.

Bond, Burnie, Esther Quintero, Leo Casey, and Matthew Di Carlo. 2015. *The state of teacher diversity in American education.* Washington, DC: Albert Shanker Institute.

Boser, Ulrich. 2011. "Teacher diversity matters: A state-by-state analysis of teachers of color." Washington, DC: Center for American Progress. Available at: https://cdn.americanprogress.org/wp-content/uploads/issues/2011/11/pdf/teacher_diversity.pdf

Bristol, Travis. 2014. "Black men of the classroom: An exploration of how the organizational conditions, characteristics, and dynamics in schools affect black male teachers' pathways into the profession." PhD dissertation, Teachers College, Columbia University.

Cherng, Hua-Yu Sebastian, and Peter F. Halpin. 2016. "The importance of minority teachers student perceptions of minority versus white teachers." *Educational Researcher* 45(7): 407–420.

Choi, Sungjoo, and Hal G. Rainey. 2010. "Managing diversity in US federal agencies: Effects of diversity and diversity management on employee perceptions of organizational performance." *Public Administration Review* 70(1): 109–121.

Clotfelter, Charles T., Helen F. Ladd, and Jacob L. Vigdor. 2010. "Teacher credentials and student achievement in high school: A cross-subject analysis with student fixed effects." *Journal of Human Resources* 45(3): 655–681.

Cole, Beverly P. 1986. "The black educator: An endangered species." *The Journal of Negro Education* 55(3): 326–334.

D'Amico, Diana, Robert J. Pawlewicz, Penelope M. Earley, and Adam P. McGeehan. 2017. "Where are all the black teachers? Discrimination in the teacher labor market." *Harvard Educational Review* 87(1): 26–49.

Dee, Thomas S. 2004. "Teachers, race, and student achievement in a randomized experiment." *Review of Economics and Statistics* 86(1): 195–210.

Dee, Thomas S. 2005. "A teacher like me: Does race, ethnicity, or gender matter?" *The American Economic Review* 95(2): 158–165.

Dee, Thomas S. 2015. "Social identity and achievement gaps: Evidence from an affirmation intervention." *Journal of Research on Educational Effectiveness* 8(2): 149–168.

Desimone, Laura. 1999. "Linking parent involvement with student achievement: Do race and income matter?" *The Journal of Educational Research* 93(1): 11–30.

Dixson, Adrienne, and Jeannine E. Dingus. 2008. "In search of our mothers' gardens: Black women teachers and professional socialization." *Teachers College Record* 110(4): 805–837.

Donovan, M. Suzanne, and Christopher T. Cross. 2002. *Minority students in special and gifted education.* Washington, DC: National Academy of Education.

Egalite, Anna J., Brian Kisida, and Marcus A. Winters. 2015. "Representation in the classroom: The effect of own-race teachers on student achievement." *Economics of Education Review* 45: 44–52.

Ehrenberg, Ronald G., Daniel D. Goldhaber, and Dominic J. Brewer. 1995. "Do teachers' race, gender, and ethnicity matter? Evidence from the National Educational Longitudinal Study of 1988." *Industrial and Labor Relations Review* 48(3): 547–561.

Erickson, Frederick. 1986. "Culture difference and science education." *The Urban Review* 18(2): 117–124.

Farkas, George, Robert P. Grobe, Daniel Sheehan, and Yuan Shuan. 1990. "Cultural resources and school success: Gender, ethnicity, and poverty groups within an urban school district." *American Sociological Review* 55(1): 127–142.

Ferguson, Ronald F. 1998. "Can schools narrow the black-white test score gap?" In *The Black-White test score gap*, edited by C. Jencks and M. Phillips (pp. 318–374). Washington, DC: Brookings Institution Press.

Foster, Michele. 1993. "Educating for competence in community and culture: Exploring the views of exemplary African-American teachers." *Urban Education* 27 (4): 370–394.

Fuller, Mary Lou. 1992. "Teacher education programs and increasing minority school populations: An educational mismatch." In *Research and multicultural education: From the margins to the mainstream*, edited by Carl A. Grant (pp. 184–200). Washington, DC: The Farmer Press.

Gershenson, Seth, Cassandra M. D. Hart, Constance A. Lindsay, and Nicholas W. Papageorge. 2017. "The long-run impacts of same-race teachers." IZA Discussion Papers, No. 10630. Bonn: Institute of Labor Economics.

Gershenson, Seth, Stephen B. Holt, and Nicholas W. Papageorge. 2016. "Who believes in me? The effect of student–teacher demographic match on teacher expectations." *Economics of Education Review* 52: 209–224.

Goldhaber, Dan, and Michael Hansen. 2010. "Race, gender, and teacher testing: How informative a tool is teacher licensure testing?" *American Educational Research Journal* 47(1): 218–251.

Grissom, Jason A. 2011. "Can good principals keep teachers in disadvantaged schools? Linking principal effectiveness to teacher satisfaction and turnover in hard-to-staff environments." *Teachers College Record* 113(11): 2552–2585.

Grissom, Jason A., S. Kabourek, and J. W. Kramer. 2020. "Exposure to same-race or same-ethnicity teachers and advanced math course-taking in high school: Evidence from a diverse urban district." *Teachers College Record.*

Grissom, Jason A., and Lael R. Keiser. 2011. "A supervisor like me: Race, representation, and the satisfaction and turnover decisions of public sector employees." *Journal of Policy Analysis and Management* 30(3): 557–580.

Grissom, Jason A., Emily C. Kern, and Luis A. Rodriguez. 2015. "The 'representative bureaucracy' in education: Educator workforce diversity, policy outputs, and outcomes for disadvantaged students." *Educational Researcher* 44(3): 185–192.

Grissom, Jason A., Hajime Mitani, and Richard S. L. Blissett. 2017. "Principal licensure exams and future job performance: Evidence from the School Leaders Licensure Assessment." *Educational Evaluation and Policy Analysis* 39(2): 248–280.

Grissom, Jason A., Jill Nicholson-Crotty, and Sean Nicholson-Crotty. 2009. "Race, region, and representative bureaucracy." *Public Administration Review* 69(5): 911–919.

Grissom, Jason A., and Christopher Redding. 2016. "Discretion and disproportionality: Explaining the underrepresentation of high-achieving students of color in gifted programs." *AERA Open* 2(1): 1–25.

Grissom, Jason A., Luis A. Rodriguez, and Emily C. Kern. 2017. "Teacher and principal diversity and the representation of students of color in gifted programs: Evidence from national data." *The Elementary School Journal* 117(3): 396–422.

Grissom, Jason A., Samantha L. Viano, and Jennifer L. Selin. 2016. "Understanding employee turnover in the public sector: Insights from research on teacher mobility." *Public Administration Review* 76(2): 241–251.

Hollins, Etta Ruth. 1982. "The Marva Collins story revisited: Implications for regular classroom instruction." *Journal of Teacher Education* 33(1): 37–40.

Holt, Stephen B., and Seth Gershenson. 2015. "The impact of teacher demographic representation on student attendance and suspensions." IZA Discussion Papers, No. 9554, Bonn: Institute for the Study of Labor.

Ingersoll, Richard M., and R. Connor. 2009. "What the national data tell us about minority and Black teacher turnover." Paper presented at the Annual Meeting of the American Educational Research Association, San Diego, CA, April.

Ingersoll, Richard M., and Henry May. 2011. "The minority teacher shortage: Fact or fable?" *Phi Delta Kappan* 93(1): 62–65.

Ingersoll, Richard M. and Henry May. 2016. *Minority teacher recruitment, employment, and retention: 1987 to 2013.* Palo Alto, CA: Learning Policy Institute.

Irvine, Jacqueline Jordan. 1988. "An analysis of the problem of disappearing Black educators." *Elementary School Journal* 88(5): 503–513.

Irvine, Jacqueline Jordan. 1989. "Beyond role models: An examination of cultural influences on the pedagogical perspectives of Black teachers." *Peabody Journal of Education* 66(4): 51–63.

Irvine, Jacqueline Jordan. 1990. *Black students and school failure.* Westport, CT: Praeger.

Johnson, Lisa S. 2008. "What it takes to be a real role model: Perspectives from new teachers of color and their students." Paper presented at the Annual Meeting of the American Education Research Association,New York City.

Kinsler, Josh. 2011. "Understanding the black–white school discipline gap." *Economics of Education Review* 30(6): 1370–1383.

Krislov, Samuel, and David H. Rosenbloom. 1981. *Representative bureaucracy and the American political system.* New York, NY: Praeger.

Ladd, Helen F. 2011. "Teachers' perceptions of their working conditions: How predictive of planned and actual teacher movement?" *Educational Evaluation and Policy Analysis* 33(2): 235–261.

LaRocque, Michelle, Ira Kleiman, and Sharon M. Darling. 2011. "Parental involvement: The missing link in school achievement." *Preventing School Failure* 55(3): 115–122.

Lim, Hong-Hai. 2006. "Representative bureaucracy: Rethinking substantive effects and active representation." *Public Administration Review* 66(2): 193–204.

Lindsay, Constance A., and Cassandra M. D. Hart. 2017. "Exposure to same-race teachers and student disciplinary outcomes for black students in North Carolina." *Educational Evaluation and Policy Analysis* 39(3): 485–510.

Lockwood, Penelope, and Ziva Kunda. 1997. "Superstars and me: Predicting the impact of role models on the self." *Journal of Personality and Social Psychology* 73(1): 91–103.

Loeb, Sussana, Linda Darling-Hammond, and John Luczak. 2005. "How teaching conditions predict teacher turnover in California schools." *Peabody Journal of Education* 80(3): 44–70.

Madkins, Tia C. 2011. "The black teacher shortage: A literature review of historical and contemporary trends." *The Journal of Negro Education* 80(3): 417–427.

Markowitz, A., Daphna Bassok, and Jason A. Grissom. 2017. "Teacher-child racial match and parental engagement with Head Start." Paper presented at the annual meeting of the Association for Public Policy Analysis and Management, Chicago, November 2–4.

Meier, Kenneth J. 1993. "Latinos and representative bureaucracy: Testing the Thompson and Henderson hypotheses." *Journal of Public Administration Research and Theory* 3(4): 393–414.

Meier, Kenneth J., and Joseph Stewart Jr. 1992. "The impact of representative bureaucracies: educational systems and public policies." *American Review of Public Administration* 22(3): 157–171.

Morris, Edward W., and Brea L. Perry. 2016. "The punishment gap: School suspension and racial disparities in achievement." *Social Problems* 63(1): 68–86.

Mosher, Frederick C. 1968. *Democracy and the public service.* New York, NY: Oxford University Press.

National Center for Education Statistics. 2017. "Digest of Education Statistics 2016, percentage of 18- to 24-year-olds enrolled in degree-granting postsecondary institutions, by level of institution and sex and race/ethnicity of student: 1970 through 2015." Table 302.60. Available at: https://nces.ed.gov/programs/digest/d16/tables/dt16_302.60.asp

National Collaborative on Diversity in the Teaching Force. 2004. "Assessment of diversity in America's teaching force: A call to action." Washington, DC: National Education Association. Available at: www.nea.org/assets/docs/HE/diversityreport.pdf

National Education Association. 2015. "NEA and teacher recruitment: An overview." Available at: www.nea.org/home/29031.htm

Nettles, Michael T., Linda H. Scatton, Jonathan H. Steinberg, and Linda L. Tyler. 2011. *Performance and passing rate differences of African American and White prospective teachers on Praxis examinations. A joint project of the National Education Association (NEA) and Educational Testing Service (ETS)*. Princeton, NJ: Educational Testing Service.

Nicholson-Crotty, Jill, Jason A. Grissom, and Sean Nicholson-Crotty. 2011. "Bureaucratic representation, distributional equity, and democratic values in the administration of public programs." *The Journal of Politics* 73(2): 582–596.

Nicholson-Crotty, Sean, Jason A. Grissom, Jill Nicholson-Crotty, and Christopher Redding. 2016. "Disentangling the causal mechanisms of representative bureaucracy: Evidence from assignment of students to gifted programs." *Journal of Public Administration Research and Theory* 26(4): 745–757.

Nieto, Sonia. 1999. *The light in their eyes: Creating multicultural learning communities.* New York, NY: Teachers College Press.

Oates, Gary L. St. C. 2003. "Teacher-student racial congruence, teacher perceptions, and test performance." *Social Science Quarterly* 84(3): 508–525.

Osborne, Jason W. 2001. "Testing stereotype threat: Does anxiety explain race and sex differences in achievement?" *Contemporary Educational Psychology* 26(3): 291–310.

Ouazad, Amine. 2014. "Assessed by a teacher like me: Race and teacher assessments." *Education Finance and Policy* 9(3): 334–372.

Page, Scott E. 2008. *The difference: How the power of diversity creates better groups, firms, schools, and societies.* Princeton, NJ: Princeton University Press.

Paluck, Elizabeth Levy, and Donald P. Green. 2009. "Prejudice reduction: What works? A review and assessment of research and practice." *Annual Review of Psychology* 60: 339–367.

Petchauer, E. 2012. "Teacher licensure exams and Black teacher candidates: Toward new theory and promising practice." *The Journal of Negro Education* 81(3): 252–267.

Pettigrew, Thomas F. 1998. "Intergroup contact theory." *Annual Review of Psychology* 49(1): 65–85.

Pettigrew, Thomas F., and Linda R. Tropp. 2000. "Does intergroup contact reduce prejudice? Recent meta-analytic findings." In *Reducing prejudice and discrimination*, edited by Stuart Oskamp (pp. 93–114). Mahwah, NJ: Lawrence Erlbaum Associates.

Pettigrew, Thomas F., and Linda R. Tropp. 2006. "A meta-analytic test of intergroup contact theory." *Journal of Personality and Social Psychology* 90(5): 751.

Pitts, David W. 2005. "Diversity, representation, and performance: Evidence about race and ethnicity in public organizations." *Journal of Public Administration Research and Theory* 15(4): 615–631.

Putman, Hannah, Michael Hansen, Kate Walsh, and Diana Quintero. 2016. *High hopes and harsh realities: The real challenges of building a diverse workforce.* Washington, DC: Brown Center on Education Policy, Brookings Institution.

Richards, Heraldo V., Ayanna F. Brown, and Timothy B. Forde. 2007. "Addressing diversity in schools: Culturally responsive pedagogy." *Teaching Exceptional Children* 39 (3): 64–68.

Richeson, Jennifer A., and Richard J. Nussbaum. 2004. "The impact of multi-culturalism versus color-blindness on racial bias." *Journal of Experimental Social Psychology* 40(3): 417–423.

Ronfeldt, Matthew, Susanna Loeb, and James Wyckoff. 2013. "How teacher turnover harms student achievement." *American Educational Research Journal* 50(1): 4–36.

Rosenthal, Robert, and Lenore Jacobson. 1968. "Pygmalion in the classroom." *The Urban Review* 3(1): 16–20.

Scafidi, Benjamin, David L. Sjoquist, and Todd R. Stinebrickner. 2007. "Race, poverty, and teacher mobility." *Economics of Education Review* 26(2): 145–159.

Schmader, Toni, Michael Johns, and Chad Forbes. 2008. "An integrated process model of stereotype threat effects on performance." *Psychological Review* 115(2): 336–356.

Selden, Sally Coleman. 1997. *The promise of representative bureaucracy: Diversity and responsiveness in a government agency.* Armonk, NY: M.E. Sharpe.

Simon, Nicole S., and Susan Moore Johnson. 2015. "Teacher turnover in high-poverty schools: What we know and can do." *Teachers College Record* 117(3): 1–36.

Steele, Claude M. 1997. "A threat in the air: How stereotypes shape intellectual identity and performance." *American Psychologist* 52(6): 613–629.

Steele, Claude M., and Joshua A. Aronson. 1995. "Stereotype threat and the intellectual test performance of African Americans." *Journal of Personality and Social Psychology* 69(5): 797–811.

Stewart, Joseph, Kenneth J. Meier, and Robert E. England. 1989. "In quest of role models: Change in black teacher representation in urban school districts, 1968–1986." *The Journal of Negro Education* 58(2): 140–152.

Tennessee Department of Education. 2017. "Preparation through partnership: Strengthening Tennessee's new teacher pipeline." Available at: http://tn.gov/assets/entities/education/attachments/Preparation_through_Partnership_report_final_web.pdf

The Century Foundation. 2017. "The benefits of socioeconomically and racially integrated schools and classrooms." Available at: https://tcf.org/content/facts/the-benefits-of-socioeconomically-and-racially-integrated-schools-and-classrooms/

Torres, Judith, Janet Santos, Nancy L. Peck, and Lydia Cortes. 2004. *Minority teacher recruitment, development, and retention.* Providence, RI: Northeast and Islands Regional Educational Laboratory LAB.

Tropp, Linda R., and Thomas F. Pettigrew. 2005. "Relationships between intergroup contact and prejudice among minority and majority status groups." *Psychological Science* 16(12): 951–957.

Uhlenberg, Jeffrey, and Kathleen M. Brown. 2002. "Racial gap in teachers' perceptions of the achievement gap." *Education and Urban Society* 34(4): 493–530.

U.S. Department of Education. 2016. *The state of racial diversity in the educator workforce.* Washington, DC: Office of Planning, Evaluation, and Policy Development, Policy and Program Studies Service.

Villegas, Ana Maria, and Jacqueline Jordan Irvine. 2010. "Diversifying the teaching force: An examination of major arguments." *The Urban Review* 42(3): 175–192.

Villegas, Ana Maria, and Tamara Lucas. 2002. "Preparing culturally responsive teachers: Rethinking the curriculum." *Journal of Teacher Education* 53(1): 20–32.

Vinopal, Katie. 2018. "Understanding individual and organizational level representation: The case of parental involvement in schools." *Journal of Public Administration and Theory* 28(1): 1–15.

Vogl, Katharina, and Franzis Preckel. 2014. "Full-time ability grouping of gifted students: Impacts on social self-concept and school-related attitudes." *Gifted Child Quarterly* 58(1): 51–68.

Wise, Lois Recascino, and Mary Tschirhart. 2000. "Examining empirical evidence on diversity effects: How useful is diversity research for public-sector managers?" *Public Administration Review* 60(5): 386–394.

# 3 Race and Policing in Modern America

*Jill Nicholson-Crotty and Sean Nicholson-Crotty*

## Practitioner Points

- Institutional routines and implicit biases are far more likely to explain disproportionate policing outcomes than overt racism among officers. Such explanations may inform effective solutions to achieve equitable outcomes.
- Policies that discourage the use of weapons and screen recruits for conflict management skills can help departments improve equity, reduce use of force complaints, and improve community relations.
- Higher levels of minority representation help to increase perceived legitimacy of the police and make some institutional reforms more effective but appear to have little direct effect on racial disproportion in arrests or use of force.
- To be effective, increases in minority representation need to be supplemented by policies and procedures that actually change police behavior.

## Introduction

On August 9, 2014, Michael Brown was shot to death by Officer Darren Wilson of the Ferguson Missouri Police Department. The incident initiated days of protest in Ferguson and a heated national debate about the treatment of Black Americans by the police, thanks in part to a number of now well-known specifics. The most salient of these included that Officer Wilson was White, Michael Brown was Black and unarmed, there was a lack of clear evidence that Brown was doing anything that would have justified his killing, videos of Brown's body lying in the street were replayed repeatedly by media around the nation, and a grand jury failed to indict Wilson for Brown's death.[1] In the twelve months following Michael Brown's death, fifteen similar incidents of an unarmed Black person being killed by police or dying in police custody under suspicious circumstances, received national media coverage. Interest groups estimate that more than 100 unarmed Black citizens were actually killed during that period (Mapping Police Violence, 2019).

Perhaps the most concerning thing about recent fatal encounters between police and the public is the *disproportionate* probability that a Black rather than a White citizen died. In 2015, 27 percent of people killed by police in the United States were Black even though only 13.3 percent of the U.S. population was Black. In cases where the person was unarmed, 34 percent of victims were Black. That means that Black Americans are more than 250 percent more likely to be killed by police when they are unarmed than we would expect, given their population proportion.[2]

The disturbing frequency of citizen-police encounters that result in the death of a Black person and the increased media and social media coverage of Black deaths at the hands of the police have dramatically raised the salience of conversations related to race and policing in recent years. Unlike the response to past surveys asking whether the country needs to continue making changes to give Blacks equal rights with Whites, the majority of White Americans now agree that more change is needed (see Lauter and Pearce, 2015). Despite renewed public concern over issues of race and policing following Ferguson, however, what happened there was nothing new. The *Washington Post* recently suggested that unarmed Black Americans were five times more likely to be shot and killed by a police officer than unarmed White Americans (*Washington Post*, 2016). The 1968 Kerner Commission Report on racial violence in American cities argued that policing practices, including the disproportionate use of fatal force on Black citizens, were a significant cause of racial unrest. The report also warned of "ominous consequences" if those practices did not change (Zelizer, 2016, p. 22).

While officer-involved homicides are the most salient and consequential outcome of biased policing, it is also important to remember that evidence of racial inequality is not limited to officer-involved fatalities. Indeed, analyses of data from major urban centers around the nation regularly find evidence of disproportion in numerous outcomes. Black Americans are far more likely to be the target of what are known as investigatory stops, where an individual is questioned based on *suspicion* of wrong-doing. Analyses of data from New York City suggests that Blacks were twice as likely as would be expected, given their population proportion, to be the target of "stop-and-frisk" encounters (New York Civil Liberties Union, 2016). Along with Hispanic drivers, Blacks are 400 percent more likely to be stopped while driving and twice as likely to have their car searched during a stop (ibid.). Black citizens are also significantly overrepresented in arrests for crimes, such as disorderly conduct, where officers have a high degree of discretion regarding whether to arrest. Finally, they are far more likely to be kicked, hit with batons, tased, or subject to other nonfatal use of police force than their population proportion or level of criminal behavior would suggest (Fryer, 2016; Headley and Wright, 2017). A recent Center for Police Equity study, which examined more than a thousand individual incidents, confirms that officers are more likely to use force on Black citizens even after carefully controlling for whether the individual was involved in criminal activity (Center for Police Euity, 2016). As mentioned above, the Kerner Commission Report provides clear evidence that these examples of disproportionality are not new.

The aim of this chapter is not to establish that policing outcomes disproportionately burden Blacks. The evidence that they do is both broad and deep. Our goal is to the review the large literature on race and policing, focusing on public administration scholarship but also including selected work from other disciplines, to better understand the causes of and solutions to this important problem. Given the persistent evidence for and consequences of racial bias in policing, it is perhaps unsurprising that scholars have explored the subject in hundreds of papers published over the last four decades. Only a small handful of these have appeared in journals explicitly focused on public administration or management, but many other studies ask complementary questions.

Even if we cast a wide net regarding work on race and policing, the insights from this long-running line of research are sometimes difficult to discern. Studies have demonstrated that cultural stereotypes affect police decision-making and that Black and White officers approach the job differently, but scholars have not provided evidence of enough systematic racism among police officers to explain commonly observed disproportions. Findings regarding institutional or environmental explanations for biased policing outcomes rest in part on implicit bias or use of stereotypes by officers, but the interaction of these factors and the relative importance of each remain underexplored. Finally, firm conclusions are difficult to reach because the growing body of research exploring changes that police departments can make to reduce racial disproportion in stops, arrests, and violent interactions offers inconsistent and sometimes contradictory findings. Despite these challenges, we believe that a systematic review of these studies will reveal patterns that can help both scholars and practitioners understand and address the issue.

Before moving on, it is important to remember that policing is only one component of a criminal justice system that includes pre-trial release, trial processes, sentencing, corrections, and post-incarceration supervision (Lynch and Sabol, 2004; Mauer and Huling, 1995; Pattillo, Western, and Weiman, 2004; Sampson and Lauritsen, 1997; Snyder and Sickmund, 2006; Spohn, 2000; Walker, Alpert, and Kenney, 2000; Zatz, 1987). Unfortunately, many of these stages are also marked by significant racial disproportion in outcomes. Blacks and Hispanics are more likely to be denied bail than White defendants (Demuth, 2003). They are likely to be sentenced to longer prison terms than Whites, even after taking a large number of case-specific factors into account (Mitchell and MacKenzie, 2004). Finally, Blacks make up 40 percent of the incarcerated population, which is more than three times the size of their share of the general U.S. population.

Despite the important questions raised by these examples of racial disproportion throughout the criminal justice system, we focus our analysis on policing for a number of reasons. First, police interactions are the beginning of the criminal justice pipeline and research suggests that small disparities in treatment here accumulate across the criminal justice system and eventually result in much higher levels of disproportion in later stages (Jaynes and

Williams, 1989). Additionally, from a public administration or management perspective, policing is the stage in the justice process that is most easily manipulated. Pre-trial release and sentencing are often a matter of policy, set by law, or of decision-making by individual judges, and not something that conscientious public administrators can easily impact. Alternatively, some researchers suggest that different hiring criteria, updated training practices, and different standard operating procedures—all things that law enforcement executives and managers can manipulate—can reduce racially biased outcomes. Finally, we focus on policing because this is the area in criminal justice where public administration scholars have focused the majority of their research. Despite our primary interest in policing, however, we will circle back to the research on sentencing and incarceration later in the chapter in order to assess how findings on causes and solutions in the study of race and policing accord with conclusions in other areas.

## Factors Contributing to Racial Disproportion in Policing

The literature on policing has long had three perspectives when attempting to explain police activities, such as the use of force. These have focused on: (1) psychological or individual factors; (2) sociological or situational factors; and (3) organizational or institutional factors (see, for example, Friedrich, 1980; Worden, 1996). The first looks to elements in an individual officer's personality, including racial identity, prejudice, and factors such as impulse control to predict behavior. The second focuses on the social dynamics of police-citizen encounters and the situational cues that officers use to decide how to handle an incident. The third approach suggests that the characteristics of departments, including the police subculture, standard operating procedures, administrative practices, and the larger legal context have a huge impact on policing outcomes.

Where public administration scholars have addressed issues of race and policing, they have often placed their work, intentionally and unintentionally, in one of these three bins. A recently published report, "Toward an Analytical Framework for the Study of Race and Police Violence" promotes a slightly more parsimonious approach, emphasizing behavioral (individual psychological) and institutional factors and makes a reasonably compelling argument that much of the work in public administration can be understood through these lenses (Rivera and Ward, 2017). Nonetheless, because we think all three perspectives can inform public administration scholarship on race and policing, we will explore individual, environmental, and institutional explanations for disproportion in the remainder of this section.

## Is It Just Racism among White Officers?

Surprisingly, many authors do not explicitly identify what they believe to be the primary reason that police outcomes often disproportionately burden Black citizens. Implicitly, however, many studies seem to begin with the assumption that disparities arise because White police officers, who make up the vast majority of most police departments across the country, hold racist or at least prejudiced views of Blacks. This is an intuitively appealing answer to the problem of race and policing for many, both because of its simplicity and because there have been periods in American history when individual members of police forces did systematically hold such views. However, evidence of widespread racist attitudes among White officers is mixed.

Policing as a way for the dominant ethnic group to maintain dominance over minority groups that are seen as dangerous or less deserving is one of the oldest explanations for police behavior (Blalock, 1967; Blumer, 1958; Chambliss, 2011). An important expectation that grows out of this "group threat" theory is that, as the minority group's share of the population increases, the perceived level of threat among members of the majority group goes up, which then motivates aggressive policing strategies as well as greater tolerance for those strategies (Liska, 1992). A further refinement suggests that aggressive police practices and the disproportion they create in outcomes really grow from a fear among members of the majority group that they will become victims of crimes perpetrated by those in the minority (Stults and Baumer, 2007). A number of empirical studies have confirmed that the size of police forces, number of arrests, and racial disproportion in the use of force correlate with larger Black populations and higher levels of Black-on-White crime (Eitle, D'Alessio, and Stolzenberg, 2002; Jacobs and O'Brien, 1998; Legewie, 2016; Liska, 1992; Smith and Holmes, 2014).

While this large and long-running literature has contributed significantly to the assumption that police officers target Black citizens because they fear their propensity for criminal behavior, it does not actually provide conclusive evidence for racism. There is, undoubtedly, some empirical evidence that White officers are more likely to target Black citizens for investigation. As an example, in an analysis of pairs of motorists and officers and controlling for a host of stop-specific variables, Antonovics and Knight (2009) demonstrate that a search of the motorist's car is more likely when the race of the officer differs from the race of the driver. They conclude that this provides evidence for "preference-based" discrimination, rather than statistical disparities in treatment that can arise in organizational level analyses. Close and Mason (2007) and Fagan et al. (2016) find very similar results.

One challenge with these studies, however, is that they are all observational in nature. In other words, they draw conclusions about officer prejudices or "preferences" based on data from stops and searches. While these are very rigorous and high quality analyses, this approach leaves open the possibility that the disproportionate targeting of minority drivers by White officers is not driven by racism, but by some other motivation.[3] There is no arguing that the *outcomes* these authors describe are racially biased, but their analyses do not conclusively demonstrate that those outcomes would change if the majority of police were less racist. In order to look for evidence that speaks to the question of whether there is systematic racism among police, we need to examine studies that assess the *attitudes* of individual officers or their *behavior* in more controlled settings.

Experimental research has offered findings regarding the attitudes of individual officers. For example, in an experimental simulation, Greenwood et al. (2002) found that officers were more likely to mistakenly shoot unarmed Black suspects compared with unarmed White suspects, regardless of officer race. Alternatively, in a far more sophisticated simulation, James et al. (2016) find that officers are *slower* to fire at Black versus White suspects, which confirmed findings from their previous experiments (James, Vila, and Daratha, 2013; James, Klinger, and Vila, 2014). Interestingly, the reduced propensity to use deadly force was observed despite the fact that officers displayed a strong implicit bias associating Black citizens with the likelihood of having a weapon. Finally, Correll et al. (2007) demonstrate that, while citizens require less negative information to prompt the decision to fire at Black versus White suspects (suggesting bias), police officers did not.

Surveys of officers regarding attitudes have revealed differences by officer race, but not always in the assumed direction. Sun (2003) finds that Black officers tend to be less focused on the punitive elements of the police role and are more likely to be supportive of legal restrictions of officer discretion and departmental problem-solving efforts. Research also shows that Black officers are more likely to support and engage in active conflict resolution activities in predominantly Black neighborhoods and are more likely to interact with these communities overall when compared to White officers (Lasley et al., 2011; Sun and Payne, 2004). Research also suggests that Black officers are more likely to believe that suspect race is a determinant of decisions by police to use force (Weisburd et al., 2000). On the other hand, however, Sun and Payne (2004) found that Black officers are more coercive when resolving conflicts among citizens. Similarly, in a study of citizen interactions with the police, Brunson and Gau (2011) found that Black and White officers both treated Black citizens with "disrespect and derision" on numerous occasions.

The evidence of racism among police officers is so mixed perhaps because the question "does disproportion arise because police are racist?" should be rephrased as "do implicit biases among police lead to disproportionate outcomes?" An implicit bias, also known as implicit stereotype, is the *unconscious* association of certain behaviors or attributes to members of a social group. In the case of policing, such biases might cause officers to assume that Black citizens are more likely to have committed a crime, to possess weapons or drugs, to act violently, or to pose a threat to officer safety. The existence of such biases fits well with anecdotes of police behavior, such as the recent shooting of Terence Crutcher in Tulsa, OK. Crutcher's family reported his car had broken down, and he was waiting for someone to pick him up. Police responded to the scene because someone had reported that the broken-down car was blocking the street. While the officer on the ground approached the scene, someone in a police helicopter hovering overhead warned her that the Black individual waiting by the car looked like "a bad dude." The officer ultimately shot Crutcher, who was unarmed and had his hands in the air, claiming she believed him to be under the influence of something and armed (Blau, Morris, and Shoichet, 2017).

While compelling, anecdotes are not conclusive, and implicit bias is hard to demonstrate empirically (hard to measure). Nonetheless, there is a growing body of experimental evidence that suggests such biases exist among police. Work using Implicit Association Tests (IATs), one of the most common methods of measuring implicit bias, finds that officers are much more likely to associate Blacks with weapons and generalized threat (see, for example, Fachner and Carter, 2015; Project Implicit, 2011). Taking another approach, Graham and Lowery (2004) find that subliminally exposing police and parole officers to the word "black" made them more likely to later identify a hypothetical suspect whose race was not identified as guilty and likely to be violent. A recent large-scale review concluded that implicit bias in policing is widespread and "occurs in the absence of explicitly 'racist' thoughts because of well-documented, pernicious stereotypes that operate largely outside of conscious awareness and control" (Spencer, Charbonneau, and Glaser, 2016). However, as the shoot/don't shoot studies cited above indicate, there is no evidence that the existence of implicit bias always leads to racially biased outcomes. Further, recent experimental work demonstrates that the existence and exercise of implicit bias are context-dependent, rather than stable or trait-like (James, 2018).

## What Other Factors Drive Disproportion?

Evidence to date regarding systematically racist views among White police or even the deleterious effects of implicit bias make it difficult to conclude that these are the only explanation for disproportions observed in stops, arrests, and more. To be sure, there are examples of egregiously racist officers, like the case of the Chicago Police Department officer John Burge as highlighted in Pegues (2017). Additionally, the evidence reviewed above does not mean that harmful stereotypes about minority groups and their members among police and the wider public do not contribute to observed disparities. However, it does suggest that overt racism or prejudice among police officers likely cannot solely explain the consistent and persistent racial disproportion in policing outcomes. What else contributes to these disproportionate outcomes? This section will review the literature that examines explanations for racial disproportion in police outcomes that do *not* depend on systematic racism among officers. Specifically, we will look at environmental explanations, which focus heavily on the reaction of police to the challenges of the job and the ways in which these reactions interact with residential segregation in order to place disproportional burdens on Black citizens. Second, we will look at institutional explanations, which focus on the ways in which the incentives of police departments as organizations interact with public policies and cultural stereotypes about different groups to create disparities.

### Environmental Factors

The key takeaway from the literature that takes an environmental or socio-logical perspective on policing is that it is context, not race, that determines the behavior of officers toward citizens. An important corollary to that perspective, however, is that residential segregation and the characteristics of neighborhoods with a high proportion of minority citizens lead to racial disproportion in policing outcomes.

Environmental explanations draw heavily on research regarding the ways in which police perceive other citizens and the ways in which they respond to events in their environment. Theories about police culture often start by recog-nizing that officers are asked to do a job that involves significant danger and risk of personal injury and that they interact with the portion of the population that is engaged in criminal behavior to a far greater degree than any other profession (McLaughlin, 2007; Westley, 1970). Furthermore, police officers are trained to be constantly aware of threats to their safety (Brown, 1981; Crank, 1997), which leads to suspicion and social isolation. Police officers consider themselves to be part of a specific social and occupational group isolated from the remainder of society who cannot understand what they face, which ultimately results in an "us-versus-them" attitude (Paoline, 2003; Westley, 1970).

Extreme vigilance regarding danger and high levels of distrust among police contribute to "community violence" explanations for aggressive policing practices. The community violence approach is a sociological perspective which proposes that police become more violent when operating in an envir-onment where considerable violence occurs. Some scholars suggest that police come to view violence as an acceptable means of conflict resolution when faced with citizens who also hold this view (Kania and Mackey, 1977). Others argue that the presence of violence simply heightens the objective threat in the environment which leads police to act more aggressively (Fyfe, 1980; Jacobs and O'Brien, 1998; Klinger et al., 2016).

In the United States, minority groups are significantly more likely to live in high poverty neighborhoods, where violent crime rates are higher, This means these groups are more likely to encounter police who perceive a high level of threat to themselves and their authority (Alexander, 2010). Policing tactics under these circumstances are likely to be more aggressive and punitive; at the same time, minority citizens in these areas are less trustful of and willing to cooperate with the police because of previous negative interactions. Social scientists argue that this combination can lead to higher levels of arrests of minority citizens and an increase in violent encounters between police and minority citizens, even in the absence of overt racism (Holmes and Smith, 2008).

Recent work on race and policing, including some by public administration scholars, has tested the community violence hypothesis but has failed to find evidence that violent crime rates correlate with police-involved homicides of Black citizens (Legewie and Fagan, 2016; Nicholson-Crotty, Nicholson-Crotty, and Fernandez, 2017). Nonetheless, work by scholars focused on questions of racial profiling has demonstrated that neighborhood context influences the types of drivers identified by officers as suspicious, which has important implications for the decision to stop a driver and the outcomes of interactions with citizens.

### Institutional and Organizational Explanations

A final category of study suggests that the characteristics of police departments, rather than individual officers, are the best predictors of policing outcomes. This perspective claims that departments set the tenor of officer behavior through the systems of incentives and disincentives they design and the content and application of rules and operating procedures (see, for example, Wilson, 1968).[4] In one of the older theories about the ways in which police departments are organized, Packer (1966) argues that departments adopt either a crime control perspective, where the end goal of reducing crime justifies a wide variety of means for reaching that goal, or a due process approach, where the rights and liberties of citizens are of paramount concern. Most important for our purposes, Packer suggests that law enforcement organizations are very good at communicating and reinforcing these norms in individual police officers. As a substantive example of this type of organizational influence, the Christopher Commission's report (ICLAPD, 1991) following the Rodney King beating blamed the high rate of violent confrontations between the Los Angeles Police Department and citizens on the fact that the department embraced a "hard-nosed" approach to law enforcement and incentivized officers to adopt "assertive" practices when dealing with the public.

Recent work by public administration scholars has put organizational factors at the center of explanations for racially biased policing outcomes, though it is important to note that widely shared cultural prejudices against certain groups often interact with organizational factors in these explanations. For example, Epp et al. (2014) consider the well-established racial disproportion in traffic stops through an explicitly institutional perspective rather than individual one. They suggest that biased outcomes arise because of the reliance on investigatory stops, where suspicion rather than observation of wrong-doing is the primary motivation for the encounter, and demonstrate that there is widespread support in the law enforcement community for these stops as a method of fighting crime; such support translates to widespread diffusion of the policies across departments, where procedures and routines are increasingly standardized. The practice is supported as constitutional following cases like *Whren v. U.S.* 517 U.S. 806 (1996)[5] and zealously incorporated into training methods and materials. As a result, investigatory stops become institutionalized as an indispensable method for achieving organizational goals.

Once enshrined as "professional policing's most 'effective crime fighting tool'" (George, 2003, as quoted in Epp, Maynard-Moody, and Haider-Markel, 2017), the adoption and implementation of investigatory stops can be driven by implicit racial stereotypes about criminality. Because these types of interventions require officers to make quick decisions about who to stop based on very incomplete information, those officers are more likely to fall back on "automatic mental processes," such as stereotypes (Blair, 2001, as cited in Epp, Maynard-Moody, and Haider-Markel, 2014). Well-documented evidence shows that negative stereotypes of Blacks as violent and prone to criminality persist among a surprisingly large swath of Americans (Bobo, 2004), and this heuristic can have a considerable influence on policing outcomes when organizations encourage practices such as investigatory stops. Further, scholars are also careful to acknowledge that this explanation does not preclude the possibility that some officers are deliberately racist in their decisions regarding who to stop but that disparities resulting from investigatory stops are still likely to arise even in the absence of systematic racism. Epp, Maynard-Moody, and Haider-Markel's (2014) account of the interaction between individual bias and institutional routines is consistent with broader social-psychological arguments about the ways in which racial discrimination can persist in modern societies, even in the absence of overt prejudice (see Dovidio et al., 1997).

Epp, Maynard-Moody, and Haider-Markel's (2014) explanation of the ways in which organizational practices create disproportionate outcomes, even in the absence of overt racism, also shares important similarities with other public administration scholarship on "institutional racism" in policing. As an example, it overlaps in important ways with Rivera and Ward's (2017) argument that racial profiling by police is best understood as an institutional phenomenon and simply one of many areas in modern service delivery where, whether intentionally or unintentionally, barriers and procedures which disadvantage ethnic minority groups are supported and maintained. Approaching the issue from the perspective of organizational socialization, Oberfield (2010; 2014) argues convincingly that rule abidance among persons who select into law enforcement occupations, combined with training and organizational norms that are at least implicitly accepting of biased outcomes in pursuit of organizational goals, can lead to racially disproportionate outcomes, regardless of the existence of individual racism.

In addition to organizational practices and norms, public administration scholars have begun to explore the ways in which technological changes in policing, and public service delivery more generally, can lead to institutionally driven disparities in outcomes. As an example, Eterno et al. (2017) examine the ways in which the adoption of CompStat by New York City, which measured and reported police performance with metrics, such as arrests and summons issued, influenced the use of investigatory techniques like "stop and frisk." The authors surveyed retired officers in order to understand how CompStat changed the incentives of officers on the street. The results are unsurprising to students of performance measurement and management but nonetheless instructive. Only 5 percent of high-ranking officers who worked before CompStat was implemented reported feeling pressure to increase investigatory stops. After implementation, this increased to 28 percent. The results were similar for pressure to produce higher arrest rates and more summonses. A survey of line officers produced almost identical results with much higher percentages reporting pressure to make more stops and arrests. Institutional pressure to meet investigatory stop quotas, combined with implicit stereotypes and lower political costs for aggressive policing in minority neighborhoods, help to explain why racial disproportion in these types of interactions exploded during the CompStat period.

The institutional approach used by scholars in public administration also accords well with similar explanations emerging from other academic disciplines. For more than two decades sociologists and legal scholars have tracked the development of a suite of techniques often classified under the heading of "New Policing." These are driven by an expressed desire on the part of departments to engage in more order maintenance policing and include aggressive suppression of minor crimes, increased use of investigatory stops to identify criminal behavior, and concentration of police resources in the highest crime neighborhoods (see, for example, Heymann 2000; Livingston, 1997). While these strategies are, on their face, racially neutral, research consistently demonstrates that they produce biased outcomes by exposing minority citizens, who live disproportionately in the neighborhoods targeted by order maintenance strategies, to more policing than an objective assessment of the probability of criminal activity would suggest is appropriate (Fagan et al., 2016). This type of "over-policing," particularly when concentrated in minority neighborhoods, can lead to disproportions in violent encounters with police, which are best predicted by simply encountering police in the first place (Fryer, 2016; Goff et al., 2016; Miller et al., 2017).

### What Are the Proposed Solutions to Reducing Disproportion?

The scholarship reviewed thus far has focused primarily on the explanations for racial disproportion in policing outcomes. However, there has also been a great deal of work, particularly in public administration, on potential solutions to the disproportions observed in policing outcomes. Sorting the literature cleanly into those that study causes or offer solutions is difficult and somewhat misleading, given that many studies are interested in both questions. Nonetheless, thinking about existing research in this way helps to identify patterns of successes or failures among proposed fixes for racial disproportion, which is one of the major points of this chapter. As such, the remainder of this section will review work on the two areas where public administration scholars have focused their attention: representational and general procedural solutions.

### Representation

The most common potential solution to issues of race and policing in public administration literature is through representation. This work is grounded in the broader theory of representative bureaucracy which has long argued that there are significant advantages to having bureaucracies that share demographic characteristics with the clients they serve (Kingsley, 1944; Meier and Nigro, 1976; Mosher, 1968). The specific nature of these advantages depends on which of the three types of representation is present in a particular situation. These include passive or demographic representation, which is simply that proportions of a group within the organization match those in the population; active representation, conceived of as administrative decisions, actions, and outputs that benefit members of the same group; and symbolic representation, where citizens view public organizations and the authority they exercise as more legitimate because those organizations look or act as representative of their interests. Even work from scholars in other disciplines that does not explicitly draw on representative bureaucracy theory tends to highlight these three different types of representation. Each are reviewed below.

One of the things that critics noted quickly after the death of Michael Brown was that while 67 percent of the population of Ferguson, MO, was Black, only 5.6 percent of the police force was Black. Far-reaching journalistic analysis confirmed that Blacks were significantly underrepresented in most police departments across the nation (Ashkenas and Park, 2015). The President's Task Force on 21st Century Policing, created by President Obama in response to the unrest in Ferguson, reached the same conclusion, arguing that, "The Federal Government should ... help communities diversify law enforcement departments to reflect the demographics of the community." A year later, the Civil Rights Division at the Department of Justice (DOJ) and the Equal Employment Opportunity Commission launched Advancing Diversity in Law Enforcement, an initiative designed to help achieve this goal.

While there is a large literature on passive representation in several types of bureaucratic organizations (see Kellough, 1990; Nachmias and Rosenbloom, 1973), there is surprisingly little work that focuses on policing. What studies there are have generally uncovered evidence of underrepresentation for minorities in the departments they examined (Cayer and Sigelman, 1980; Stokes and Scott, 1996). However, these studies lack a careful assessment of *how* representation should be conceived or what factors consistently predict the representativeness of police departments.[6] The Advancing Diversity in Law Enforcement initiative speculated about several plausible causes of under-representation, including distrust of law enforcement among potential minority applicants, screening and testing procedures that disadvantage minority appli-cants, and organizational requirements or norms such as residency restrictions and strong unions but left these suppositions untested.

Recently, Kennedy et al. (2017), in providing the most comprehensive treatment of passive racial representation in law enforcement organizations to date, undertook a two-part analysis that first examines trends in minority representation over a 20-year period in departments across the nation and then tests hypotheses about the predictors of those levels of representation. Their results show that minority representation in police organizations *decreased* significantly between 1993 and 2013. The decrease was especially steep in large cities and particularly acute for Blacks relative to other minority groups. The authors show that the decline in representation correlates with significant population growth, and was most pronounced in areas that experienced that growth. As such, it is not that fewer total Blacks are working as police officers but rather that the number doing so is not keeping pace with population growth.

Kennedy et al. also consider a number of factors that can explain variation in the degree of passive representation across jurisdictions. Specifically, they test the degree to which minority representation among local political leaders, residency requirements imposed on potential officers, and whether officers are unionized influence the representativeness of the force. In an analysis of large cities, they find that the mayor's racial identity is associated with an increase in the representation of that group in the police force. Residency requirements are correlated with improved representativeness overall, but the impact is driven by changes in the number of White, Hispanic, and Asian officers. Residency requirements are not associated with an increase in Black representation. Union presence has the opposite effect, with changes again driven by increases in Whites and Hispanics, rather than African Americans.

Next, the hypothesized relationship between passive and active representation rests on several key assumptions (Meier and Nigro, 1976). First, members of a social group undergo similar socialization experiences that set them apart from members of other groups. Second, socialization experiences strongly influence attitudes, which means that members share attitudes that are distinct from those of members of other social groups. Finally, attitudes influence behavior. Thus, a member of a social group who becomes a bureaucrat with discretionary authority will be inclined to act in ways that reflect and advance the interests of his or her social group. Whether those actions occur and are meaningful is contingent on certain preconditions being met (Keiser et al., 2002; Meier, 1993; Meier and Nicholson-Crotty, 2006; Meier and Stewart, 1992; Thompson, 1976). These include that bureaucrats should have discretion when implementing policies and that the policies bureaucrats implement should be salient or meaningful to the demographic group in question, which means that the issue bureaucrats are dealing with has clear and direct implications for them and members of their social group. Finally, the decisions and actions of bureaucrats must be able to directly affect the demographic group in question.

All of these conditions are met in the case of policing and racial disproportion in police outcomes, which is why public administration scholars routinely hypothesize that an increase in minority representation will lead to improved outcomes for historically underserved groups. The potential benefits of representation in policing have also been carefully delineated by scholars of other disciplines; criminologists, sociologists, economists, and political scientists have all suggested that more minority officers should reduce racial disproportion in policing outcomes.

Unfortunately, the findings from this body of work have been decidedly mixed, regardless of the outcome measured. In the case of arrest behavior, some studies suggest that Black officers may treat Black citizens more harshly (Brown and Frank, 2006; Thompson, 1976) while others find no correlation between race congruence and officer behavior (Holmes and Smith, 2008). Similarly, in the case of racial profiling, Antonovics and Knight (2009) find that White officers are more likely to stop and search Black motorists while Wilkins and Williams (2008) find that a higher proportion of Black officers makes Black motorists more likely to be profiled. The authors suggest that the unique police culture and the effectiveness of departments in socializing members to organizational norms likely interfere with the translation of demographic representation into bureaucratic actions that benefit minority groups. Recent work by Baumgartner et al. (2017) finds that Black drivers are 75 percent more likely to be searched than Whites, 5 percent less likely to be ticketed, and 43 percent more likely to be arrested. In jurisdictions where there are higher levels of Black political power, Baumgartner et al. (ibid.) find that Black motorists receive more tickets and are subject to more investigatory stops.

In a recent study of use of force complaints against police, Hong (2017) finds that increased representation of ethnic minorities does not reduce the rate of complaints among all minority citizens but does result in a decreased rate of complaints by Black citizens.[7] In analyzing individual level data from two major cities, Headley and Wright (2017) find that White officers have an increased likelihood of using more severe force on Black citizens relative to when the race of the officer and the citizen match.

Research on representation and fatal encounters with police have similarly reached contradictory conclusions. Nicholson-Crotty et al. (2017) return to work that suggests that given the high degree of socialization in police departments, the concept of critical mass may offer the most accurate model of the passive-to-active representation process in these organizations. Critical mass can be viewed as an extension of representative bureaucracy theory, which suggests that individuals will adhere closely to organizational rather than be active advocates for their preferences until people who share their characteristics and beliefs become a sufficiently large proportion of organizational members (see Henderson, 1979; Kanter, 1976; Meier, Wrinkle, and Polinard, 1999; Thompson, 1976). Examining police-involved homicides of Black citizens in large cities, Nicholson-Crotty et al. (2017) find some evidence for this assertion. The rate of Black citizens killed is positively associated with the percentage of Black officers until Black officers reach approximately 42 percent of the organization, at which point the positive linkage begins to decline. The apparent reduction is not statistically significant, however; this is likely because the number of departments consisting of at least 42 percent Black officers is small. In analyses of a different data source, the authors see a similar relationship between percentage of Black officers and Black citizens' deaths, but the relationship never reaches statistical significance.

Other very recent work on officer race and police-involved homicides has also reached conditional conclusions. Legewie and Fagan (2016) find that an increase in the percentage of officers who are Black does not have a direct impact on the rate of Black citizens killed by police. They do show, however, that representation *moderates* other factors that contribute to fatal encounters. Specifically, they show that the impact of the Black-on-White homicide rate, which the authors use as a proxy for group threat theory (see discussion above), is reduced as the percentage of the force that is Black increases.

The mixed and conditional results on active representation cited above accord well with conclusions from research in criminology which has asked similar questions about officer race and policing outcomes. Bradbury and Kellough's (2011) review of this literature uncovered evidence supporting expectations related to active representation. For example, Close and Mason (2006; 2007) and Gilliard-Matthews, Kowalski, and Lundman (2008) found minority officers treated minority drivers more favorably compared to White officers. However, they also point to other policing studies (e.g., Anbarci and Lee, 2008; Brown and Frank, 2006) where the results showed minority officers were less lenient toward minorities and more likely to arrest them.

Beyond passive and active representation, we also consider symbolic representation. One of the potential benefits of representation is not that it changes the behavior of government actors, but rather that it changes the perceptions of citizens regarding those actors. In the case of policing, the key question relates to how Black officers change the views of the Black community regarding police and the criminal justice system more broadly. To answer this question, we first need a baseline for the community's perceptions. Unfortunately, the findings from this research have been tremendously mixed. Some research in criminal justice has found that Black communities generally have a positive perception of the police but note that it is lower than that of White citizens (Alpert and Dunham, 1988). Other work has argued, however, that the race of the citizen is not significantly related to confidence in the police when controlling for other characteristics such as the level of crime in a neighborhood, and still other research suggests that Black communities generally perceive the criminal justice system as unfair and the application of laws as inequitable.

Work which explores whether more Black officers change those perceptions or if race match in individual interactions with police matters also remains inconclusive. In criminal justice, older work found a positive relationship between force diversity and citizen attitudes (Skogan, 1979), but newer scholarship suggests a more complicated picture in which attitudes of middle-class Blacks might be positively related to representation while those of lower socioeconomic status tend to hold negative views of police officers regardless of race. The most recent work by criminal justice scholars on the subject also finds a null or negative association between officer race and citizen attitudes, concluding that "shared racial background fails to guarantee positive interactions between police and citizens and that Black citizens can in fact be very dissatisfied with Black officers" (Brunson and Gau, 2011).

Conclusions from public administration reflect a similar lack of consistency. Theobald and Haider-Markel (2008) find that, in the context of specific interactions with Black officers, Black citizens are more likely to perceive police actions as legitimate if the officer is Black or if there is at least a Black officer present. Interestingly, the authors found that White citizens viewed interactions as more legitimate when the police officer shared their race. Alternatively, Epp et al. (2014) do not find a significant impact for officer race on the perceptions of Black citizens stopped by police.

### Generalized Benefits of Diversity

A portion of research on police force diversity has investigated whether increasing passive minority representation reduces overall levels of violent encounters with citizens of any race. This is important from a representation perspective because recent research shows that the killing of White citizens is the best predictor of fatal encounters with Black citizens (Nicholson-Crotty, Nicholson-Crotty, and Fernandez, 2017). Smith (2003) was the first paper to examine the impact of police force demographics on total fatal encounters and found that there was not a significant correlation between the racial composition of the police force and the number of reported killings of felons. Several studies have confirmed the finding that the level of minority officers does not correlate with a reduction in the killing of citizens (see, for example, Holmes and Smith, 2008; Smith and Holmes, 2014). Alternatively, some work has shown that total use of lethal force increases with Black officer representation (Kennedy et al., 2017. Ochs, 2011) while other studies find that White officers are more likely to use deadly force than their Black or Hispanic counterparts (e.g., McElvain and Kposowa, 2008).

Scholars have also investigated whether passive representation can make departments more likely to change the norms and institutions that contribute to bias. This work might be thought of as assessing the indirect, rather than direct, effect of representation. Here the results are more consistently encouraging. Research suggests that increased diversity can make law enforcement agencies more open to reform, more willing to initiate cultural and systemic changes, and more responsive to the residents they serve. Kennedy et al. (2017) find that more representative departments are more likely to have written policies regarding citizen complaints and to have adopted civilian review boards.

## Influence of Policies

While research has devoted more attention to investigating the relationship between force demographics and racial disproportion in policing outcomes, a number of scholars have also explored the impact of department policies and procedures. This line of research extends from a theoretical argument that suggests that the behavior of police can and should be controlled by explicit organizational rules that provide guidance to officers and set boundaries on the use of their discretion (Wilson, 1968). Empirical tests of this assertion have at times been mixed, but a number of studies have suggested that policy and procedural changes can have a significant impact on disproportion. Work in this area has, broadly speaking, examined policies restricting officer discretion and/or requiring certain training for officers as well as recruitment and screening procedures used by departments.

Research on policies limiting officer discretion have typically focused on police use of force. This work has often not focused explicitly on racial bias in these encounters though, as noted before, departments that are more aggressive generally are also those that exhibit higher levels of disproportion. Though perhaps outdated, Fyfe (1982) found some evidence that the city of Memphis was able to limit police-involved shootings by implementing standard operating procedures for the use of weapons. Subsequent research confirmed this result for policies specifically related to firearm use or for the level of discretion afforded officers more generally (Walker, 1993; Worden, 1996).

The most recent work by public administration scholars finds that policies which require a report to be filed each time an officer draws a weapon as well as when the weapon is fired, are associated with lower rates of police-involved gun deaths (Jennings and Rubado, 2017). The authors speculate that discouraging officers from drawing their weapon (via the cost of filing paperwork) means reduced opportunities for firing it and, by extension, a decline in fatal encounters. It is important to note, however, that Jennings and Rubado do not find an effect for community policing training on police-involved homicides despite expectations that they should help accomplish this goal through improved police/community relations (Cordner, 2014).

Finally, two papers have found that policies requiring more in-service or field training correlate positively with both the total number of police-involved homicides and the number involving Black citizens (Bailey, 1990; Smith, 2004). Smith (2004) notes that this may be because field training for police is often focused not on avoiding violent confrontations but on how to survive and prevail when one arises (see also Fyfe, 1986).

The body of work on the impact of officer recruitment and screening has found somewhat more consistent evidence that these policies can reduce police violence and racial disproportion in use of force and other outcomes. Requiring a higher level of education among recruits has been shown to correlate with lower use of force rates in a number of studies (Terrill and Mastrofski, 2002; Worden, 1996), though Smith (2004) fails to confirm this relationship in his larger sample of cities. Current research by public administration scholars also suggests that other screening criteria have a significant impact on policing outcomes. Nicholson-Crotty et al. (2017) analyzed more than 500 police departments between 2002 and 2008 and found that screening recruits for conflict management skills reduced racial disproportion in discretionary arrests, particularly in departments that are more representative of the communities they serve. The analyses also suggest that conflict management screening, when combined with recruit screening for sensitivity to diverse cultures, reduces the lethal use of force by police. The authors suggest that these new types of "community relations" screenings can help departments overcome problems that lead to overly aggressive and discriminatory policing. They also suggest that these are the same problems that law enforcement organizations are hoping to address by hiring more minority officers.

## What Have We Learned and What's Next?

We began with the assertion that it is sometimes difficult to discern definitive patterns in the very large literature on race and policing, both by public administration scholars and those from other disciplines. We believe, however, that the admittedly incomplete review of that literature presented above does permit reasonable inference regarding which causes of and solutions to racial disparity in policing outcomes are most plausible. It also suggests that further research in some areas is needed to help more precisely and confidently identify what works.

The first thing that stands out is that overt racism among White police, who make up the vast majority of officers in most departments, is probably not the primary source of disparities in policing outcomes. There are undoubtedly examples of individual police who are racist in the classic sense—that is who intentionally discriminate against Black citizens or believe that Blacks are inherently inferior to Whites. There is no evidence, however, that such officers exist in large enough numbers to explain observed racial disproportionality in stops, arrests, and lethal encounters. It is important to remember, however, that some of the best research on police attitudes shows that they do hold stereotypes of Blacks similar to those held by the American public, and these stereotypes associate Blacks with violence and criminality.

These implicit biases are often an important component of institutional explanations for racial disproportion in policing outcomes. An institutional lens suggests that disparities worsen when organizations embrace routines and procedures that accentuate, rather than moderate, the role of implicit biases and stereotypes in officer decision-making. Practices such as investigatory stops, which encourage officers to act on suspicions rather than observed wrong-doing; gang sweeps, in which the neighborhood and its demographic composition are substituted for individual level probable cause; or performance measurement strategies that reward high numbers of arrests offer the most compelling explanation for the widespread racial disparities in encounters between police and citizens. Moreover, the exposure model suggests that racial disproportion in those encounters is one of the best predictors of disproportion in the use of force by and fatal encounters with police; more contacts and lower levels of trust increase the likelihood that interactions between police and Black citizens will end in violence.

This story of institutional accretion both contributes to and accords well with explanations for racial bias in the rest of the criminal justice system. Generally speaking, that literature has concluded that overt discrimination does occasionally occur and that racial stereotypes continue to inform the decision-making of key actors in the process. It also suggests, however, that the major factor in producing disparities is that these stereotypes inform and are magnified by institutionalized practices such as the pretrial release system, the public defender system, and drug sentencing guidelines, all of which then combine to create meaningful differences in the way Black and White citizens are treated in the criminal justice system. These differences in treatment accumulate across the criminal justice system and, over time, result in higher levels of racial disparity in outcomes than can be explained by criminality or widespread racism (Rosich, 2007; Sampson and Laurestin, 1997).

Fixes for the institutional contributors to racial disproportion are difficult to identify. Epp et al. (2014), among others, suggest that police need to abandon investigatory techniques, only stopping or searching citizens when they actually observe wrong-doing. Even Walker (1999) a strong advocate of "order maintenance" policing, eventually suggested that stops on the basis of suspicion, especially when race was used as a proxy for that suspicion, should be curtailed. These authors admit, however, that this is unlikely to occur as these techniques are widely considered as effective by police organizations and have diffused widely among them. An alternative might be procedural changes that can offset the negative consequences of bias in organizations. One of the most widely touted of these is community policing, though research reviewed here suggests that the empirical evidence for these suppositions is somewhat limited. Nonetheless, a great deal more research is necessary to determine if community policing strategies can indeed reduce racial disproportion because of the myriad techniques and approaches that fall under that conceptual umbrella. For example, a small number of departments have made participation in community problem-solving partnerships part of their performance evaluation systems and, given widespread evidence that people focus on what is being measured, this may be a good place to see reductions in biased outcomes. More research is also needed because of widespread evidence that even departments that loudly pledge their support for the community approach often make important decisions based on other, less race-neutral, criteria (Beckett, Nyrop, and Pfingst, 2006).

There are other policy solutions, however, which do seem to show promise of at least preventing interactions between police and Black citizens from deteriorating into violent or fatal encounters. In the parlance of drug policy, these might be considered "harm reduction" strategies. For example, a small number of studies have shown that policies which discourage officers from using their weapons or carefully delineate the conditions under which they do so can reduce both overall levels of violence and racial disparities in those incidents. Similarly, recent work suggests that screening recruits for conflict resolution skills can also reduce levels of violence and even racial disproportion in arrests. Moving forward, researchers should examine the impact of more potential harm reduction practices such as body cameras or civilian review boards.

Additionally, if we believe that institutional factors that accentuate the role of implicit bias in decision-making are unlikely to disappear, then we need a better understanding of the degree to which careful recruit screening can reduce negative stereotypes of Black citizens among police. Recent work suggests that cultural sensitivity screening, when combined with conflict management screening, can reduce lethal use of force by police. Future research should test whether other "community relations" screenings, including those for volunteering/community service history or proficiency in a second language, can reduce racial disparity in outcomes. Additionally, scholars should empirically test for the effectiveness of training programs designed to reduce implicit bias among officers. Scholars, the U.S. Department of Justice, and the officers who participate in the trainings all suggest that they can be a powerful tool to raise awareness, and thereby reduce the influence, of implicit racial bias and stereotypes (see Kahn and Martin, 2016; Smith, 2015). To date, however, research has not determined whether this type of training actually decreases disproportions in outcomes.

Of course, the most common solution offered for reducing implicit racial bias and overt racism among police is increasing the proportion of minority officers. Work on police attitudes reveals important differences between Black and White officers in terms of their perceptions of minority citizens, levels of community engagement, and perceived role. Further, empirical work suggests that policy changes intended to overcome institutionalized practices that contribute to biased outcomes are more impactful in more representative departments, likely because the levels of implicit bias among officers has been reduced.

For this and other reasons, the literature suggests that it would be a mistake to dismiss representation as a solution to the problem of racial disproportion in policing outcomes, despite the inconsistent results regarding a direct influence. To this point, it is important to remember that representational approaches to race and policing rest on assumptions that Black officers view Black citizens differently than their White peers *and* that more representative organizations behave differently toward and have different relationships with the communities they police. Thus, more representative departments may produce fewer racial disparities because of reduced officer biases, differing environmental conditions and reactions to those conditions, or because they moderate the impact of institutionalized practices that contribute to bias.

There is some evidence that suggests these potential mechanisms are at work. For example, the findings on symbolic representation in policing suggest that increased force diversity may in some cases change the way the public views interactions with the police, increasing perceived legitimacy, and reducing the likelihood that interactions between police and citizens escalate unnecessarily. Research also suggests that representation reduces perceived racial threat, which decreases the potential for violent police actions as well as the disparities in who is affected by such violence. Again, however, more research is needed to understand the ways in which representation, however subtly, reshapes both the environment in which police officers work as well as the response by police officers to their environment.

We argue that work on representation, race, and policing has yet to answer the foundational question regarding *who* Black police officers feel they should represent. Noting research suggesting that Black officers are sometimes more aggressive toward Black suspects, Bradbury and Kellough (2011) suggest that minority officers may be tougher on minority citizens because they feel that it is the best way to protect minority communities, which suffer under the highest rates of crime and victimization. Others have argued more forcefully that failing to address the relatively high probabilities of victimization and violence faced by urban minorities represents a type of racism (DiIulio, 1996). If we accept these premises and combine them with evidence regarding the generalized mistrust with which police view those they interact with in the course of their jobs, then findings that Black officers are more punitive toward Black citizens whom they view as potential criminals could actually be consistent with, rather than contrary to, active representation. We need to determine the degree to which this is the case before we draw conclusions about the impact of representation on racial disparities in police outcomes. Answering this question may also take us a good distance toward understanding the interaction of officer attitudes and environmental or institutional features of policing and the ways in which those interactions facilitate or mitigate against biased outcomes.

## Discussion Questions

1   What is the difference between racism and implicit bias among police officers? Is one more problematic than the other? Why or why not?
2   Does the evidence, overall, suggest that Black citizens are treated differently by police officers? What can future research do to help answer this question in a way that is useful to practitioners?
3   Will diversity in the composition of a police force improve the relationship between officers and Black citizens? What about other types of under-represented groups?
4   Consider the mixed evidence provided in this chapter. If you were a chief of police, what screenings or other factors would be most important to you in recruiting individuals to serve as police officers? What would be the greatest challenges in recruiting new officers?
5   Which factor do you feel is likely to shape disparities in policing outcomes more—environmental, institutional, or individual-level characteristics? What does this mean for finding solutions to current racial inequities in the criminal justice system?

## Notes

1 Despite those circumstances, however, it remains somewhat of a mystery as to why this particular event was so incendiary. These events, along with advocacy efforts such as #blacklivesmatter started after the death of Trayvon Martin and

the increasing ease with which everyday citizens can video police-citizen inter-actions may help to explain the national attention that has become focused on police-caused homicides in the wake of Ferguson.

2  Calculations made using data from "The Counted" database maintained by the *Guardian*, which is arguably the most comprehensive data on fatal encounters with police. Calculations using the data gathered by mappingpoliceviolence.org or the *Washington Post* are very similar.

3  Close and Mason (2007) try to account for this by offering counterfactuals regarding what their results would look like if police were motivated by efficiency or public safety concerns, but their conclusions are nonetheless highly constrained because of their observational approach.

4  It should be noted that a body of work has argued for decades that formal rules and structures have little power to influence the "police culture" that leads to excessive use of force and other undesirable outcomes (see Brown 1981; Manning 1977).

5  *Whren v. United States*, 517 U.S. 806, was a unanimous United States Supreme Court decision that "declared that any traffic offense committed by a driver was a legitimate legal basis for a stop."

6  Though see Warner et al. (1989) for a discussion of these factors in the context of female representation on police forces, which also touches on the issue of racial group representation.

7  Although the mixed conclusions are consistent with work in the U.S. context, it is important to remember Hong's findings come from an analysis of departments in the UK and Wales, where constructions of race and the nature of policing are very different than in American cities.

# References

Alexander, Peter. 2010. "Rebellion of the poor: South Africa's service delivery protests–a preliminary analysis." *Review of African Political Economy* 37(123): 25–40.

Alpert, Geoffrey P., and Roger G. Dunham. 1988. *Policing urban America*. Prospect Heights, IL:Waveland Press.

Anbarci, Nejat, and Jungmin Lee. 2008. "Speed discounting and racial disparities: Evidence from speeding tickets in Boston." IZA Discussion Papers, No. 3903. Bonn: Institute for the Study of Labor.

Antonovics, Kate, and Brian G. Knight. 2009. "A new look at racial profiling: Evidence from the Boston Police Department." *Review of Economics and Statistics* 91(1): 163–177.

Ashkenas, Jeremy, and Haeyoun Park. 2015. "The race gap in America's police departments." *The New York Times*, April 8, 2015.

Bailey, William C. 1990. "Murder, capital punishment, and television: Execution publicity and homicide rates." *American Sociological Review* 55: 628–633.

Bailey, William C. 1996. "Less-than-lethal weapons and police-citizen killings in US urban areas." *Crime & Delinquency* 42(4): 535–552.

Baumgartner, Frank, Derek Epp, and Kelsey Shoub. 2017. *Suspect citizens: What 20 million traffic stops tell us about policing and race*. New York, NY: Cambridge University Press.

Beckett, K., Nyrop, K., and Pfingst, L. 2006. "Race, drugs, and policing: Under-standing disparities in drug delivery arrests." *Criminology* 44(1), 105–137.

Blair, Irene V. 2001. "Implicit stereotypes and prejudice." In *Cognitive social psychology: The Princeton Symposium on the legacy and future of social cognition*, edited by Gordon B. Moskowitz (pp. 359–374). Mahwah, NJ: Lawrence Erlbaum.

Blalock, Hubert M. 1967. *Toward a theory of minority-group relations.* New York, NY: Wiley.

Blau, Max, Jason Morris, and Catherine E. Shoichet. 2017. "Tulsa police shooting investigated by Justice Department." Available at: amsterdamnews.com/news/2016/sep/21/tulsa-police-shooting-investigated-justice-department

Blumer, Herbert. 1958. "Race prejudice as a sense of group position." *The Pacific Sociological Review* 1(1): 3–7.

Bobo, Lawrence D. 2004. "Inequalities that endure? Racial ideology, American politics, and the peculiar role of social sciences." In *The changing terrain of race and ethnicity*, edited by Maria Krysan and Amanda E. Lewis (pp. 13–42). New York, NY: Russell Sage Foundation.

Bradbury, Mark, and J. Edward Kellough. 2011. "Representative bureaucracy: Assessing the evidence on active representation." *The American Review of Public Administration* 41(2): 157–167.

Brown, Michael. K. 1981. *Working the street: Police discretion and the dilemmas of reform.* New York, NY: Russell Sage Foundation.

Brown, Robert A., and James Frank. 2006. "Race and officer decision making: Examining differences in arrest outcomes between black and white officers." *Justice Quarterly* 23(1): 96–126.

Brunson, Rod, and Jacinta Gau. 2011. "Officer race versus macro-level context." *Crime and Delinquency* 61(2): 213–242.

Cayer, N. Joseph, and Lee Sigelman. 1980. "Minorities and women in state and local government: 1973–1975." *Public Administration Review* 40(5): 443–450.

Center for Police Equity. 2016. "Race arrests." Available at: https://policingequity.org/images/pdfs-doc/CPE_SoJ_Race-Arrests-UoF_2016-07-08-1130.pdf

Chambliss, William J. 2001. *Power, politics, and crime.* Boulder, CO: Westview Press.

Chambliss, William J. (Ed.). 2011. *Police and law enforcement*, vol. 2. Thousand Oaks, CA: Sage Publications.

Close, Billy R., and Patrick L. Mason. 2006. "After the traffic stops: Officer characteristics and enforcement actions." *BE Journal of Economic Analysis & Policy* 6(1): 1–43.

Close, Billy R., and Patrick L. Mason. 2007. "Searching for efficient enforcement: Officer characteristics and racially biased policing." *Review of Law & Economics* 3(2): 263–321.

Cordner, Gary. 2014. "Community policing." In *The Oxford handbook of police and policing*, edited by Michael D. Reisig, and Robert J. Kane (pp. 148–171) . New York, NY: Oxford University Press.

Correll, Joshua, Bernadette Park, Charles M. Judd, and Bernd Wittenbrink. 2007. "Stereo-types and racial bias in the decision to shoot." *European Journal of Social Psychology* 37(6): 1102–1117.

Crank, John P.. 1997. "Celebrating agency culture: Engaging a traditional cop's heart in organizational change." In *Community policing in a rural setting*, edited by Quint C. Thurman and Edmund F. McGarrell (pp. 49–57). Cincinnati, OH: Anderson Publishing.

Demuth, Stephen. 2003. "Racial and ethnic differences in pretrial release decisions and outcomes: A comparison of Hispanic, Black, and White felony arrestees." *Criminology* 41(3): 873–908.

DiIulio, John. J. 1996. "Help wanted: Economists, crime and public policy." *Journal of Economic Perspectives* 10(1): 3–24.

Dovidio, John F., Kerry Kawakami, Craig Johnson, Brenda Johnson, and Adaiah Howard. 1997. "On the nature of prejudice: Automatic and controlled processes." *Journal of Experimental Social Psychology* 33(5):510–540.

Eitle, David, Stewart J. D'Alessio, and Lisa Stolzenberg. 2002. "Racial threat and social control: A test of the political, economic, and threat of black crime hypotheses." *Social Forces* 81(2): 557–576.

Epp, Charles R., Steven Maynard-Moody, and Donald Haider-Markel. 2014. *Pulled over: How police stops define race and citizenship.* Chicago: University of Chicago Press.

Epp, Charles R., Steven Maynard-Moody, and Donald Haider-Markel. 2017. "Beyond profiling: The institutional sources of racial disparities in policing." *Public Administration Review* 77(2): 168–178.

Eterno, John A., Christine S.Barrow, and Eli B. Silverman. 2017. "Forcible stops: Police and citizens speak out." *Public Administration Review* 77(2): 181–192.

Fachner, George, and Stephen Carter. 2015. *An assessment of deadly force in the Philadelphia Police Department (collaborative reform initiative).* Washington, DC: Office of Community Oriented Policing Services, U.S. Department of Justice.

Fagan, Jeffrey, Anthony A. Braga, Rod K. Brunson, and April Pattavina. 2016. "Stops and stares: Street stops, surveillance, and race in the new policing." *Fordham Urban Law Journal* 43: 539–614.

Friedrich, Robert J. 1980. "Police use of force: Individuals, situations, and organizations." *The Annals of the American Academy of Political and Social Science* 452(1): 82–97.

Fryer, Roland G. 2016. "An empirical analysis of racial differences in police use of force." Working paper. Washington, DC: National Bureau of Economic Research. Available at: www.nber.org/papers/w22399.pdf

Fyfe, James J. 1980. "Geographic correlates of police shooting: A microanalysis." *Journal of Research in Crime and Delinquency* 17(1): 101–113.

Fyfe, James J. 1982. "Blind justice: Police shootings in Memphis." *The Journal of Criminal Law and Criminology* 73(2): 707–722.

Fyfe, James J. 1986. "The split-second syndrome and other determinants of police violence." In *Violent transactions*, edited by Anne Campbell and John J. Gibbs (pp. 583–598). New York, NY: Basil Blackwell.

Gau, Jacinta, and Rod K. Brunson. 2010. "Procedural justice and order maintenance policing: A study of inner-city young men's perceptions of police legitimacy." *Justice Quarterly* 27(2): 255–279.

Georges, William P. 2000. "Traffic safety strategies yield tangible benefits." *Police Chief* 67(7): 53–55.

Gilliard-Matthews, Stacia, Brian R. Kowalski, and Richard J. Lundman. 2008. "Officer race and citizen-reported traffic ticket decisions by police in 1999 and 2002." *Police Quarterly* 11(2): 202–219.

Goff, Phillip Atiba, Tracey Lloyd, Amanda Geller, Steven Raphael, and Jack Glaser. 2016. *The science of justice: Race, arrests, and police use of force.* New York, NY: Center for Policing Equity.

Graham, Sandra, and Brian S. Lowery. 2004. "Priming unconscious racial stereotypes about adolescent offenders." *Law and Human Behavior* 28(5): 483–504.

Greenwood, Peter W., Jan M. Chaiken, and Joan Petersilia. 2002. *The criminal investigation process.* Lexington, MA: Heat.

Headley, Andrea, and James E. Wright II. 2017. "Does representation matter? A study of police use of force in Indianapolis." Paper presented at the Annual Meeting of the Midwest Political Science Association,Chicago.

Henderson, Lenneal J. 1979. *Administrative advocacy: Black administrators in urban bureaucracy*. Palo Alto, CA: R&E Research Associates.

Heymann, Philip B. 2000. "The new policing." *Fordham Urban Law Journal* 28: 407.

Holmes, Malcolm D., and Brad W. Smith. 2008. *Race and police brutality: Roots of an urban dilemma*. Albany, NY: State University of New York Press.

Hong, Sounman. 2017. "Does increasing ethnic representativeness reduce police misconduct?" *Public Administration Review* 77(2): 195–205.

ICLAPD (Independent Commission on the Los Angeles Police Department). 1991. "Report of the Independent Commission on the Los Angeles Police Department." Los Angeles: R. R. Donnelly Financial International.

Jacobs, David, and Robert M. O'Brien. 1998. "The determinants of deadly force: A structural analysis of police violence." *American Journal of Sociology* 103(4): 837–862.

James, L., 2018. "The stability of implicit racial bias in police officers." *Police Quarterly* 21(1): 30–52.

James, Lois, Stephen M.James, and Bryan Vila. 2016. "The reverse racism effect." *Criminology & Public Policy* 15(2): 457–479.

James, Lois, David Klinger, and Bryan Vila. 2014. "Racial and ethnic bias in decisions to shoot seen through a stronger lens: Experimental results from high-fidelity laboratory simulations." *Journal of Experimental Criminology* 10(3): 323–340.

James, Lois, Bryan Vila, and Kenn Daratha. 2013. "Results from experimental trials testing participant responses to White, Hispanic and Black suspects in high-fidelity deadly force judgment and decision-making simulations." *Journal of Experimental Criminology* 9(2): 189–212.

Jaynes, G., and Williams, R. 1989. *A common destiny: Blacks and American society*. Washington, DC: National Academy Press.

Jennings, Jay T., and Meghan E. Rubado. 2017. "Preventing the use of deadly force: The relationship between police agency policies and rates of officer-involved gun deathsv" *Public Administration Review* 77(2): 217–226.

Kahn, K. B., and Martin, K. D. 2016. "Policing and race: Disparate treatment, perceptions, and policy responses." *Social Issues and Policy Review* 10(1): 82–121.

Kania, Richard R. E., and Wade C. Mackey. 1977. "Police violence as a function of community characteristics." *Criminology* 15(1): 27–48.

Kanter, Rosabeth Moss. 1976. "The impact of hierarchical structures on the work behavior of women and men." *Social Problems* 23(4): 415–430.

Keiser, Lael R., Vicky M. Wilkins, Kenneth J. Meier, and Catherine A. Holland. 2002. "Lipstick and logarithms: Gender, institutional context, and representative bureaucracy." *American Political Science Review* 96(3): 553–564.

Kellough, J. Edward. 1990. "Integration in the public workplace: Determinants of minority and female employment in federal agencies." *Public Administration Review* 50(5): 557–566.

Kennedy, Brandy A., Adam M. Butz, Nazita Lajevardi, and Matthew J. Nanes. 2017. *Race and representative bureaucracy in American policing*. Basingstoke, UK: Palgrave Macmillan.

Kingsley, John Donald. 1944. *Representative bureaucracy*. Yellow Springs, OH: Antioch Press.

Klinger, David, Richard Rosenfeld, Daniel Isom, and Michael Deckard. 2016. "Race, crime, and the micro-ecology of deadly force." *Criminology & Public Policy* 15(1):193–222.

Lasley, James R., James Larson, Chandrika Kelso, and Gregory Chris Brown. 2011. "Assessing the long-term effects of officer race on police attitudes towards the community: A case for representative bureaucracy theory." *Police Practice and Research* 12(6): 474–491.

Lauter, David, and Matt Pearce. 2015. "After a year of high-profile killings by police, Americans' views on race have shifted." *Los Angeles Times*, August 5, 2015. Available at: www.latimes.com/nation/la-na-race-poll-20150805-story.html#page=1

Legewie, Joscha. 2016. "Racial profiling and use of force in police stops: How local events trigger periods of increased discrimination." *American Journal of Sociology* 122(2): 379–424.

Legewie, Joscha, and Jeffrey Fagan. 2016. "Group threat, police officer diversity and the deadly use of police force." *Columbia Public Law Research Paper* 14: 512.

Liska, Allen E. 1992. *Social threat and social control.* Albany, NY: State University of New York Press.

Livingston, Debra. 1997. "Police discretion and the quality of life in public places: Courts, communities, and the new policing." *Columbia Law Review* 551: 573–591.

Lynch, James P., and William J. Sabol. 2004. "Effects of incarceration on informal social control." In *Imprisoning America: The social effects of mass incarceration*, edited by Mary Pattillo, Bruce Western, and David Weiman (pp. 135–164). New York, NY: Russell Sage Foundation.

Manning, P. K. 1977. *Police work: The social organization of policing.* Cambridge, MA: MIT Press.

Mapping Police Violence. 2019. "Unarmed victims." Retrieved from https://mapp ingpoliceviolence.org

Mauer, Marc, and Tracy Huling. 1995. *Young black Americans and the criminal justice system: Five years later.* Washington, DC: The Sentencing Project.

McElvain, James P., and Augustine J.Kposowa. 2008. "Police officer characteristics and the likelihood of using deadly force." *Criminal Justice and Behavior* 35(4): 505–521.

McLaughlin, Eugene. 2007. *The new policing.* London: Sage.

Meier, Kenneth J. 1993. "Representative bureaucracy: A theoretical and empirical exposition." *Research in Public Administration* 2(1): 1–35.

Meier, Kenneth J., and Jill Nicholson-Crotty. 2006. "Gender, representative bureaucracy, and law enforcement: The case of sexual assault." *Public Administration Review* 66(6): 850–860.

Meier, Kenneth J., and Lloyd G. Nigro. 1976. "Representative bureaucracy and policy preferences: A study in the attitudes of federal executives." *Public Administration Review* 36(4): 458–469.

Meier, Kenneth J., and Joseph Stewart Jr. 1992. "The impact of representative bureaucracies: Educational systems and public policies." *The American Review of Public Administration* 22(3): 157–171.

Meier, Kenneth J., Robert D.Wrinkle, and Jerry L.Polinard. (1999). "Representative bureaucracy and distributional equity: Addressing the hard question." *The Journal of Politics* 61(4): 1025–1039.

Miller, Ted R., Bruce A.Lawrence, Nancy N.Carlson, et al. 2017. "Perils of police action: A cautionary tale from US data sets." *Injury Prevention* 23(1): 27–32.

Mitchell, O., & MacKenzie, D.L. (2004). "The relationship between race, ethnicity, and sentencing outcomes: A meta-analysis of sentencing research." Washington, DC: U.S. Department of Justice.

Mosher, Frederick C. 1968. *Democracy and the public service*. New York, NY: Oxford University Press.

Nachmias, David, and David H. Rosenbloom. 1973. "Measuring bureaucratic representation and integration." *Public Administration Review* 33(6): 590–597.

New York Civil Liberties Union. 2016. "Stop-and-frisk data." Available at: www.nyclu.org/ content/stop-and-frisk-data

Nicholson-Crotty, Sean, Jill Nicholson-Crotty, and Sergio Fernandez. 2017. "Will more black cops matter? Officer race and police-involved homicides of black citizens." *Public Administration Review* 77(2): 206–216.

Oberfield, Zachary W. 2010. "Rule following and discretion at government's frontlines: Continuity and change during organization socialization." *Journal of Public Administration Research and Theory* 20(4): 735–755.

Oberfield, Zachary W. 2014. *Becoming bureaucrats: Socialization at the front lines of government service*. Philadelphia, PA: University of Pennsylvania Press.

Ochs, Holona Leanne. 2011. "The politics of inclusion: Black political incorporation and the use of lethal force." *Journal of Ethnicity in Criminal Justice* 9(3): 238–265.

Packer, Herbert. 1966. "The courts, the police, and the rest of us." *Journal of Criminal Law and Criminology* 57(3): 238–243.

Paoline, Eugene A. 2003. "Taking stock: Toward a richer understanding of police culture." *Journal of Criminal Justice* 31(3): 199–214.

Pegues, Jeff. 2017. *Black and blue: Inside the divide between the police and Black America*. Amherst, NY: Prometheus Books.

Project Implicit. 2011. "Education." Available at: https://implicit.harvard.edu/imp licit/education.html

Rivera, Mario A., and James D. Ward. 2017. "Toward an analytical framework for the study of race and police violence." *Public Administration Review* 77(2): 242–250.

Rosich, Katherine J. 2007. *Race, ethnicity, and the criminal justice system*. Washington, DC: American Sociological Association.

Sampson, Robert J., and Janet L. Lauritsen. 1997. "Racial and ethnic disparities in crime and criminal justice in the United States." *Crime and Justice* 21: 311–374.

Sklansky, David Alan. 2005. "Not your father's police department: Making sense of the new demographics of law enforcement." *Journal of Criminal Law & Criminology* 96: 1209.

Skogan, Wesley G. 1979. "Crime in contemporary America." In *Violence in America*, edited by H. Graham and T.R. Gurr (pp. 375–391). Newbury Park, CA: Sage Publications.

Smith, Brad W. 2003. "The impact of police officer diversity on police-caused homicides." *Policy Studies Journal* 31(2): 147–162.

Smith, Brad W. 2004. "Structural and organizational predictors of homicide by police." *Policing: An International Journal of Police Strategies & Management* 27(4): 539–557.

Smith, Brad W., and Malcolm D. Holmes. 2014. "Police use of excessive force in minority communities: A test of the minority threat, place, and community accountability hypotheses." *Social Problems* 61(1): 83–104.

Smith, Robert. J. 2015. "Reducing racially disparate policing outcomes: Is implicit bias training the answer?" *University of Harvard Law Review* 37: 295.

Snyder, Howard N. and Melissa Sickmund. 2006. "Juvenile offenders and victims: 2006 national report." Washington, DC: Office of Juvenile Justice and Delinquency Prevention, U.S. Department of Justice.

Spencer, Katherine B., Amanda K. Charbonneau, and Jack Glaser. 2016. "Implicit bias and policing." *Social and Personality Psychology Compass* 10(1): 50–63.

Spohn, Cassia. 2000. "Thirty years of sentencing reform: The quest for a racially neutral sentencing process." *Criminal Justice* 3(1): 427–501.

Stokes, Larry D., and James F. Scott. 1996. "Affirmative action and selected minority groups in law enforcement." *Journal of Criminal Justice* 24(1): 29–38.

Stults, Brian J., and Eric P. Baumer. 2007. "Racial context and police force size: Evaluating the empirical validity of the minority threat perspective." *American Journal of Sociology* 113(2): 507–546.

Sun, Ivan Y. 2003. "A comparison of police field training officers' and non-training officers' conflict resolution styles: Controlling versus supportive strategies." *Police Quarterly* 6(1): 22–50.

Sun, Ivan Y., and Brian K. Payne. 2004. "Racial differences in resolving conflicts: A comparison between Black and White police officers." *Crime & Delinquency* 50(4): 516–541.

Terrill, William, and Stephen D. Mastrofski. 2002. "Situational and officer-based determinants of police coercion." *Justice Quarterly* 19(2): 215–248.

Theobald, Nick A. and Donald P. Haider-Markel. 2008. "Race, bureaucracy, and symbolic representation: Interactions between citizens and police." *Journal of Public Administration Research and Theory* 19(2): 409–426.

Thompson, Frank J. 1976. "Minority groups in public bureaucracies: Are passive and active representation linked?" *Administration & Society* 8(2): 201–226.

Walker, Samuel. 1993. *Taming the system: The control of discretion in criminal justice, 1950–1990.* New York, NY: Oxford University Press.

Walker, Samuel. 1999. *Police in America: An introduction,* 3rd edn. Boston: McGraw-Hill College.

Walker, Samuel, Geoffrey P. Alpert, and Dennis J. Kenney. 2000. "Early warning systems for police: Concept, history, and issues." *Police Quarterly* 3(2): 132–152.

Ward, James D., and Mario A. Rivera. 2014. *Institutional racism, organizations and public policy.* New York, NY: Peter Lang.

Warner, Rebecca L., Brent S. Steel, and Nicholas P. Loverich. 1989. "Conditions associated with the advent of representative bureaucracy: The case of women in policing." *Social Science Quarterly* 70(3): 562–578.

*Washington Post.* 2016. "Aren't more white people than black people killed by police? Yes, but no." July 11. Available at: www.washingtonpost.com/news/post-nation/wp/2016/07/11/arent-more-white-people-than-black-people-killed-by-police-yes-but-no/

Weisburd, David, Rosann Greenspan, Edwin E. Hamilton, Hubert Williams, and Kellie A. Bryant. 2000. *Police attitudes toward abuse of authority: Findings from a national study* Washington, DC: National Institute of Justice.

Westley, William A. 1970. *Violence and the police: A sociological study of law, custom, and morality.* Cambridge, MA: MIT Press.

Wilkins, Vicky M., and Brian N. Williams. 2008. "Black or blue: Racial profiling and representative bureaucracy." *Public Administration Review* 68(4): 654–664.

Wilson, James Q. 1968. *Varieties of police behavior: The management of law and order in eight communities.* Cambridge, MA: Harvard University Press.

Worden, Robert. 1996. "The causes of police brutality: Theory and evidence on police use of force." In *Police violence*, edited by William A. Geller, and Hans Toch (pp. 23–51). New Haven, CT: Yale University Press.

Zatz, Marjorie S. 1987. "The changing forms of racial/ethnic biases in sentencing." *Journal of Research in Crime and Delinquency* 24(1): 69–92.

Zelizer, J. 2016. *The Kerner report*. Princeton, NJ: Princeton University Press.

# 4 Public Administration and Racial Disparities in Health and Health Care

## Toward New Health Inequality Research

*Ling Zhu and Kenicia Wright*

### Practitioner Points

- Policy should ensure health care access for individuals with lower socioeconomic status. Barriers to health care access are one of the leading reasons why poor individuals in many countries have worse health outcomes compared to those who are more affluent.
- Expanded coverage of publicly funded health insurance programs (e.g. Medicaid and SCHIP) is recommended. Lower-income individuals have improved health outcomes in states with more generous Medicaid/SCHIP programs and/or greater public health expenditures. This is particularly important for large, diverse states.
- To properly manage heterogeneous effects, policymakers and public managers need to give more attention to racial inequality in access to health care resources, improve the cultural competence training of medical health professionals, and increase efforts to recruit and retain minority health care professionals. Neutrally designed public health policies might have disparate effects (whether intended or not) on different racial and ethnic groups.
- Both scholars and policymakers should take account of intersectionality in order to improve awareness of how public policy affects citizens across crosscutting social identities. Intersectionality is a useful theoretical tool that offers insights on how overlapping social identities affect health disparity.
- The integration of the different parts of government involved in health care provision must be improved. Although health care services and health interventions increasingly involve complex policy networks, involving both government agencies and private sector organizations, it is imperative to promote cross-sector collaboration and to improve co-production with targeted populations.

# Introduction

Social inequalities in population health and access to health care resources are prevalent in many industrialized democracies (Marmot, 2005). The Institute of Medicine defines health care disparities as differences in treatment between population groups that are not justified by differences in preferences for services or health. Health inequality, meanwhile, refers to group differences in preventable health risks and access to health care (Nelson, Stith, and Smedley, 2002). Health-related inequality is a major form of social inequality and affects the lives of many people in both developed and developing countries, and potentially undermines democracy (Tilly, 2007; Wilkinson and Pickett, 2009).

The term "inequality" was first used to describe health policy and outcomes in Great Britain in the Black Report (Black, 1980). Published in 1980, the report revealed widespread health inequality in the UK, discussed contributing social factors, and offered recommendations for reducing health inequality. Health care scholars and federal agencies made similar efforts to improve the understanding and awareness of health-related inequality in the U.S. (Hofrichter and Bhatia, 2010; Nelson, Stith, and Smedley, 2002). The United States distinguishes itself from many other western countries by the evident social inequality in access to health care and social disparities in health outcomes (Barr, 2007; LaVeist, 2005).

Academic scholars play a key role in producing research that contributes to our understanding of health inequality. In this chapter, we discuss the history of racial bias and mistrust of minorities in the modern-day health care system. We review the existing literature on health inequality in the U.S. and consider how race factors into the policy and political processes that produce health inequality. From a review of the growing literature on race and public administration in the area of health inequality, it appears that the stark pattern of health inequality may be attributed to various policy factors, including failure to provide generous redistributive health care benefits (Gray et al., 2010), the privatization of government responsibilities in health care (Amirkhanyan, 2008; Hacker, 2004; Soss, Hacker, and Mettler, 2007), partisan politics that yield unequal representation (Zhu and Clark, 2015), and government inaction in the face of market-based inequality and insecurity (Hacker, 2006). We also compare trends in racial and ethnic diversity in the U.S. population to the diversity of U.S. health care workers and find a significant gap between these groups. We offer insights on why this gap could contribute to health inequality by reviewing flaws in the design of public policy and patterns of racial bias in the policy implementation process. More specifically, we discuss how race-neutral health policies may be structured and implemented in a way that reproduces racial disparity. Next, we turn to two types of emerging studies—those on race, representative bureaucracy, and health inequality and those on intersectionality theory and health inequality—to highlight potential benefits of a more diverse and representative bureaucracy in the health care arena. We conclude by acknowledging important questions that remain unanswered.

## The History of Minority Distrust in Health Care

Before exploring inequalities in both health and health care, it is important to note that minorities have long experienced discrimination, racial bias, and prejudicial treatment from those providing care in the medical industry in the U.S. Systematic discrimination dates back at least to the Flexner Report and the American Medical Association's effort to close Black medical schools and restrict minority admissions to AMA-accredited medical schools in the early 1900s (Steinecke and Terrell, 2010). Discrimination in health care reflected and continues to reflect general levels of discriminatory treatment present in the United States. The Tuskegee Syphilis Study (also referred to as the Tuskegee Experiment) is an example of the experiences Blacks have had in the health care context. The experiment began in 1932 and involved doctors from the U.S. Public Health Service and 600 Black men (399 with latent syphilis and a "control group" of 201). The Black men did not receive factual information about the study or provide informed consent for their participation. During treatment, subjects were given placebos by the doctors instead of penicillin, which was the recommended treatment for syphilis at the time. Doctors continued giving the Black men placebos even after they went blind, insane, or experienced other effects from untreated syphilis, citing a need for increased insight on the full progression of the disease (Centers for Disease Control and Prevention, 2015b). Congress ultimately concluded the Tuskegee Experiment was unethical and rewarded surviving participants and the heirs of the deceased participants a $10 million settlement. Although many improvements and changes have occurred in the health care context since the Tuskegee Experiments, Blacks in particular continue to face racial bias, racial tension, and limited representation in the health care context. We examine each of these factors in the coming sections of this chapter.

Black women have faced many unique and very troubling experiences in the health care arena as well. Events during slavery established a foundation for the treatment and, in many ways, negative attitudes and stereotypes surrounding Black women. Although the United States abolished slavery in 1865, events during subsequent eras significantly shaped the experiences of Black women and influence the levels of distrust present in this subpopulation (e.g., Prather et al., 2018). Examples abound; reproductive surgeries were performed without anesthesia on female slaves, compulsory sterilization was often enforced during the Jim Crow era, nonconsensual medical experiments continued into the Civil Rights era, and targeted abortions continue into the twenty-first century (ibid., p. 251).

Of course, negative experiences in the health care system and the subsequent development of distrust are not limited to Blacks. For example, the "Latino Paradox" refers to the fact that Latino Americans commonly have better health outcomes than non-Hispanic White Americans despite unequal experiences in obtaining health care. Latinos consistently assign lower ratings to clinicians than other racial and ethnic groups in the U.S. (Blair et al., 2012), report poorer communication with their doctor or health care provider (Ashton et al., 2003; Morales et al., 1999), and experience implicit bias that shapes their health care experiences (Blair et al., 2012). Some of this may be related to the "chilling effect" which argues that policies restricting immigrant access to public welfare and social programs also reduce the take-up of social policy benefits by eligible Latinos (Padraza and Zhu, 2015). In other words, this effect highlights the potential for contemporary discourse surrounding immigrants and related exclusionary policies to result in eligible Latinos being hesitant, fearful, and/or unwilling to accept available public health benefits.

Interestingly, while many of the stereotypes surrounding Asians are *positive,* this racial group is far from immune from negative experiences in obtaining health care. For example, one of the most common stereotypes of Asians is that of the "model minority," or that Asians are affluent, hard-working, and generally healthy. Yet, views about skin color and texture also shape projections and perceptions of the health of Asians (Tan, Tiddeman, and Stephen, 2018), and cultural incompetence can lead to misinterpretation of the behavior of Asian patients. Language and cultural differences in general make it more difficult for a positive and trusting relationship to develop between minorities and their health care providers (Alpers, 2016). Such differences and the nature of health care-related experiences of Asians may also contribute to negative relationships between Asian patients and their physicians (Sung, 1999), unmet health care needs of Asians (Jang et al., 2018), reduced cancer screenings among Asian populations (Hong, Tauscher, and Cardel, 2018), and poor cardiovascular-related health of Asians (Kalra et al., 2019).

Understanding the history and experiences of racial minorities when seeking care for health as well as the distrust minorities often develop toward providers is important because of how these factors ultimately shape minority health outcomes (Williams and Mohammed, 2009). Such consequences also include increased anxiety while waiting to see a physician (Abdou and Fingerhut, 2014), disparities in health screenings for cancer for minority women (Mouton et al., 2010), and increased risk for hypertension (Brondolo et al., 2011).

## What We Know about Health Inequality

Health inequality, one of the major forms of social inequality, can be understood as group differences in preventable health risks and access to health care. While "health disparity" is used to refer to disparate group-based health outcomes, "health care inequality" refers to inequality in access to health care resources and services. Health inequality is not only a problem in the U.S.; there is widespread health inequality around the world. Global health care access and quality have improved since 1990, yet inequalities in differences in health care access and quality between the best- and worst-performing countries have grown. According to a 2017 Global Burden of Disease study, even countries with similar development levels have vastly different health care inequality (GBD 2015 Healthcare Access and Quality Collaborators, 2017). Several examples make this pattern clear. According to a 2015 World Health Organization (WHO) factsheet, 830 women die due to complications of pregnancy and childbirth every day; nearly all of these deaths occur in low-resource environments and could have been prevented (Alkema et al., 2017). The Global Health Observatory (GHO) reports that there is a needs-based shortage of health care workers as 44 percent of WHO Member States report having less than one physician per 1,000 people, with the greatest shortages in the South East Asian and African regions (Global Health Observatory, 2017). The Black Report contained information on the health status of those in Great Britain and revealed marked differences in mortality rates, chronic sickness, and preventative services across races (Gray, 1982). More recent data from the UK Health Department suggests that these differences still exist and largely occur along lines of social class. Despite efforts to reduce these inequalities, many have actually widened.

Health inequality is particularly salient in the United States. The U.S. ranks near the bottom of 35 countries in a recent Organization for Economic Cooperation and Development (OECD) report on most standard measures of health, such as infant mortality rates, maternal mortality rates, and life expectancy (Centers for Disease Control and Prevention, 2006). Similar patterns exist for health care disparities. Getting high quality health care requires access to the health care system; because health insurance coverage is a key determinant of having access to health care, the uninsured are particularly vulnerable (Levy and Meltzer, 2008). From 2000 to 2010, the percentage of Americans between 18 and 64 who reported not having health insurance coverage increased from 18.7 percent to 22.3 percent (AHRQ, 2015). Since the enactment of the Patient Protection and Affordable Care Act of 2010 (ACA), there has been a reduction in uninsured rates and other types of health care inequality (Abdus, Mistry, and Selden, 2015), though debates around the ACA and what provisions should be offered to the public continue (Starr, 2013).

### Key Takeaways from Health Inequality Research

Health disparities among individuals in the U.S. exist across numerous indicators. For example, there are significant income- and race-based differences in birth-related outcomes (Atkins and Wilkins, 2013; Bitler and Currie, 2004; Devaney, Bilheimer, and Schore, 1992; Zimmerman and Gager, 1997), asthma (Collard, 2006), smoking (Joyce, Racine, and Yunzal-Butler, 2008), hospitalization rates (Kaestner and Khan, 2012), and mortality rates (Kim and Jennings, 2009).

Scholars have studied the factors that affect both inequality in access to health care and disparities in health outcomes. On the one hand, scholars attribute disparate health outcomes to various determinants, including biological and genetic factors, individual health behavior, the social environment, the physical environment, and access to health services (e.g., access to health insurance and health care utilization). On the other hand, scholars have paid attention to the role of politics in shaping health inequality. For example, government inaction in the face of market-based inequality and insecurity (Hacker, 2006) has important effects on social inequality as does partisan politics that yield unequal representation (Zhu and Clark, 2015). Additionally, the privatization of government responsibilities in health care significantly shapes health inequality in the U.S. (Amirkhanyan, 2008; Hacker, 2004; Soss, Hacker, and Mettler, 2007), including distributive effects on access to health care and the health status of different social groups. Other policy factors, such as the failure to provide generous, redistributive health care benefits can significantly curtail efforts at improving inequality through health reform (Gray et al., 2010).

There is an important connection between public policy and health disparities whereby scholars focus on the health status of welfare participants. Welfare programs comprise the safety net that provides and improves recipients' access to health care. More inclusive and generous welfare programs are often associated with improved health outcomes. For example, participation in Women, Infants, and Children (WIC) programs improves the health of low-income women by reducing risks during pregnancy and improving birth outcomes (Bitler and Currie, 2004; Devaney, Bilheimer, and Schore, 1992). Relatedly, the longer the period an individual is enrolled in WIC, the lower the smoking rate, the better the weight gain during pregnancy, the better the birth outcomes, and the greater the likelihood of breastfeeding (Joyce, Racine, and Yunzal-Butler, 2008). In the aggregate population, teen birth rates are lower in states with higher welfare payments (Zimmerman and Gager, 1997). A generous social welfare system also has promising effects for the elderly population, such as lower mortality rates, less frequent outpatient visits, and lower probability of hospitalization (Kaestner and Khan, 2012; Kim and Jennings, 2009). The connection between public policy and health disparities highlights the fact that poverty and poor health are often strongly related. This reflects a "resource-based" explanation of health disparities (Lopoo, 2004; Ram and Hou, 2003). There is a strong correlation between an individual's income and his/her racial and ethnic background. Because racial and ethnic minorities tend to have lower levels of income and wealth than Whites, they also have more health-related problems.

The more recent comparative health research suggests that social class is an important determinant of health inequality in many other countries outside of the United States (van Doorslaer et al., 1997, van Doorslaer and Koolman, 2004. In both developed and developing countries, individuals with high socioeconomic status have better health outcomes than other groups. Although income-based differences in health exist for most individuals in middle- to high-income countries, the U.S. has one of the largest income-based health disparities in the world (Hero, Zaslavsky, and Blendon, 2017). Exponential increases in income inequality in OECD countries has been observed in recent years such that it is at its highest level in the past half-century. Simply put, those with lower incomes are likely to live shorter, sicker lives than those with higher incomes.

### Key Takeaways from Health Care Inequality Research

Recognizing the connection between health care access and health-related inequality, many wealthy nations offer some types of universal health care, with the U.S. being an exception. Universal health coverage means that all citizens have access to quality medical services and, in part, the lack of universal health care in the U.S. has resulted in a strong link between income inequality and inequality in health outcomes. Most Americans gain access to health care through health insurance, but there has been growing inequality in both employment-based health insurance coverage and publicly funded coverage, such as Medicaid and the Children's Health Insurance Program (Buchmueller and Carpenter, 2012; Ettner, 1997; Fossett and Thompson, 2006; Ketsche et al., 2007; Zhu and Johansen, 2014; Zhu and Xu, 2015).

Cross-nationally, health care spending is another factor commonly expected to affect health status, but the U.S. is an exception to this generalization. Indeed, a staggering amount of spending in the U.S. is dedicated to health care. National health expenditures as the percentage of GDP were 17.8 percent in 2015, and spending on health care has increased steadily since the mid-1950s (CDC, 2015a). Data from the World Bank and the Institute for Health Metrics and Evaluation show that the U.S. has the highest per capita health care spending compared to countries with similar life expectancy. In fact, the OECD reports that per capita health care spending was slightly more than $9,000 in the U.S. in 2015 while per capita spending in Switzerland, the country with the second highest spending and universal health care, was $6,787. This reflects an interesting paradox; one would expect promising health outcomes given the high amounts of money the U.S. spends on health care, but that is not the case.

Recently, scholars have focused on studying the inclusiveness of health care services; this research provides useful insights on key differences in health care access in the United States. First, income- and race-based differences in the use of health care services contribute to growing health care inequality (DeSoto, Tajalli, and Hofer, 2001). It is well documented that there are significant differences in the health care access for different sub-groups, and racial and ethnic minorities tend to have lower health insurance coverage rates than White Americans (Lillie-Blanton and Hoffman, 2005). Disparities in children's mental health care use are persistent and driven by disparities in initiation for health care services (Cook, Barry, and Busch, 2013), which means policies that aim to reduce health care disparities need to focus on improving initial access, particularly for those with low socioeconomic status.

Second, studies have found significant health care inequality based on income, employment, and citizenship status (Lillie-Blanton and Hoffman, 2005). For example, legal immigrants must reside in the U.S. for at least five continuous years before possibly being eligible for Medicare, and undocumented immigrants are not eligible for any of the federal programs that offer individuals health care services (i.e. Medicare, Medicaid, etc.). While the ACA has initiated reform efforts to increase health insurance coverage for low-income Americans, many of the policy reforms benefit citizens and legal immigrants (Thompson, 2013) and do not extend insurance coverage to undocumented immigrants (Siskin, 2011). Most immigrants—both undocumented and documented—work in low-wage jobs and often do not receive job-related benefits such as medical insurance (Chavez, 2012). Non-citizens and their children are less likely to have health insurance and a regular source of care compared with individuals born in the U.S. (Pitkin Derose et al., 2009). The lack of protection under the ACA and the lack of employer-covered health care can result in undocumented immigrants using medical services disproportionately less than legal immigrants and citizens (Chavez, 2012). Instead, undocumented immigrants rely more heavily on free health clinics and hospital emergency rooms for their health care services than other sub-groups (Liebert and Ameringer, 2013) or delay or forgo health care treatment altogether (Heyman, Núñez, and Talavera, 2009).

There are also policy factors that shape unequal access to health care and disparities in health outcomes. With awareness of the relationship between health care access and health outcomes, understanding health-related inequality requires consideration of health care coverage. Health care coverage and the institutional characteristics of health care systems have important consequences for health-related inequality. For example, the generosity of Medicaid benefits affects low-income elderly participation in Medicaid (Ettner, 1997). Despite the benefits of publicly funded health care on health care access, there also exist negative stereotypes concerning beneficiaries of social welfare programs. Because these stereotypes are widespread, the stigma of publicly funded health care programs results in families that receive State Children's Health Insurance Programs (SCHIP) and Medicaid benefits perceiving differences in how they are treated by network providers, their access to health care services, and their satisfaction with care (Ketsche et al., 2007).

Federalism plays a major role in health access and equity. Although there is a set of federal health policies that govern American citizens, there are major differences in how policies are further defined and implemented at the state and local levels. U.S. citizens and immigrants again provide a good example. The design of a state's Medicaid eligibility rules toward immigrants significantly accounts for the varying participation gaps across the 50 states (Zhu and Xu, 2015). Bureaucratic responsiveness also shapes the health care inequality faced by economically disadvantaged members of society. In fact, SCHIP participation is largely explained by states' varying administrative responsiveness (Fossett and Thompson, 2006). Internet availability (Rethemeyer, 2007), and information flow regarding available health services (Figlio, Hamersma, and Roth, 2015) both shape health care inequality. Of course, health care inequality would still exist if an individual had health care access (i.e. health insurance) without the available facilities providing health care services. As a result, the existence of free clinics is important for improving low-income minority and particularly immigrant access to and use of health care service (Liebert and Ameringer, 2013).

This understanding of the determinants of health care inequality offers valuable information on how the design and implementation of health care policies have profound distributional consequences. It also demonstrates the fruitfulness of applying major public administration concepts (e.g., dimensional publicness, bureaucratic responsiveness, policy feedback) in health care inequality research. Studying various health behaviors and health outcomes (e.g. mothers' self-reported health status, alcohol and drug use, smoking, mental health, body mass index, children's health conditions) highlights that low-income individuals who live in public housing residences are less likely to have access to efficient care and more likely to experience bad health outcomes (Fertig and Reingold, 2007). Similarly, improved health care coverage for children from poor and near-poor families through Medicaid expansion is associated with improved health status (Lykens and Jargowsky, 2002). In other words, equal and inclusive health care coverage is associated with better overall population health outcomes including counts of chronic and acute illness and functional limitations (e.g., school or work absentee days) due to illness.

Inequality research in the educational context reveals a racial gradient in the policy implementation process and the importance of administrative factors that contribute to inequality (Hicklin and Meier, 2008; Meier, Stewart, and England, 1989). Most of these studies focus on the social identities of street-level bureaucrats and how frontline public employees affect racial inequality. However, there has been limited attention to how race matters in shaping health and health care inequality. To date, most health inequality research focuses on the efficiency and effectiveness of health services, health care reform, the management of health care organizations and inter-organizational networks (e.g., connections among hospitals, nursing homes, mental health and substance abuse facilities), and government health care spending. While there was an uptick in attention to health disparities and health care inequality during the initial roll-out of the ACA in 2010, health inequality in general (either inequality in access to health care, disparities in health outcomes, or both) is the focus of only a small body of scholarly research, despite long-standing scholarly interest in inequality research and the persistent nature and serious effects of this inequality. The remaining sections of this chapter explain why consideration of race and ethnicity is critically important to our understanding of health inequality and offer promising avenues that warrant additional attention.

## Health Inequality in the U.S.: Why Race Is Important

While the policy determinants of health disparities and health care inequality are fairly well understood, it is also important to give attention to the nexus of race and health inequality. The importance of accounting for race in order to understand health disparities is not surprising given the legacy of racial divides in the U.S. Complex issues shape health care, and racism remains one of the most challenging issues in trying to improve public health. Health care disparities have an extensive history, and often minorities disproportionately suffer from treatable, curable, or altogether preventable diseases. Racial and ethnic health disparities refer to "racial or ethnic differences in the quality of health care that are not due to access-related factors or clinical needs, preferences, and appropriateness of intervention" (Nelson, Stith, and Smedley, 2002). Racial minorities continue to suffer from a disproportionate burden of disease when compared to Whites.

There are many examples of health inequality along lines of race and ethnicity. Some of the most commonly reported health disparities occur in cardiovascular disease, cancer, and diabetes (Baldwin, 2003). Blacks, specifically, have higher lung cancer mortality rates than Whites (AHRQ, 2008). In 2003, the rate of new AIDS cases was three times higher among Hispanics and ten times higher among Blacks than Whites (26 and 75 per 100,000 vs. 7 per 100,000, respectively). Considering the intersection of race and gender reveals additional layers of health-related inequality. A few examples are that the infant mortality rate is higher for Black women than women of all other racial and ethnic groups, Black female Medicaid beneficiaries have longer wait times for their health care services than White women, and Black women are less likely than White women to receive chemotherapy within 6 months of a cancer diagnosis (ibid.). Even when socioeconomic status is considered, health-related disparities persist. For example, college-educated Black women have a higher infant mortality rate (11.5 per 1,000 live births) than White women with similar education (4.2 per 1,000 live births).

Similar patterns on the influence of race on health disparities and inequality exist in countries outside of the U.S. Race and ethnicity shape the nature of health inequality in the United Kingdom (Nazroo, 2003) and New Zealand (Harris et al., 2006). Similarly, although the Brazilian conceptualization of "race" is quite different than that in the U.S. (see Chapter 7), it also shapes the health-related experiences of Brazilians as discrimination continues to plague the health care system there (Ikawa and Mattar, 2008). The seriousness of the effects of racism on global health motivated the U.S. and Brazil to form the U.S.-Brazil Joint Action Plan to Eliminate Racial and Ethnic Discrimination and Promote Equality, a bilateral agreement targeting racism, in 2008. According to the Centers for Disease Control and Prevention (CDC), the plan is a unique partnership between civil society and private sector committees that targets racial discrimination, provides a platform for cooperation against discrimination, and shares information on addressing discrimination in various areas. The widespread nature of this problem ultimately led to the U.S. signing a comparable plan with Columbia in January 2010.

What makes finding avenues for addressing health inequality even more critical is that the U.S. population is becoming increasingly diverse. Organizations such as Physicians for Human Rights and the American Medical

Association recognize the severity of racial and ethnic health inequality and have made eliminating health disparities a priority. Congress even directed the Agency for Health Care Research and Quality (AHRQ) to develop the National Health Care Disparity Report (NHDR) and annually track prevailing disparities in health care delivery as they relate to racial and socioeconomic factors in the segments of the population suffering from the most adverse health disparities.

Why are race and ethnicity key to understanding health inequality in a plural society such as the United States? We offer four reasons. First, the race of health care providers has important effects on health inequality, so we apply representative bureaucracy theory to the health care context. In other words, a more racially and ethnically diverse bureaucracy may help to mitigate health-related disparities. Second, health inequality is shaped by the design of health policy and health service programs. Policy design can be shaped in important ways by race, such that programs have racialized effects. Third, there is racial bias in the policy implementation process. Though many health policies are race-neutral, these policies may be structured and implemented in ways that reinforce racial disparities. Fourth, health-related inequality exists around more than one social identity. As the U.S. becomes more diverse, a comprehensive understanding of health inequality requires extending the focus beyond a single social identity to consider the inter-sections of race/ethnicity, gender, and immigration status.

## Race, Representative Bureaucracy, and Health Inequality Research

There are benefits of health care providers and their patients sharing the same racial identity. A common understanding is that a more diverse body of health care professionals is an effective way to reduce health inequality, however, the diversity of the U.S. population does not match the diversity of health care professionals. According to data from the Association of American Medical Colleges (AAMC), in 2015, Blacks comprised 12 percent of the U.S. population but only 6 percent of new medical school graduates, and Hispanics were approximately 18 percent of the population but were only 5 percent of new medical school graduates (AAMC, 2015). Interestingly, Asians comprise 6 percent of the U.S. population but are 22 percent of new medical school graduates while Native Americans comprise nearly 1 percent of the U.S. population and of new medical school graduates (ibid.). In 2043, current racial minorities are expected to become the majority in the U.S., which makes understanding and identifying ways to eliminate racial and ethnic health-related disparities even more important.

Health care providers are street-level bureaucrats responsible for the implementation of local, state, and federal policies. These providers have direct interactions with patients and often determine their positive or negative experiences with health care systems. Many important positive consequences accrue from health care providers and their patients sharing the same racial identity. This is often referred to as patient-physician concordance (by race); and while the mechanism that results in concordance improving health outcomes is largely unclear (Street et al., 2008), the theory of representative bureaucracy may help to better clarify this relationship. Representative bureaucracy theory posits that public bureaucracies should reflect the populations they serve (Krislov, 2012), and it is used to study different administrative, political, and social problems across national contexts (Groeneveld and van de Walle 2010, p. 240). The logic driving this theory is that "if the attitudes of administrators are similar to the attitudes held by the general public, the decisions administrators make will in general be responsive to the desires of the public" (Meier and Nigro, 1976). There are two types of representation. Passive representation refers to similarity in the demographic characteristics of bureaucrats and their clients, while active representation concerns the actual actions of bureaucrats to address the needs of a particular group of people (Pitkin, 1967). Explained differently, passively representative bureaucracies employ women, minorities, and other groups in percentages close to the size of these groups in the general public while actively representative bureaucracies employ bureaucrats who pursue the interests of clients in the public who share their social identity (Mosher, 1968).

Representative bureaucracies have promising effects in non-health policy contexts, so under-represented minority health professionals may be key in meeting the needs of disadvantaged patients and reducing racial and ethnic health disparities (Saha and Shipman, 2008). Representative bureaucracies improve education-related outcomes of minority students (Keiser et al., 2002; Meier and Stewart ,1991; Meier, Stewart, and England, 1989; Meier, Wrinkle, and Polinard, 1999; Nicholson-Crotty et al., 2016; Pitts, 2005; see also Chapter 2), environmental health sanctions and outcomes (Liang, 2016), and criminal justice-related effects (Meier and Nicholson-Crotty, 2006; Riccucci, Van Ryzin, and Lavena, 2014; see Chapter 3). Interestingly, though these linkages have been less studied in terms of health outcomes, Atkins and Wilkins (2013) find that as the percentage of Black teachers in Georgia public schools approaches 20 percent, there is a reduction in the teen pregnancy rates for Black female students. Further, the negative effects of implicit bias or stereotyping are reduced when a patient and clinician share the same race (i.e. a Black patient having a Black clinician) (Cooper et al., 2012). A representative bureaucracy yields national benefits as well. For example, increases in minority health care professionals and teachers led to a reduction in the teen birth rates of minorities across U.S. states from 1990–2006 (Zhu and Walker, 2013).

There are several theories about the mechanisms that result in a more representative bureaucracy alleviating racial or ethnic health disparities. Theories of representative bureaucracy suggest minority health care providers are more likely to practice in under-served areas (Williams and Jackson, 2005, p. 332). Studies also find that health care providers from minority groups will bring greater awareness of the health inequalities from which minorities suffer and will be motivated to serve the minority community by promoting minority health. Relatedly, shared racial and ethnic identity between health care providers and their clients promotes trust in providers by patients. As a result, minority patients may become more compliant and more likely to cooperate. There are mixed findings for this expectation, but some support does exist. Trust in physicians moderates the negative effects of racial discrimination for Black men and women (Cuffee et al., 2013). Overall, though several mechanisms are possible, the conclusion is fairly consistent: a more representative health care workforce generally leads to improved health outcomes of minorities. The understanding of a positive relationship of racial concordance between health care providers and their patients has led to scholars exploring how greater racial and ethnic representation in other sectors affects health-related outcomes (Atkins and Wilkins, 2013).

## Race and the Design of Public Policy

As racial and ethnic disparities in health persist and America becomes increasingly diverse, it is important to consider how the design of health care policies and health service programs affect the take-up of health care benefits and services. Race is a social construct, but it also acts as "a marker for differential exposure to multiple disease-producing" factors (Williams and Jackson 2005, p. 325). Some conclusions about the role of race in the production of health disparities have been inappropriate or even erroneous, but attention to race and health disparity in the U.S. is warranted and necessary (LaVeist, 1996) because relationships exist among race, policy design, and health disparity. Health policy has heterogeneous effects on different groups in society (Berkman, 2009). For example, even having one set of health policies in a given state, it is common to observe racial disparity in the quality and intensity of medical treatment, preventative services for cancer, and quality of care for Medicaid patients (Williams and Jackson, 2005). Similar racial disparities have been noted in the service use of Medicaid beneficiaries following mandatory enrollment in managed care (Tai-Seale, Van Ryzin, and Lavena, 2001). Recently, the Institute of Medicine's Subcommittee on Standardized Collection of Race/Ethnicity Data for Health Care Quality emphasized the importance of accounting for and exploring race and ethnicity in all efforts targeting racial disparities in health. There has also been a specific call for more attention to the role of race during policy development, policy implementation, and the dissemination of policy information (Bleich et al., 2012; Williams and Sternthal, 2010).

Attention to the structure of bills targeting racial and ethnic health disparities has been particularly insightful in existing research. Ladenheim and Groman (2006) consider statutes, laws, and bills introduced in four states with sizable minority populations and note variation in the trends of disparity legislation. Key terms and the language used to discuss racial and ethnic health disparities also vary across the U.S. states (Young, Pollack, and Rutkow, 2015). Although these policies do not explicitly discriminate along racial lines, they tend to affect racial groups differently. For example, the structure of federal and state-imposed "barriers" for Medicaid eligibility—requirements for legal immigration status and residency, limited eligibility according to disability requirements, and income and benefit limits—affect some racial and ethnic minority beneficiaries more than others (Morin et al., 2002). Recognizing and accounting for the interplay of race and the design of health policies across different states are important to our understanding of health inequality.

### Racial Bias in the Policy Implementation Process

Existing explanations—such as unequal health care access or inclusiveness of health care services—do not completely explain the health disparity that exists in the U.S. For example, a 2003 report by the Institute of Medicine reveals significant racial and ethnic disparities in health care quality, even when factors such as health insurance coverage, socioeconomic status, stage and severity of disease, and the type of health care facility are accounted for (Nelson, Stith, and Smedley, 2002). This suggests that there are other factors at play.

In light of the extensive history of racial divides in America, it is likely that racial bias affects policy implementation in a manner that contributes to racial and ethnic disparities in health. Health care providers are responsible for policy implementation, and we argue that how the race of these providers affects their behaviors is generally overlooked. Of course, past legislation targets instances of unfair treatment. For example, a leading legislative accomplishment of the Civil Rights movement was the passage of the Civil Rights Acts of 1964 (CRA), which banned discrimination and segregation based on race, religion, national origin, and gender in schools, the workplace, public accommodations, and in federally assisted programs. While this important piece of legislation outlaws explicit racial bias or discrimination, it does not mention implicit racial bias, or the subconscious bias that affects the attitudes or stereotypes that shape an individual's perceptions, decisions, and actions. Though the CRA is associated with a reduction in explicit racial bias, there are reasons to suspect that implicit racial bias continues to plague the health policy implementation process.

Implicit racial bias may be triggered by "cues" such as a person's race or accent (Blair, Steiner, and Havranek, 2011) and is particularly problematic because it may operate without a provider being aware of it. While the implicit bias of most health care providers generates positive attitudes toward White patients, it results in negative attitudes toward people of color (Hall et al., 2015). Even well-meaning physicians may have implicit racial bias that inadvertently infiltrates their behavior during policy implementation. The effects of implicit bias are grave. Subconscious biases or attitudes can influence the implementation process and contribute to differences in treatment according to race, gender, age, language, and a host of other factors. For example, when asked about their experiences with primary care providers and community members, Latinos and Blacks perceive significant levels of implicit bias from both primary care providers and community members but do not report any experiences of explicit bias with these health care providers (Blair et al., 2012). A separate study exploring the connection between explicit and implicit bias and patient perceptions of their clinicians found that while there are very low levels of explicit bias among clinicians, clinicians vary in the level of their implicit bias (Blair, Steiner, and Havranek, 2011). Recent research in political science also reveals a "spillover" effect of racial attitudes on the general public's health care attitudes (Tesler, 2012) and suggests that clinicians are influenced by race, racial attitudes, and even racial bias at a level that is comparable to members of the public (Blair, Steiner, and Havranek. 2011).

We offer an example from Blair et al. (2012) to further demonstrate the possible detrimental effects of race, implicit bias, and policy implementation. Because of implicit bias or pre-existing stereotypes, a physician may view a Black patient who suffers from hypertension as unlikely to follow an intensive treatment regimen. The effects of the bias may result in the physician unintentionally behaving in a manner (via certain facial expressions, voice tone, etc.) that makes the patient feel uncomfortable, which then disrupts the flow of information and creates tension or discomfort in the physician-patient interaction. This would weaken the patient's likelihood of following the treatment recommended by the physician. From this example, it is clear that attention to the behaviors of health care workers in examining the potential for racial bias in implementing policy is vital. Physicians (and other health care providers) are the street-level bureaucrats responsible for implementing health care policy and providing health care services to the public. Given their central role in service provision, studying implicit racial bias in the behavior of these providers is crucial.

### Intersectionality Theory and Health Inequality Research

As America becomes increasingly diverse, policymakers and bureaucrats must consider the overlaps that occur among multiple social identities to fully understand the dynamics of health inequality. This requires moving beyond understanding health-related disparities as differences in the health outcomes and health care access between Whites and minorities and focusing on differences across multiple social identities. Here, social identity refers to how individuals identify themselves relative to others. Examples of social groups include but are not limited to one's racial/ethnic identity, gender, and class. Intersectionality and related frameworks were originally developed by Black feminist scholars (Crenshaw ,1991; hooks, 1982) and emphasize the importance of considering multiple social identities in order to fully understand the nature of social inequality. After all, individuals have multiple social identities (for example, Black women, White males, high-income Latinos, etc.). The central principle of intersectionality theory is that the concurrent presence of multiple social identities can result in interlocking systems of oppression or privilege. In other words, the intersectional effects of social identities may offer important insights about the dynamics of social inequality that would be overlooked by focusing on the isolated effects of single social identities.

As most current discussions of health-related inequality focus on social identities such as race, gender, and class as separate categories, applying intersectionality theory to health-related inequality can likely enhance awareness of how to conceptualize, investigate, analyze, and address persistent and troubling inequalities (Bowleg, 2012). Using an intersectionality approach also allows researchers to integrate institutionalized racial bias theory, which refers to the policies, practices, and procedures of institutions that have a disproportionately negative effect on the access and quality of goods, services, and opportunities of minorities, and study/understand health-related inequality.

There are several ways this recommendation can be achieved in research moving forward. For the intersection of race and gender, for example, we can move beyond the standard comparison of the health access and outcomes of racial/ethnic minorities to Whites to focusing on White women, Black women, Latinas, Asian women, and other minority women (as well as comparing the outcomes of these women to men, when appropriate). As mentioned earlier in this chapter, there are disparities in health outcomes and health care access of individuals that are particularly stark when accounting for race/ethnicity *and* gender. This includes major differences in HIV-related health indicators. In 2009, Blacks were only 13 percent of the U.S. population but accounted for 52 percent of new HIV cases. Applying the intersectional approach reveals an additional layer of key differences. For 2009, while Black men comprised 42 percent of new cases among all men, Black women comprised 66 percent of new cases among all women (CDC, 2009). This approach also helps to reveal that minority women have a higher incidence of parity-related obesity than White women (Davis et al., 2009) and shows gaps in the early detection of cancer rates for nine groups of minority women compared to White women (Glanz et al., 2003). These disparities become even more complicated when the intersection of gender and sexual orientation is taken into account (Operario et al., 2015; Przedworski et al., 2014).

Promising avenues for improving the health status of minority women can also extend from health inequality research that works through the lens of intersectionality. It seems that there is also a need for greater cultural sensitivity and competence in education and health care delivery structures in reducing health inequality for minority women (Kritek et al., 2002) as well as strategies that account for the sociocultural importance of body appearance (Versey, 2014) if the health inequality that minority women suffer from is to be reduced.

Intersectionality theory can also be useful for exploring how ethnicity and immigration status affects health inequality. For example, major variations exist in health outcomes across Hispanic subgroups (Williams and Jackson, 2006). There are differences in the inclusiveness of immigrant eligibility policies for Temporary Assistance for Needy Families (TANF) and Medicaid (Filindra, 2012) and gaps in the health care coverage rates of the native and foreign-born populations. Further, immigrants' access to health insurance is influenced by immigrant population density and Medicaid eligibility rules (Zhu and Xu, 2015).

## New Research on Health Inequality: A Comparative Perspective

Although the dynamics of health-related inequality in other countries are not of the same nature of inequality in the U.S. (i.e. the high levels of health care spending in the U.S. and poorer health outcomes than other countries), major differences in the health status and in health care access among different sub-population groups exist across countries. Ethnicity refers to cultural differences that are the result of common geographical origin, linguistic, and/or religious differences (Bartley, 2017). A World Health Organization (WHO) report estimates that there are nearly one billion migrants across the world (WHO, 2014). Many countries have experienced increased levels of immigration and ethnic diversity, which have contributed to rising ethnic health disparities in a variety of places (Karlsen and Nazroo, 2002). For example, there are major differences in many of the health outcomes of native-born and foreign-born populations in Canada (Siddiqi et al., 2013) and the United Kingdom (Marmot, Adelstein, and Bulusu, 1984). Lorant and Bhopal (2011) highlight the connection between immigration levels, increased ethnic diversity, and health inequality in Europe. There are also major gaps in other health indicators—such as satisfaction with health-related quality of life—for immigrants and native-born Germans (Nesterko et al., 2013) as well as for Māori, an indigenous group, and Europeans in New Zealand (Harris et al., 2006).

Several factors have been highlighted as important levers in attempts to reduce health-related inequality. One factor that receives a significant amount of attention is health-related spending. Across countries, there is an expectation that increased health-related spending will improve the health outcomes of citizens. In most countries, ethnicity and income have a strong, yet complicated relationship. The nature of this relationship makes it important for public health scholars and managers to consider how ethnicity shapes health status (Nazroo, 1998) and results in socioeconomic indicators being very important for understanding health-related inequality in a comparative context (Stronks and Kunst, 2009). A second factor is the level of competition. A common argument is that competition can increase the efficiency of health care systems. However, there is not a clear relationship between competition, efficiency, responsiveness to patients, and thus health-related inequality, because competition does not affect health care inequality in the United Kingdom (Cookson et al., 2010) but has important benefits in other countries. Increasing the efficiency of a health care system can be a lengthy and complicated process that depends on various factors (Schut and Van de Ven, 2005). Recognizing the difficulty of attaining the conditions that promote a relationship between competition, efficiency, and reduced health-related inequality, many countries outside of the U.S. commonly use hospital accountability agreements. Governments employ these agreements in an effort to ensure public funding is achieving its desired performance in hospitals. These types of structures have been shown to reduce health inequalities in countries (see Reeleder et al., 2008 for an example from Canada).

## Unanswered Questions and New Policy Challenges

There are several questions that current and future health care providers, public managers, and public policy and public administration students should consider. Three lines of policy inquiry regarding racial bias and health inequality are highlighted here. First, given the nature of implicit bias, exploring how different social identities of health care professionals affect their level of implicit bias (if this can be measured well) will be important. Conducting surveys or interviewing health care providers who do not have high levels of implicit bias can also offer crucial insight on the delivery of health care services. Second, how biases affect specific components of health care provider assessments of patients is important. This includes attention to the effects of the demographic patterns of states and structure of health care systems on these dynamics. Lastly, our understanding of health inequality would benefit from information on ways to reduce the negative effects of implicit bias on policy structure and implementation. Some social psychologists have started studying this (Burgess et al., 2007), but concrete steps to mitigating these effects are still lacking.

Questions relating to race and health policy design also warrant greater attention. What are the common themes in legislation that targets racial and ethnic disparities? For example, guidelines for pharmaceutical testing from the National Institute of Health (NIH) now require more racially inclusive populations. These guidelines were likely revised because, although drug testing policies are not inherently racialized, there is a racial bias that can occur if public policies are not implemented in a universal manner (Becker et al., 2014; Kunins et al., 2007). It is important to examine the wording and themes of this type of legislation. Relatedly, examining how effective legislation is in actually reducing these disparities across different social contexts will also be insightful. Of course, there are not different health policies for members of different racial groups; that is, individuals in the same area are regulated by the same health policies. Greater attention should be given to identifying community or societal level factors that result in differences in the take-up rates of health care services by members of different racial groups. There has also been attention to the social determinants of health (e.g., Williams and Jackson, 2005) that can consider important questions such as whether there are major differences in the locations of health delivery systems for members of different racial and ethnic groups. Students should think critically about the role race plays in the design of health policy—even if inadvertently—and how these dynamics contribute to health inequality. Extending the focus beyond state-level health policy and considering community-level efforts are necessary. What community-based initiatives exist? Have these efforts been successful at reducing racial and ethnic disparities?

Several unanswered questions remain regarding race, representative bureaucracy, and racial disparities in health. Overall, there are many benefits of having minority health care providers and a representative bureaucracy.

What remains unclear is whether there are limits to the beneficial effects of representative bureaucracy on health disparity. That is, are the expected benefits of a representative bureaucracy limited by health care or organizational contexts? Do these benefits vary according to health care professional type (i.e. clinicians, nurses, doctors)? Is there a minimum threshold that must be attained before the benefits of minority representation are realized? Will potential effects also impact members of different minority groups in comparable ways? We also need to consider the demand for representative bureaucracy from those who suffer from poor health (Thielemann and Stewart, 1996). In other words, do individuals with poor health express an interest in having a health care clinician who shares their race? Are these individuals more likely to comply with the instructions they are given when they have the same race as their health care clinician? Increasing the diversity of the health care workforce is a complicated and lengthy process, and it may be the case that cultural competency could serve as a temporary alternative for addressing health inequality. Culturally competent health care providers understand that cultural differences matter and adapt their communication with patients accordingly. It will be worthwhile studying the prevalence and variation in this training as well as whether such training has any short- or long-term effects.

Our first recommendation centers on the use of intersectional approaches by scholars and policymakers alike. For research to be as useful as possible, scholars must ensure that research being produced captures real-world complexities. Considering intersectionality moves research in that direction as studying how multiple social identities interactively shape health disparities offers a more comprehensive understanding on the nature of health disparity as well as how health policy design may affect the social constructions of the targeted populations. Policymakers should also adopt an intersectional approach more effectively in the policymaking process. Applying this approach can contribute to a better, more informed policymaking process.

In a related point, greater attention should be given to the dynamics surrounding the health of minorities and particularly to groups other than Black Americans. For example, the Latino Paradox is a term used to describe an interesting phenomenon—that (first-generation) Latino and Hispanic Americans tend to have comparable, and sometimes better, health outcomes (particularly, lower mortality rates, see Abraido-Lanza, Chao, and Florez, 2005, p. 1243) than non-Hispanic White Americans though, on average, Latinos and Hispanics have less education and lower incomes. It seems that community networks (McGlade, Saha, and Dahlstrom, 2004), and neighborhood context (Cagney, Browning, and Wallace, 2006) explain a portion of this phenomenon. While there is general consensus that the paradox will erode over time (Viruell-Fuentes, 2007), the mechanisms that contribute to this paradox are still poorly understood (Abraido-Lanza et al., 1999).

Lastly, health inequality in a comparative context should also receive greater attention as an increasing number of industrialized countries face similar challenges. Greater attention to health-related inequality across countries by public administration students, public managers, and those interested in public health can offer promising insight. For example, considering health disparities in different nations will shed light on the effects of universal health care on health-related inequality, the nature of health inequality for different sub-groups, and a host of additional important questions.

## Conclusion

This chapter offers a critical synopsis of the emerging literature on racial and ethnic disparities in health. Health-related inequality (health inequality and health disparities) is problematic given its nature (existing along social constructs that are widespread, and many that are largely preventable) and the seriousness of its effects. What makes health inequality particularly peculiar in the U.S. is that the U.S. spends more money on health care than any other country in the world. What mechanisms explain how the nation that spends the most on health care also has a population that suffers from some of the worst health outcomes?

We split our discussion of these important questions into two sections: the first focusing on health inequality and disparity in general and the second centering on health inequality and disparity that exist along lines of race and intersectional social identities. Our review uncovered many factors that have serious effects on health inequality. For example, the design, delivery, and management of health policy have had profound effects on disadvantaged groups' access to care, service utilization, and health status.

The second half of our review began by noting the limited racial and ethnic diversity of health care providers. We highlighted how racial bias affects both policy design and implementation. After reviewing the current understanding of the effects of race/ethnicity on health-related inequality, we called for more attention to intersectionality theory. This will allow us to better account for the intersectional effects of multiple social identities on health-related inequality. Finally, the chapter considered unanswered questions that should be addressed in order to expand our understanding of health inequality globally and in the U.S.

## Discussion Questions

1   What is health inequality? How would you describe racial and ethnic disparities in health?
2   Discuss the nature of health inequality both globally and in the U.S. context specifically. What dynamics make health inequality so puzzling in the American context?
3   Diversity can exist along many characteristics, including race, ethnicity, gender, age, religion, and socioeconomic status, to name a few. What is the trend in the diversity of health care professionals in the U.S.? Discuss state-wide initiatives aimed at increasing workforce diversity and other factors you think may increase the diversity of health care professionals.

4    Which suggestions made in this chapter are most promising? Do any seem problematic?
5    What is intersectionality theory? Which intersections of social identities are most important for our understanding of health inequality in the U.S.? Do you think different intersectional identities are important in countries outside of the U.S.?

# References

AAMC (Association of American Medical Colleges). 2015. "Total graduates by US Medical School and race and ethnicity, 2014–2015." Available at: www.aamc.org/data-reports/students-residents/report/facts

Abdou, Cleopatra M., and Adam W. Fingerhut. 2014. "Stereotype threat among Black and White women in health care settings." *Cultural Diversity and Ethnic Minority Psychology* 20(3): 316–323.

Abdus, Salam, Kamila B. Mistry, and Thomas M. Selden. 2015. "Racial and ethnic disparities in services and the Patient Protection and Affordable Care Act." *American Journal of Public Health* 105(S5): S668–S675.

Abraido-Lanza, Ana F., Maria T. Chao, and Karen R. Florez. 2005. "Do healthy behaviors decline with greater acculturation?: Implications for the Latino mortality paradox." *Social Science & Medicine* 61(6): 1243–1255.

Abraido-Lanza, Ana F., Bruce P. Dohrenwend, Daisy S. Ng-Mak, and J. Blake Turner. 1999. "The Latino mortality paradox: A test of the 'salmon bias' and healthy migrant hypotheses." *American Journal of Public Health* 89(10): 1543–1548.

Adler, Nancy E. and David H. Rehkopf. 2008. "US disparities in health: Descriptions, causes, and mechanisms." *Annual Review of Public Health* 29: 235–252.

AHRQ (Agency for Healthcare Research and Quality). 2008. *Reducing racial and ethnic disparities in health care: Program brief.* Bethesda, MD: AHRQ. Available at: www.ahrq.gov/professionals/quality-patient-safety/index.html.

AHRQ (Agency for Healthcare Research and Quality). 2015. *Key findings.* Bethesda, MD: AHRQ. Available at: www.ahrq.gov/research/findings/nhqrdr/nhqdr14/key1.html.

Alkema, Leontine, Doris Chou, Daniel Hogan, et al. 2017."Global, regional, and national levels and trends in maternal mortality between 1990 and 2015, with scenario-based projections to 2030: A systematic analysis by the UN Maternal Mortality Estimation Inter-Agency Group." *The Lancet* 387(10017): 462–474.

Alpers, Lise-Merete. 2016. "Distrust and patients in intercultural healthcare: A qualitative interview study." *Nursing Ethics* 25(3): 313–323.

Amirkhanyan, Anna. 2008. "Privatizing public nursing homes: Examining the effects on quality and access." *Public Administration Review* 68(4): 665–680.

Ashton, Carol M., Paul Haidet, Debora A. Paterniti, et al. 2003. "Racial and ethnic disparities in the use of health services: bias, preferences, or poor communication?" *Journal of General Internal Medicine* 18(2): 146–152.

Atkins, Danielle N., and Vicky M. Wilkins. 2013. "Going beyond reading, writing, and arithmetic: The effects of teacher representation on teen pregnancy rates." *Journal of Public Administration Research and Theory* 23(4): 771–790.

Baldwin, Dee M. 2003. "Disparities in health and health care: Focusing efforts to eliminate unequal burdens." *Online Journal of Issues in Nursing* 8(1): 231–266.

Barr, Donald. 2007. *Health disparities in the United States: Social class, race, ethnicity, and health.* Baltimore, MD: The Johns Hopkins University Press.

Bartley, Mel. 2017. *Health inequality: An introduction to concepts, theories and methods.* Malden, MA: Polity Press.

Becker, William C., Salimah Meghani, Jeanette M. Tetrault, and David A. Fiellin. 2014. "Racial/ethnic differences in report of drug testing practices at the workplace level in the US." *The American Journal on Addictions* 23(4): 357–362.

Berkman, Lisa F. 2009. "Social epidemiology: Social determinants of health in the United States: Are we losing ground?" *Annual Review of Public Health* 30: 27–41.

Bitler, Marianne P., and Janet Currie. 2004. "Does WIC work? The effects of WIC on pregnancy and birth outcomes." *Journal of Policy Analysis and Management* 24(1): 73–91.

Black, Douglas. 1980. *Inequalities in health: Report of a research working group.* London: DHSS.

Blair, Irene V., Edward P. Havranek, David W. Price, Rebecca Hanratty, Diane L. Fairclough, et al. 2012. "Assessment of biases against Latinos and African Americans among primary care providers and community members." *American Journal of Public Health* 103(1): 92–98.

Blair, Irene V., John F. Steiner, and Edward P. Havranek. 2011. "Unconscious (implicit) bias and health disparities: Where do we go from here?" *The Permanente Journal* 15(2): 71–78.

Bleich, Sara N., Marian P. Jarlenski, Caryn N. Bell, and Thomas A. LaVeist. 2012. "Health inequalities: Trends, progress, and policy." *Annual Review of Public Health* 33: 7–40.

Bowleg, Lisa. 2012. "The problem with the phrase Women and Minorities: Intersectionality- An important theoretical framework for public health." *American Journal of Public Health* 102(7): 1267–1273.

Braveman, Paula. 2012. "Health inequalities by class and race in the US: What can we learn from the patterns?" *Social Science & Medicine* 74(5): 665–667.

Brondolo, Elizabeth, Erica E. Love, Melissa Pencille, Antoinette Schoenthaler, and Gbenga Ogedegbe. 2011. "Racism and hypertension: A review of the empirical evidence and implications for clinical practice." *American Journal of Hypertension* 24 (5): 518–529.

Buchmueller, Thomas C., and Christopher S. Carpenter. 2012. "The effect of requiring private employers to extend health benefit eligibility to same-sex partners of employees: Evidence from California." *Journal of Policy Analysis and Management* 31 (2): 388–403.

Burgess, Diana, Michelle Van Ryn, John Dovidio, and Somnath Saha. 2007. "Reducing racial bias among health care providers: Lessons from social-cognitive psychology." *Journal of General Internal Medicine* 22(6): 882–887.

Cacari-Stone, Lisa, Nina Wallerstein, Analilia P. Garcia, and Meredith Minkler. 2014. "The promise of community-based participatory research for health equity: A conceptual model for bridging evidence with policy." *American Journal of Public Health* 104(9): 1615–1623.

Cagney, Kathleen A., Christopher R. Browning, and Danielle M. Wallace. 2006. "The Latino paradox in neighborhood context: The case of asthma and other respiratory conditions." *American Journal of Public Health* 97(5): 919–925.

CDC (Centers for Disease Control and Prevention). 2006. *Centers for Disease Control and Prevention: Health e-stats.* Atlanta, GA: CDC. Available at: www.cdc.gov/nchs/products/pubs/pubd/hestats/prelimdeaths04/preliminarydeaths04.htm.

CDC (Centers for Disease Control and Prevention). 2009. *Centers for Disease Control and Prevention: HIV surveillance report.* Atlanta, GA: CDC. Available at: www.cdc.gov/hiv/surveillance/resources/reports/2009report/pdf/2009SurveillanceReport.pdf.

CDC (Centers for Disease Control and Prevention). 2015a. *Centers for Disease Control and Prevention: Health, United States, 2016, Table 93.* Atlanta, GA: CDC. Available at: www.cdc.gov/nchs/data/hus/2016/093.pdf

CDC (Centers for Disease Control and Prevention). 2015b. *US Public Health Service Syphilis Study at Tuskegee.* Atlanta, GA: CDC. Available at: www.cdc.gov/tuskegee/timeline.htm.

Chavez, Leo R. 2012. "Undocumented immigrants and their use of medical services in Orange County, California." *Social Science & Medicine* 74(6): 887–893.

Collard, Erin. 2006. "Collaboration to address the asthma problem among Native Americans." *Public Administration Review* 66(S1): 157–158.

Collison, David, Colin Dey, Gwen Hannah, and Lorna Stevenson. 2007. "Income inequality and child mortality in wealthy nations." *Journal of Public Health* 29(2): 114–117.

Cook, Benjamin Lê, Colleen L. Barry, and Susan H. Busch. 2013. "Racial/ethnic disparity trends in children's mental health care access and expenditures from 2002 to 2007." *Health Services Research* 48(1): 129–149.

Cookson, Richard, Mark Dusheiko, Geoffrey Hardman, and Stephen Martin. 2010. "Competition and inequality: Evidence from the English National Health Service 1991–2001." *Journal of Public Administration Research and Theory* 20(Suppl. 2): i181–i205.

Cooper, Lisa A., Debra L. Roter, Kathryn A. Carson, Mary Catherine Beach, Janice A. Sabin, et al. 2012. "The associations of clinicians' implicit attitudes about race with medical visit communication and patient ratings of interpersonal care." *American Journal of Public Health* 102(5): 979–987.

Crenshaw, Kimberle. 1991. "Mapping the margins: Intersectionality, identity politics, and violence against women of color." *Stanford Law Review* 43(6): 1241–1299.

Cuffee, Yendelela L., J. Lee Hargraves, Milagros Rosal, Becky A. Briesacher, Antoinette Schoenthaler, et al. 2013. "Reported racial discrimination, trust in physicians, and medication adherence among inner-city African Americans with hypertension." *American Journal of Public Health* 103(11): e55–e62.

Davis, Esa M., Stephen J. Zyzanski, Christine M. Olson, Kurt C. Stange, and Ralph I. Horwitz. 2009. "Racial, ethnic, and socioeconomic differences in the incidence of obesity related to childbirth." *American Journal of Public Health* 99(2): 294–299.

DeSoto, William, Hassan Tajalli, and Kay Hofer. 2001. "Health care in rural Texas." *Policy Studies Journal* 29(1): 154–164.

Devaney, Barbara, Linda Bilheimer, and Jennifer Schore. 1992. "Medicaid costs and birth outcomes: The effects of prenatal WIC participation and the use of prenatal care." *Journal of Policy Analysis and Management* 11(4): 573–592.

Dong, XinQi. 2018. "Achieving health equity in the Asian population." *Gerontology and Geriatric Medicine* 4: 1–4.

Ettner, Susan L. 1997. "Medicaid participation among the eligible elderly." *Journal of Policy Analysis and Management* 16(2): 237–255.

Fertig, Angela R., and David A. Reingold. 2007. "Public housing, health, and health behaviors: Is there a connection?" *Journal of Policy Analysis and Management* 26(4):831–859.

Figlio, David N., Sarah Hamersma, and Jeffrey Roth. 2015. "Information shocks and the take-up of social programs." *Journal of Policy Analysis and Management* 34(4): 781–804.

Filindra, Alexandra. 2012. "Immigrant social policy in the American states: Race politics and state TANF and Medicaid eligibility rules for legal permanent residents." *State Politics & Policy Quarterly* 13(1): 26–48.

Ford, Chandra L., and Collins O. Airhihenbuwa. 2010. "Critical race theory, race equity, and public health: Toward antiracism praxis." *American Journal of Public Health* 100(S1): S30–S35.

Fossett, James, and Frank J. Thompson. 2006. "Administrative responsiveness to the disadvantaged: The case of children's health insurance." *Journal of Public Administration Research and Theory* 16(3): 369–392.

Frederickson, H. George. 1989. "Minnowbrook II: Changing epochs of public administration." *Public Administration Review* 49(2): 95–100.

Frederickson, H. George. 1990. "Public administration and social equity." *Public Administration Review* 50(2): 228–237.

Gaskin, Darrell J., Roland J. Thorpe Jr., Emma E. McGinty, Kelly Bower, Charles Rohde, et al. 2014. "Disparities in diabetes: The nexus of race, poverty, and place." *American Journal of Public Health* 104(11): 2147–2155.

GBD 2015 and Healthcare Access and Quality Collaborators. 2017. "Healthcare access and quality index based on mortality from causes amenable to personal health care in 195 countries and territories, 1990–2015: A novel analysis from the global burden of disease .study 2015." *Lancet* 390(10091): 231–266.

Gee, Gilbert C. 2002. "A multilevel analysis of the relationship between institutional and individual racial discrimination and health status." *American Journal of Public Health* 92(4): 615–623.

Glanz, Karen, Robert T. Croyle, Veronica Y. Chollette, and Vivian W. Pinn. 2003. "Cancer-related health disparities in women." *American Journal of Public Health* 93 (2): 292–298.

Global Health Observatory. 2017. *Global Health Observatory health workforce.* Geneva: World Health Organization. www.who.int/gho/healthworkforce/en/.

Gooden, Susan, and Shannon Portillo. 2011. "Advancing social equity in the Minnowbrook tradition." *Journal of Public Administration Research* 21(Suppl. 1): i61–i76.

Gray, Alastair McIntosh. 1982. "Inequalities in health. The Black Report: A summary and comment." *International Journal of Health Services* 12(3): 349–380.

Gray, Virginia, David Lowery, James Monogan, and Erik K. Godwin. 2010. "Incrementing toward nowhere: Universal health care coverage in the States." *Publius: The Journal of Federalism* 40(1): 82–113.

Green, Alexander R., Dana R. Carney, Daniel J. Pallin, Long H. Ngo, Kristal L. Raymond, et al. 2007. "Implicit bias among physicians and its prediction of thrombolysis: Decisions for black and white patients." *Journal of General Internal Medicine* 22(9): 1231–1238.

Groeneveld, Sandra, and Steven Van de Walle. 2010. "A contingency approach to representative bureaucracy: Power, equal opportunities, and diversity." *International Review of Administrative Sciences* 76(2): 239–258.

Hacker, Jacob S. 2004. "Privatizing risk without privatizing the welfare state: The hidden politics of social policy retrenchment in the United States." *American Political Science Review* 98(2): 243–260.

Hacker, Jacob S. 2006. *The great risk shift: The new economic insecurity and the decline of the American dream.* New York, NY: Oxford University Press.

Hall, William J., Mimi V. Chapman, Kent M. Lee, Yesenia M. Merino, Tainayah W. Thomas, et al. 2015. "Implicit racial/ethnic bias among health care professionals and its influence on health care outcomes: a systematic review." *American Journal of Public Health* 105(12): e60–e76.

Harris, Ricci, Martin Tobias, Mona Jeffreys, Kiri Waldegrave, Saffron Karlsen, et al. 2006. "Effects of self-reported racial discrimination and deprivation on Māori health and inequalities in New Zealand: cross-sectional study." *The Lancet* 367 (9527): 2005–2009.

Hero, Joachim O., Alan M. Zaslavsky, and Robert J. Blendon. 2017. "The United States leads other nations on differences by income in perceptions of health and health care." *Health Affairs* 36(6): 1032–1040.

Heyman, Josiah McC, Guillermina Gina Núñez, and Victor Talavera. 2009. "Healthcare access and barriers for unauthorized immigrants in El Paso County, Texas." *Family & Community Health* 32(1): 4–21.

Hicklin, Alisa, and Kenneth J. Meier. 2008. "Race, structure, and state governments: The politics of higher education." *The Journal of Politics* 70(3): 851–860.

Hofrichter, Richard, and Rajiv Bhatia. 2010. *Tackling health inequalities through public health practice.* New York, NY: Oxford University Press.

Hong, Young-Rock, Justin Tauscher, and Michelle Cardel. 2018. "Distrust in health care and cultural factors are associated with uptake of colorectal cancer screening in Hispanic and Asian Americans." *Cancer* 124(2): 335–345.

hooks, bell. 1982. *Ain't I a woman? Black women and feminism.* New York, NY: Routledge.

Humphries, Karin H., and Eddy van Doorslaer. 2000. "Income-related health inequality in Canada." *Social Science & Medicine* 50(5): 663–671.

Ikawa, Daniela, and Laura Mattar. 2008. "Racial discrimination in access to health: The Brazilian experience." *Kansas Law Review* 57: 949–970.

Jang, Yuri, Nan Sook Park, Hyunwoo Yoon, Ya-Ching Huang, Min-Kyoung Rhee, et al. 2018. "The risk typology of healthcare access and its association with unmet healthcare needs in Asian Americans." *Health and Social Care in the Community* 26(1): 72–79.

Joyce, Ted, Andrew Racine, and Cristina Yunzal-Butler. 2008. "Reassessing the WIC effect: Evidence from the pregnancy nutrition surveillance system." *Journal of Policy Analysis and Management* 27(2): 277–303.

Kaestner, Robert, and Nasreen Khan. 2012. "Medicare Part D and its effect on the use of prescription drugs and use of other health care services of the elderly." *Journal of Policy Analysis and Management* 31(2): 253–279.

Kalra, Rajat, Nirav Patel, Pankaj Arora, and Garima Arora. 2019. "Cardiovascular health and disease among Asian-Americans (from the National Health and Nutrition Examination Survey)." *The American Journal of Cardiology* 124(2): 270–277.

Kaplan, Sherrie H., Sheldon Greenfield, and John Ware. 1989. "Assessing the effects of physician-patient interactions on the outcomes of chronic disease." *Medical Care* 27(3): S110–S127.

Karlsen, Saffron, and James Y. Nazroo. 2002. "Relation between racial discrimination, social class, and health among ethnic minority groups." *American Journal of Public Health* 92(4): 624–631.

Kawachi, Ichiro, Norman Daniels, and Dean E. Robinson. 2005. "Health disparities by race and class: Why both matter." *Health Affairs* 24(2): 343–352.

Keiser, Lael, Vicky M. Wilkins, Kenneth J. Meier, and Catherine A. Holland. 2002. "Lipstick and logarithms: Gender, institutional context and representative bureaucracy." *American Political Science Review* 96(3): 553–564.

Ketsche, Patricia, E. Kathleen Adams, Angela Snyder, Mei Zhou, Karen Minyard, and Rebecca Kellenberg. 2007. "Discontinuity of coverage for Medicaid and SCHIP children at a transitional birthday." *Health Services Research* 42(62): 2410–2423.

Kim, Ae-Sook, and Edward T. Jennings. 2009. "Effects of US states' social welfare systems on population health." *Policy Studies Journal* 37(4): 745–767.

Kim, Wooksoo and Robert H. Keefe. 2010. "Barriers to healthcare among Asian Americans." *Social Work in Public Health* 25(3–4): 286–295.

Krislov, Samuel. 2012. *Representative bureaucracy*. New Orleans, LA: Quid Pro Books.

Kritek, Phyllis Beck, Martha Hargraves, Ernestine H. Cuellar, Florence Dallo, Donna M. Gauthier, et al. 2002. "Eliminating health disparities among minority women: A report on conference workshop process and outcomes." *American Journal of Public Health* 92(4): 580–587.

Kunins, Hillary Veda, Eran Bellin, Cynthia Chazotte, Evelyn Du, and Julia Hope Arnsten. 2007. "The effect of race on provider decisions to test for illicit drug use in the peripartum setting." *Journal of Women's Health* 16(2): 245–255.

Ladenheim, Kala, and Rachel Groman. 2006. "State legislative activities related to elimination of health disparities." *Journal of Health Politics, Policy and Law* 31(1): 153–184.

LaVeist, Thomas A. 1996. "Why we should continue to study race… but do a better job: An essay on race, racism and health." *Ethnicity & Disease* 6(1–2): 21–29.

LaVeist, Thomas A. 2005. *Minority populations and health: An introduction to health disparities in the United States*. San Francisco, CA: Jossey-Bass.

Levy, Helen, and David Meltzer. 2008. "The impact of health insurance on health." *Annual Review Public Health* 29: 399–409.

Liang, Jiaqi. 2016. "The shadow of the politics of deservedness? The implications of group- centric policy context for environmental policy implementation inequalities in the United States." *Journal of Public Administration Research and Theory* 26(3): 552–570.

Liebert, Saltanat, and Carl F. Ameringer. 2013. "The health care safety net and the Affordable Care Act: Implications for Hispanic immigrants." *Public Administration Review* 73(6): 810–820.

Lillie-Blanton, Marsha, and Catherine Hoffman. 2005. "The role of health insurance coverage in reducing racial/ethnic disparities in health care." *Health Affairs* 24(2): 398–408.

Lopoo, Leonard M. 2004. "Maternal employment and teenage childbearing: Evidence from the PSID." *Journal of Policy Analysis and Management* 24(1): 23–46.

Lorant, Vincent, and Raj S. Bhopal. 2011. "Ethnicity, socio-economic status and health research: Insights from an implications of Charles Tilly's theory of durable inequality." *Journal of Epidemiology & Community Health* 65(8): 671–675.

Lykens, Kristine A., and Paul A. Jargowsky. 2002. "Medicaid matters: Children's health and Medicaid eligibility expansions." *Journal of Policy Analysis and Management* 21(2): 219–238.

Marmot, Michael. 2005. "Social determinants of health inequalities." *Lancet* 365: 1099–1104.

Marmot, Michael Gideon, Abraham Manie Adelstein, and Lak Bulusu. 1984. *Immigrant mortality in England and Wales 1970–78: Causes of death by country of birth.* London: MSO.

McGlade, Michael S., Somnath Saha, and Marie E. Dahlstrom. 2004. "The Latina paradox: An opportunity for restructuring prenatal care delivery." *American Journal of Public Health* 94(12): 2062–2065.

Meier, Kenneth J., and Jill Nicholson-Crotty. 2006. "Gender, representative bureaucracy, and law enforcement: The case of sexual assault." *Public Administration Review* 66(6): 850–860.

Meier, Kenneth J., and Lloyd G. Nigro. 1976. "Representative bureaucracy and policy preferences: A study in the attitudes of federal executives." *Public Administration Review* 36(4): 458–469.

Meier, Kenneth J., and Joseph Stewart. 1991. *The politics of Hispanic education: Un paso pa'lante y dos pa'tras.* Albany, NY: State University of New York Press.

Meier, Kenneth J., Joseph Stewart, and Robert E. England. 1989. *Race, class and education: The politics of second-generation discrimination.* Madison, WI: University of Wisconsin Press.

Meier, Kenneth J., Robert D. Wrinkle, and Jerry L. Polinard. 1999. "Representative bureaucracy and distributional equity: Addressing the hard question." *The Journal of Politics* 61(4): 1025–1039.

Morales, Leo S., William E. Cunningham, Julie A. Brown, Honghu Liu, and Ron D. Hays. 1999. "Are Latinos less satisfied with communication by health care providers?" *Journal of General Internal Medicine* 14(7): 409–417.

Morin, Stephen F., Sohini Sengupta, Myrna Cozen, T. Anne Richards, Michael D. Shriver, et al. 2002. "Responding to racial and ethnic disparities in use of HIV drugs: Analysis of state policies." *Public Health Reports* 117(3): 263–272.

Mosher, Frederick C. 1968. *Democracy and the public service.* New York, NY: Oxford University Press.

Mouton, Charles P., Pamela L. Carter-Nolan, Kepher H. Makambi, Teletia R. Taylor, Julie R. Palmer, et al. 2010. "Impact of perceived racial discrimination on health screening in black women." *Journal of Health Care for the Poor and Undeserved* 21(1): 287–300.

Nazroo, James Y. 1998 "Genetic, cultural or socio-economic vulnerability? Explaining ethnic inequalities in health." *Sociology of Health & Illness* 20(5): 710–730.

Nazroo, James Y. 2003. "The structuring of ethnic inequalities in health: Economic position, racial discrimination, and racism." *American Journal of Public Health* 93(2): 277–284.

Nelson, Alan R., Adrienne Y. Stith, and Brian D. Smedley. 2002. *Unequal treatment: Confronting racial and ethnic disparities in health care.* Washington, DC: National Academies Press.

Nesterko, Yuriy, Elmar Braehler, Gesine Grande, and Heide Glaesmer. 2013 "Life satisfaction and health-related quality of life in immigrants and native-born Germans: The role of immigration-related factors." *Quality of Life Research.* 22(5): 1005–1013.

Nicholson-Crotty, Sean, Jason A. Grissom, Jill Nicholson-Crotty, and Christopher Redding. 2016. "Disentangling the causal mechanisms of representative bureaucracy: Evidence from assignment of students to gifted programs." *Journal of Public Administration Research and Theory* 26(4): 745–757.

O'Leary, Rosemary. 2011. "Minnowbrook tradition, idea, spirit, event, challenge." *Journal of Public Administration Research and Theory* 21(suppl. 1): i1–i6.

Operario, Don, Kristi E. Gamarel, Benjamin M. Grin, Ji Hyun Lee, Christopher W. Kahler, et al. 2015. "Sexual minority health disparities in adult men and women in the United States: National Health and Nutrition Examination Survey, 2001–2010." *American Journal of Public Health* 105(10): e27–e34.

Padraza, Francisco I., and Ling Zhu. 2015. "Immigration enforcement and the 'chilling effect' on Latino Medicaid enrollment." The Robert Wood Johnson Foundation Scholars in Health Policy Research Program. Available at: https://pdfs.semantic scholar.org/4f6f/3ac412800f26ac8bf6b00f23e0f797d9c835.pdf

Pandey, Sanjay K., Joel C. Cantor, and Kristen Lloyd. 2014. "Immigrant health care access and the Affordable Care Act." *Public Administration Review* 74(6): 749–759.

Paradies, Yin, Mandy Truong, and Naomi Priest. 2014. "A systematic review of the extent and measurement of healthcare provider racism." *Journal of General Internal Medicine* 29(2): 364–387.

Pitkin, Hannah Fenichel. 1967. *The concept of representation.* Berkeley, CA: University of California Press.

Pitkin Derose, Kathryn, Benjamin W. Bahney, Nicole Lurie, and José J. Escarce. 2009. "Immigrants and health care access, quality, and cost." *Medical Care Research and Review* 66(4): 355–408.

Pitts, David W. 2005. "Diversity, representation, and performance: Evidence about race and ethnicity in public organizations." *Journal of Public Administration Research and Theory* 15(4): 615–631.

Prather, Cynthia, Taleria R. Fuller, William L. Jeffries IV, Khiya J. Marshall, A. Vyann Howell, et al. 2018. "Racism, African American women, and their sexual and reproductive health: A review of historical and contemporary evidence and implications for health equity." *Health Equity* 2(1): 249–259.

Przedworski, Julia M., Donna D. McAlpine, Pinar Karaca-Mandi, and Nicole A. Van Kim. 2014. "Health and health risks among sexual minority women: An examination of 3 subgroups." *American Journal of Public Health* 104(6): 1045–1047.

Quinn, Sandra Crouse, Supriya Kumar, Vicki S. Freimuth, Donald Musa, Nestor Casteneda-Angarita et al. 2011. "Racial disparities in exposure, susceptibility, and access to health care in the US H1N1 influenza pandemic." *American Journal of Public Health* 101(2): 285–293.

Ram, Bali, and Feng Hou. 2003. "Changes in family structure and children outcomes: Roles of economic and familial resources." *Policy Studies Journal* 31(3): 309–330.

Reeleder, David, Vivek Goel, Peter A. Singer, and Douglas K. Martin. 2008. "Accountability agreements in Ontario hospitals: Are they fair?" *Journal of Public Administration Research and Theory* 18(1): 161–175.

Reidpath, Daniel D., and Pascale Allotey. 2003. "Infant mortality rate as an indicator of population health." *Journal of Epidemiology & Community Health* 57(5): 344–346.

Rethemeyer, R. Karl. 2007. "Policymaking in the age of internet: Is the internet tending to make policy networks more or less inclusive?" *Journal of Public Administration Research and Theory* 17(2): 259–284.

Riccucci, Norma M., Gregg G. Van Ryzin, and Cecilia F. Lavena. 2014. "Representative bureaucracy in policing: Does it increase perceived legitimacy?" *Journal of Public Administration Research and Theory* 24(3): 537–551.

Sabin, Janice A., and Anthony G. Greenwald. 2012. "The influence of implicit bias on treatment recommendations for 4 common pediatric conditions: Pain, urinary tract infection, attention deficit hyperactivity disorder, and asthma." *American Journal of Public Health* 102(5): 988–995.

Saha, Somnath, and Scott A. Shipman. 2008. "Race-neutral versus race-conscious workforce policy to improve access to care." *Health Affairs* 27(1): 234–245.

Schroeder, Steven A. 2007. "We can do better improving the health of the American people." *New England Journal of Medicine* 357(12): 1221–1228.

Schut, Frederik T., and Wynand P.M.M. Van de Ven. 2005. "Rationing and competition in the Dutch health-care system." *Health Economics* 14(S1): S59–S74.

Shavers, Vickie L., Pebbles Fagan, Dionne Jones, William M.P. Klein, Josephine Boyington, et al. 2012. "The state of research on racial/ethnic discrimination in the receipt of health care." *American Journal of Public Health* 102(5): 953–966.

Siddiqi, Arjumand, India J. Ornelas, Kelly Quinn, Dan Zuberi, and Quynh C. Nguyen. 2013. "Societal context and the production of immigrant status-based health inequalities: A comparative study of the United States and Canada." *Journal of Public Health Policy* 34(2): 330–344.

Siskin, Alison. 2011. *Treatment of noncitizens under the Patient Protection and Affordable Care Act. Report # R41714.* Washington, DC: Congressional Research Service.

Soss, Joe, Jacob S. Hacker, and Susanne Mettler. 2007. *Remaking America: Democracy and public policy in an age of inequality.* New York, NY: The Russell Sage Foundation.

Starr, Paul. 2013. *Remedy and reaction: The peculiar American struggle over health care reform.* New Haven, CT: Yale University Press.

Steinecke, Ann, and Charles Terrell. 2010. "Progress for whose future? The impact of the Flexner Report on medical education for racial and ethnic minority physicians in the United States." *Academic Medicine* 85(2): 236–245.

Stewart, Moira A. 1984. "What is a successful doctor-patient interview? A study of interactions and outcomes." *Social Science and Medicine* 19(2): 167–175.

Street, Richard L., Kimberly J. O'Malley, Lisa A. Cooper, and Paul Haide. 2008. "Understanding concordance in patient-physician relationships: Personal and ethnic dimensions of shared identity." *The Annals of Family Medicine* 6(3): 198–205.

Stronks, Karien, and Anton E. Kunst. 2009. "The complex interrelationship between ethnic and socio-economic inequalities in health." *Journal of Public Health* 31(3): 324–325.

Sung, Chen-Li. 1999. "Asian patients' distrust of western medical care: One perspective." *The Mount Sinai Journal of Medicine* 66(4): 259–261.

Tai-Seale, Ming, Deborah Freund, and Anthony LoSasso. 2001. "Racial disparities in service use among Medicaid beneficiaries after mandatory enrollment in managed care: A difference-in-differences approach." *INQUIRY: The Journal of Health Care Organization, Provision, and Financing* 38: 49–59.

Tan, Kok Wei, Bernard Tiddeman, and Ian D. Stephen. 2018. "Skin texture and colour predict perceived health in Asian faces." *Evolution and Human Behavior* 39(3): 320–335.

Tesler, Michael. 2012. "The spillover of racialization into health care: How President Obama polarized public opinion by racial attitudes and race." *American Journal of Political Science* 56(3): 690–704.

Thielemann, Gregory S., and Joseph Stewart. 1996. "A demand-side perspective on the importance of representative bureaucracy: AIDS, ethnicity, gender, and sexual orientation." *Public Administration Review* 56(2): 168–173.

Thompson, Frank J. 2013. "Health reform, polarization, and public administration." *Public Administration Review* 73: S3–S12.

Tilly, Charles. 2007. *Durable inequality.* Oakland, CA: University of California Press.

Van Doorslaer, Eddy, and Xander Koolman. 2004. "Explaining the differences in corre-lated health inequalities across European countries." *Health Economics* 13(7): 609–628.

Van Doorslaer, Eddy, Adam Wagstaff, Han Bleichrodt, et al. 1997. "Income-related inequalities in health: Some international comparisons." *Journal of Health Economics* 16 (1): 93–112.

Versey, H. Shellae. 2014. "Centering perspectives on Black women, hair politics, and physical activity." *American Journal of Public Health* 104(5): 810–815.

Viruell-Fuentes, Edna A. 2007. "Beyond acculturation: Immigration, discrimination, and health research among Mexicans in the US." *Social Science & Medicine* 65(7): 1524–1535.

Viruell-Fuentes, Edna A., Patricia Y. Miranda, and Sawsan Abdulrahim. 2012. "More than culture: Structural racism, intersectionality theory, and immigrant health." *Social Science and Medicine* 75(12): 2099–2106.

WHO (World Health Organization). 2014. *Migrant health.* Geneva: WHO.

Wilkinson, Richard, and Kate Pickett. 2009. *The spirit level: Why greater equality make societies better.* New York, NY: Bloomsbury.

Williams, David R. 2008. "Racial/ethnic variations in women's health: The social embeddedness of health." *American Journal of Public Health* 98(Suppl. 1): S38–S47.

Williams, David R., and Chiquita Collins. 1995. "US socioeconomic and racial differ-ences in health: Patterns and explanations." *Annual Review of Sociology* 21(1): 349–386.

Williams, David R., and Pamela Braboy Jackson. 2005. "Social sources of racial disparities in health." *Health Affairs* 24(2): 325–334.

Williams, David R., and Pamela Braboy Jackson. 2006. "Explaining racial and ethnic disparities in health care." *Medical Care* 44(5): I64–I72.

Williams, David R., and Selina A. Mohammed. 2009. "Discrimination and racial disparities in health: Evidence and needed research." *Journal of Behavioral Medicine* 32(1): 20–47.

Williams, David R., and Michelle Sternthal. 2010. "Understanding racial-ethnic disparities in health: Sociological contributions." *Journal of Health and Social Beha-vior* 51(1S): S15–S27.

Xu, Ke Tom. "State-level variations in income-related inequality in health and health achievement in the US." *Social Science & Medicine* 63(2): 457–464.

Young, Jessica L., Keshia Pollack, and Lainie Rutkow. 2015. "Review of state legisla-tive approaches to eliminating racial and ethnic health disparities, 2002–2011." *American Journal of Public Health* 105(3): S388–S394.

Zhu, Ling, and Jennifer H. Clark. 2015. "'Rights without Access': The political context of inequality in health care coverage in the US states." *State Politics & Policy Quarterly* 15(2): 239–262.

Zhu, Ling, and Morgen Johansen. 2014. "Public responsibility and inequality in health insurance coverage: An examination of American state health care systems." *Public Administration* 92(2): 422–439.

Zhu, Ling, and Meredith B.L. Walker. 2013. "'Too much too young': Race, descriptive representation, and heterogeneous policy responses in the case of teenage childbearing." *Politics, Groups and Identities* 1(4): 528–546.

Zhu, Ling, and Ping Xu. 2015. "The politics of welfare exclusion: Immigration and disparity in Medicaid coverage." *Policy Studies Journal* 43(4): 456–483.

Zimmerman, Shirley L., and Constance T. Gager. 1997. "A potential case of social bankruptcy: States' AFDC payments and their teen birth rates." *Policy Studies Journal* 25(1): 109–123.

# 5 Race, Place, and Digital Governance

*Adrian Brown, Karen Mossberger, and Seong K. Cho*

## Practitioner Points

- Information should be oriented toward the needs of all residents and neighborhoods, including multilingual information and open data. It should be available through multiple channels, both online and offline.
- Programs of outreach to residents and neighborhood organizations are important. Local governments need to find out what information citizens care about. In terms of data, what do community groups and residents need, and what kinds of visualization or other assistance would help them to use it?
- Mobile-friendly platforms and mobile apps can help governments connect with residents. Mobile use is increasingly important in low-income Black and Latino communities, particularly for those who rely on mobile devices as their primary form of Internet access.
- Local governments play an important role in addressing the digital divide by providing public access and assistance in libraries and other community spaces. These spaces should be identified and marketed to residents.
- Discounted broadband offered by the private sector or nonprofits (such as Comcast Internet Essentials or Connect2Compete) can widen access options and should be advertised. Some communities are more directly involved in providing affordable options through municipal broadband or public-private partnerships.

## Introduction

One of the major developments in public administration over the past few decades has been the evolution of digital government, from the emergence of government websites in the early days of the Internet to more recent use of social media, mobile apps, open data portals, big data gathered from sensors, crowdsourcing of information, and more. Today local governments employ technology for a range of "smart city" strategies for transportation, energy, public safety, and sustainability. As technologies evolve, governments must understand how their use affects equity and democratic governance. Like access to health and education, as governments move more information online, inclusive digital governance represents access to fundamental services and opportunities.

A central premise of digital government is the potential to influence relationships between government and citizens by enabling information sharing, government-to-citizen interaction, and participatory governance. Digital government can offer solutions to public administrators for enhanced governance, connecting them to and building relationships with diverse constituents by expanding access to information, government, and the policy process and by offering new and multiple pathways to participation and influence in community decision-making. However, recent research suggests that access to and the use of these resources are uneven, particularly within communities of color. Accordingly, this chapter explores how digital governance, or the use of technology to connect citizens and government, may be a mechanism to create more inclusive and equitable systems of governance.

We focus on the local level of government, where citizens often have the most direct experience with government for their daily needs, where participation is most likely to occur, and where participation has the greatest impact (Nabatchi, 2012; Oates, 1972). Within cities, racial and ethnic conflicts often develop over concerns with policing, schools, or neighborhood services. The local level is also the context for concentrated poverty and segregation, creating visible disparities across neighborhoods, and wide inequalities in resources and services across cities (Dreier, Mollenkopf and Swanstrom, 2004; Hendrick, 2012; Kneebone and Holmes, 2016; Lewis and Hamilton, 2011). Poverty and segregation may affect government relationships with citizens as well as the potential for community engagement through digital government because of race and place-based differences in technology access and use. Accordingly, we address the implications of racial, ethnic, and spatial differences in technology access and use, and the implications of these trends for creating inclusive digital governance.

This chapter begins with a discussion of inequalities in Internet access and use, and how these differences are patterned across U.S. cities and communities of color. We then discuss the implications of these trends for participatory governance, focusing on how digital inequalities may influence the relationship between government and communities of color. The chapter concludes with a discussion of practical and actionable recommendations for practitioners, including practical examples of jurisdictions making strides in digital equality and digital citizenship.

## Digital Inequalities and Digital Citizenship

Differences in Internet access matter for what people do online; this includes digital citizenship, or the ability to participate in society online (Mossberger, Tolbert, and McNeal, 2008) and activities that require information literacy, or the ability to find, evaluate, and apply online information (Mossberger, Tolbert, and Stansbury, 2003). With the growth of open data portals, this increasingly includes the ability to use data or data literacy, even with aids such as visualization. What government does to promote transparency, responsiveness, and openness matters, but the ability of citizens to use these resources is also critical.

Digital citizenship requires regular and effective access to the Internet and the skills to use it (Mossberger, Tolbert, and McNeal, 2008). The U.S. trails many other nations in terms of the percentage of the population with home Internet access (fixed broadband subscriptions), ranking 17th among OECD nations in June 2018 (OECD, 2019). Twenty-seven percent of the population does not have home Internet access (Pew Research Center, 2019a),[1] and disparities are driven by race and ethnicity even when controlling for other significant factors, such as age, income, and education (Mossberger, Tolbert, and Franko, 2013).

According to 2019 Pew Research Center data, 79 percent of non-Hispanic Whites had broadband at home, compared with 66 percent of Blacks/African Americans and 61 percent of Latinos (Pew Research Center, 2019b), as shown in Table 5.1. There are more modest racial and ethnic differences, however, in smartphone use: 80 percent of Blacks/African Americans and 79 percent of Latinos have smartphones compared to 82 percent of non-Hispanic Whites (Pew Research Center, 2018). In recent years, growth in home broadband adoption has slowed while mobile use has increased. As a result, there is a small but growing percentage of "smartphone-only" Internet users, who do not have home broadband; and they tend to be young, low-income, less-educated, Black/African American, and Latino (Mossberger, Tolbert, and Franko, 2013; Smith, 2015). In 2019, this represented 17 percent of the U.S. population but 25 percent of Latinos, 23 percent of Blacks/African Americans, and 12 percent of non-Hispanic Whites (Pew Research Center 2019a). Although Pew does not track Internet use for American Indians and Alaska Natives, federal data show that this group also lags in broadband adoption at home and is more likely to rely on smartphones for Internet access (Parkhurst et al., 2015). While there are differences across Asian populations, data for Asian Americans overall show rates of access similar to or higher than non-Hispanic Whites (Mossberger, Tolbert, and Franko, 2013).

*Table 5.1* Comparison of broadband access by race (%)

|  | Broadband at home | Smartphone | Smartphone-only |
|---|---|---|---|
| Non-Hispanic Whites | 79 | 82 | 12 |
| Blacks/African Americans | 66 | 80 | 23 |
| Latinos | 61 | 79 | 25 |

Source: Pew Research Center (2018; 2019b).

But aggregate statistics by race and ethnicity obscure the extent of disparities for low-income Blacks and Latinos, particularly in areas of concentrated poverty. Because geography matters for political representation, access to services, and relationships with local government, it is important to examine how access and activities online vary by place.

### Place and Digital Citizenship

Neighborhood segregation and spatially-concentrated poverty diminish the probability of Internet access and use and magnify barriers to use (Mossberger, Tolbert, and Gilbert, 2006; Mossberger et al., 2012). In fact, neighborhood-level income explains the disparities between Blacks and non-Hispanic Whites; in other words, Blacks who reside outside high-poverty communities do not differ significantly from Whites in their Internet access. Neighborhood income is significant for predicting Internet access and use for Latinos as well but does not entirely account for gaps for this group (Mossberger, Tolbert, and Gilbert, 2006).

There is little data on Internet use and activities online available at the neighborhood level, with the exception of estimates drawn from citywide surveys in Chicago between 2008 and 2013. Chicago is a socially and economically diverse city with patterns of Internet use that mirror the rest of the nation (Mossberger, Tolbert, and Franko, 2013), and it is useful to examine Chicago as a case study in digital government use and technology disparities.

Neighborhood-level differences in access are visible in activities online. Chicago shows wide gaps in digital government use across the city's 77 official community areas. The percentage of the population ever having used a government website in 2013 was 61 percent citywide (Mossberger, Tolbert, and Anderson, 2015).[2] However, government website usage varies widely across neighborhoods, ranging from just 31 percent in Gage Park, a neighborhood with a Hispanic population of 92 percent, to 83 percent in the O'Hare community area, where 76 percent of residents are White (Chicago Metro Agency for Planning, 2017; Mossberger, Tolbert, and Anderson, 2015). Such disparities are replicated across predominantly Black and Hispanic communities on Chicago's south and west sides, representing unequal access to government services, information, and communication.

### Smartphones, Place, and Digital Citizenship

The shift toward wireless Internet platforms has resulted in new forms of access for mobile phone users (Cooper and Shah, 2000). Mobile phones often require a smaller upfront investment than laptops and desktop computers (Kang, 2011). Kraut and Kiesler (2006) suggest that the salience of mobile phone utility and value is more widespread among users. Thus, there may be a level of comfort with the device that does not exist with home computers. Infrastructure may also be a problem. In some rural areas, fixed line infrastructure for broadband is not available. Therefore, the only option is some form of wireless or mobile Internet technology (Srinuan, Srinuan, and Bohlin, 2011). Popular media suggest that smartphones may help close the digital divide, reducing unequal access to important information. But are smartphones closing gaps in Internet access and digital government? With smaller screens and keyboards, some functions are difficult to perform on smartphones. Additionally, data caps can restrict use. When we look at the effects of smartphone access on digital citizenship, or activities online, we can see that mobile technologies have clearly improved access for those who were lacking personal access in the past. However, the shortcomings of mobile Internet technology as a primary form of Internet access are also apparent.

The 2013 survey of Chicago, mentioned above, reveals wide differences in activities online based on the type of Internet access (Mossberger, Tolbert, and Anderson, 2017). Table 5.2 shows the percentage of Chicago residents with broadband at home and mobile Internet access who engage in various activities online related to government and community with the number of survey respondents shown. The "mobile" column includes anyone who has mobile access (whether or not they have broadband), but "mobile-only" Internet users do not have fixed broadband connections at home. Broadband and mobile Internet users are quite similar, as might be expected, given the substantial overlap between the groups. But mobile-only Internet users who rely on smartphones stand apart, engaging in these activities at much lower rates, with differences from more than 12 to over 32 percentage points.

*Table 5.2* Percentages and numbers of citizens performing activity online by forms of access

| Online activities | Broadband | Mobile | Mobile-Only |
|---|---|---|---|
| Get information about politics (%) | 75.85 | 73.03 | 41.33 |
| Total number | 1167 | 1004 | 85 |
| Get public transportation schedule online (%) | 79.96 | 80.00 | 64.24 |
| Total number | 1230 | 1100 | 132 |
| Get government information online (%) | 76.57 | 74.10 | 44.26 |
| Total number | 1178 | 1019 | 91 |
| Find property tax online (%) | 44.34 | 43.77 | 31.06 |
| Total number | 682 | 602 | 64 |
| Use Chicago website (%) | 70.52 | 70.01 | 57.17 |
| Total number | 1085 | 962 | 117 |
| Read news online (%) | 90.26 | 89.03 | 66.76 |
| Total number | 1389 | 1224 | 137 |
| Get neighborhood information online (%) | 68.06 | 68.87 | 49.90 |
| Total number | 1047 | 947 | 102 |
| Column Total Respondents | 1539 | 1375 | 205 |

Source: Mossberger, Tolbert, and Anderson (2017).

Smartphone-only users do less online, but analysis shows Blacks and Hispanics use smartphones for government and community-related activities online at a significantly higher rate than non-Hispanic Whites. These effects were most pronounced for Latinos living in predominantly Hispanic neighborhoods (ibid.). Previous research has shown that residents of these immigrant gateway communities are least likely to be online and that they perceive the most barriers to Internet use (Mossberger, Tolbert, and Franko, 2013). The diffusion of smartphones is benefitting those who were least likely to have regular access, and it is making a difference in their ability to access digital citizenship, including the use of digital government. This is a step forward, though these smartphone-only Internet users are still disadvantaged in comparison with fully-connected Internet users, who have a mobile in addition to home connections.

### Inequality across Cities

Disparities in Internet access are surprisingly stark across cities, reflecting differences in race, concentrated poverty, and regional economic health. Given that metropolitan areas have some type of broadband provision, these differences in Internet access demonstrate the impact of social inequality rather than a lack of infrastructure. Comparing the 50 most populous cities in the U.S., the five highest-ranked cities for Internet use in 2017 have at least 90 percent of residents with home broadband or mobile connectivity, according to the 5-year estimates of the American Community Survey (Table 5.3). The highest-ranked cities—which include Silicon Valley and the Raleigh research triangle—also have high concentrations of technology firms. In all these cities, Blacks and Latinos lag behind non-Hispanic Whites in broadband adoption, even when smartphone use is counted.

In contrast, the five major cities with the lowest rates of broadband adoption have majority-minority populations and are mostly in the South or Midwest. Rates of fixed and cell internet subscription vary between 66–73 percent compared to over 90 percent for the five highest-ranked cities (Table 5.4).

*Table 5.3* Five highest rates of broadband subscription (fixed broadband and cellphone), from 50 largest U.S. cities, by race/ethnicity, 2017 (%)

| City | Total | White | Black | Hispanic | Asian |
|------|-------|-------|-------|----------|-------|
| Raleigh, NC | 92.4 | 93.0 | 80.5 | 78.1 | 92.4 |
| San Diego, CA | 91.5 | 93.2 | 83.3 | 83.0 | 93.6 |
| San Jose, CA | 91.4 | 92.0 | 87.4 | 85.7 | 94.6 |
| Seattle, WA | 91.3 | 92.9 | 75.7 | 85.1 | 87.9 |
| Virginia Beach, VA | 90.9 | 91.3 | 82.0 | 90.2 | 92.3 |

Source: American Community Survey, 5-year estimates, 2013–2017 (as cited in Tolbert and Mossberger 2015).

*Table 5.4* Five lowest rates of broadband subscription (fixed broadband and cellphone), from 50 largest U.S. cities, by race/ethnicity, 2017 (%)

| City | Total | White | Black | Hispanic | Asian |
|------|-------|-------|-------|----------|-------|
| Miami, FL | 65.9 | 86.1 | 51.9 | 68.1 | 78.0 |
| Detroit, MI | 67.5 | 71.5 | 57.2 | 57.7 | 72.2 |
| Philadelphia, PA | 71.6 | 82.4 | 68.8 | 72.4 | 86.3 |
| Memphis, TN | 71.8 | 83.5 | 59.5 | 55.0 | 84.7 |
| Milwaukee, WI | 73.1 | 81.3 | 64.7 | 68.0 | 84.0 |

Source: American Community Survey, 5-year estimates, 2013–2017 (as cited in Tolbert and Mossberger 2015).

There is a 26-point percentage difference between Miami and Raleigh for the total population. Blacks have rates of broadband adoption ranging between 52 percent and 69 percent in the lowest-ranked cities, and Latinos fare little better at 55–73 percent. Broadband adoption for non-Hispanic Whites and Asians is also lower in these places in comparison with high-ranked cities, suggesting a broader context of poverty and disadvantage. Still, the gap between Blacks and non-Hispanic White residents is nearly 35 percentage points in Miami, and in double-digits in all five lowest-ranked cities.

### Segregation and Concentrated Poverty

Digital inequality is place-based, reflecting segregation and concentrated poverty; it is accompanied by other forms of social inequality experienced in such communities. Discrimination and racial preferences in the housing market help explain residential patterns and may constrain mobility for Blacks and Hispanics, hindering their ability to escape poverty and build wealth (Iceland and Wilkes, 2006). Decades after the passage of the Fair Housing Act, progress in racial integration has been steady yet slow, especially for Blacks (Logan and Stults, 2011). Latinos experience less segregation than Blacks, but segregation has grown in recent years in some areas with higher proportions of Latinos (Lewis and Hamilton, 2011; Logan and Stults, 2011). Such segregation is not merely the result of individual choice; the United States Department of Housing and Urban Development (HUD) (2012) reports that people of color continue to experience discrimination in their search for housing.

Racial and ethnic segregation is highly correlated with concentrated poverty. After declining throughout the economic growth of the 1990s, the prevalence of spatially concentrated poverty grew rapidly during the first decade of the new millennium, especially after the 2008 recession. Five-year census estimates for 2010–2014 showed 14 million people living in extremely poor neighborhoods, with poverty rates of 40 percent or more. This was double the incidence in 2000 (Kneebone and Holmes, 2016). Growth in the proportion of poor residents living in extremely poor communities is higher for Blacks and Latinos than for non-Hispanic Whites. In 2010–2014, for example, poor Blacks were five times more likely than poor Whites to live in areas of concentrated poverty, and poor Latinos were three times more likely than low-income non-Hispanic Whites to live in such neighborhoods (ibid.).

Areas of concentrated poverty may offer fewer opportunities to learn about technology through the workplace, social networks, or public institutions. In addition to having limited incomes, residents in poor communities must contend with environments with fewer job opportunities and less upward mobility (ibid.). Segregation and spatially concentrated poverty perpetuate gaps in access to educational opportunities, particularly for Blacks, because of the local property tax that finances the lion's share of public education in most cities. Municipalities with a greater proportion of low-income residents have higher needs for many municipal services, yet they generate less tax wealth to support services such as schools and libraries (Dreier, Mollenkopf, and Swanstrom, 2004; Hendrick, 2012). Implementation of digital government is more challenging in such communities because of lower rates of technology use, yet the needs and potential benefits may be greatest in these low-income communities of color, where technology could enhance access to services and information, as well as relationships between government and community.

## Implications for Digital Governance

### *Trust and Digital Governance*

Trust in government is a key component of governance (Yang and Holzer, 2006) and the basis for the fundamental democratic legitimacy of government. However, trust in government is currently dismal with just 20 percent of adults stating they trust government to do what is right (Doherty, Kiley, and Johnston, 2017; Kellar, 2014). Surveys showing that Americans trust local governments more than other levels of government reflect more positive attitudes toward local government among non-Hispanic Whites. Blacks are most likely to say that they *hardly ever* trust local governments to do what is right (at 40 percent). Hispanics are also somewhat more likely to exhibit such distrust in local government (at 35 percent), in comparison with a 32 percent probability for non-Hispanic Whites, holding other variables constant (Nunnally 2012, pp. 215–216). Local governments are closest to citizens, and racial and ethnic differences in trust at the local level indicate troubling differences in how people feel about government in the communities where they live. A history of discriminatory laws and actions underpins inequalities in access to wealth-building resources, government, and democratic processes for communities of color. Historical discrimination may also contribute to negative perceptions and feelings of alienation, leading to potential distrust of government among people of color.

Digital government has long been viewed as a remedy for declining trust and confidence in government (United Nations Public Administration Network and American Society for Public Administration, 2002), because it can enhance transparency and communications with citizens as well as the delivery of services. The information and communication capacities of digital technologies offer public administrators ways to connect and share information with citizens and involve them in policy processes. While trust and confidence in government reflect factors such as judgments about incumbents, the party in power, and government responses to recent events (Craig, Niemi, and Silver, 1990; Levi and Stoker, 2000; Nye, Zelikow, and King, 1997), many studies suggest that technology has a positive effect on citizen attitudes toward government, including trust and confidence (e.g., Gauld, Gray, and McComb, 2009; Kim and Lee, 2012; Reddick and Roy, 2013; Tolbert and Mossberger, 2006; Welch, Hinnant, and Moon, 2005; West, 2004). Some scholars have found a relationship between digital government and positive attitudes toward government but not trust (McNeal, Hale, and Dotterweich, 2008; West, 2004). Tolbert and Mossberger (2006) found evidence that digital government use increased trust at the local level only but was related to other positive perceptions for government at all levels. Research has also linked specific properties of e-government to trust and confidence in government, including transparency (Kim and Lee, 2012), communication and responsiveness (Gauld, Gray, and McComb, 2009; Hung et al., 2009), and effectiveness and efficiency (Kim and Lee, 2012).

How might digital government help to improve trust and confidence in government for communities of color? Thomas (1998) argues that trust in government is both process- and institution-based. Process-based trust results from direct experience or interactions with government. In contrast, institution-based trust is an expectation of whether or not institutions will do what is right. It may be a perception of how fair and equitable processes and outcomes are as well as the direct experience of individuals or their social networks. Digital government can influence process-based trust through better experiences with government and institution-based trust through the image that digital government conveys (Tolbert and Mossberger, 2006).

In general, trust in government has been attributed to perceptions that government is fair, responsive, and open (Craig, Niemi, and Silver, 1990; Donovan and Bowler, 2004; Hibbing and Theiss-Morse, 2002). Government use of technologies communicates equity and inclusiveness, an important potential benefit for communities of color (Bertot, Jaeger, and Grimes, 2010; Roman and Miller, 2013; Tolbert and Mossberger, 2006; Verdegem and Verleye, 2009; Yang and Rho, 2007).[3] We argue that several factors traditionally related to e-government are relevant for building trust in government at the local level in communities of color: transparency, responsiveness, and government openness to participation are discussed in the next section.

## Transparency and Access to Information

Transparency refers to the extent to which to governments disclose information about decision processes, enabling citizens to monitor government actions and performance (Bertot, Jaeger, & Grimes, 2010; Grimmelikhuijsen, et al., 2013; Wong & Welch, 2004). Access to government information is needed to create an educated citizenry and awareness of public issues, which can be enhanced with the use of digital government technologies. Digital government enhances transparency by providing various ways for the public to monitor government processes and performance (Andersen, 2009; , Jaeger, and Grimes, 2010; Relly & Sabharwal, 2009; Shim & Eom, 2008; 2009). The concept of open government, which includes transparency, citizen participation on issues of importance, and collaboration to resolve issues, has guided efforts to increase public access to government information through digital government platforms (Bonsón et al., 2012; Chun et al., 2010; Noveck, 2009). Digital government allows for access to timely information and permits citizens to view and monitor government activities (Bertot, Jaeger, and Grimes, 2010). Technologies enable information to be shared more quickly, are updated frequently to ensure accuracy and relevance, and made available around the clock.

Online information promoting transparency could be used by residents or community organizations to monitor government performance, identify needs, or intervene in policy processes. Performance data are available through many city websites or open data portals. Neighborhood information is also common on local websites. Chicago, for example, has an extensive amount of searchable data on its portal, which includes affordable rental housing, problem landlords, building code scofflaw lists, vacant and abandoned buildings, graffiti removal requests, public health data, 311 service requests (potholes, abandoned vehicles, sanitation, street lights, and more), languages spoken in neighborhoods, and maps of grocery stores. Additionally, local government websites offer information about regulations and procedures, boards and commissions, the organization of city government, elected and appointed officials, and public hearings (Mossberger and Jimenez, 2009; Mossberger and Wu, 2012).

Prior research has shown, however, that transparency does not necessarily lead to greater trust in government or even more positive attitudes toward government. In fact, transparency can lead to greater criticism of government and perceptions that it is ineffective (Grimmelikhuijsen and Meijer, 2012; Grimmelikhuijsen et al., 2013), or it may expose inequities that lead to more distrust, especially if they are not addressed. However, a lack of transparency and openness may be a greater danger in the long run, particularly in communities where distrust already exists.

### Responsiveness

Responsiveness through digital government could improve citizen perceptions that government cares about them. In addition to making data on neighborhoods available online, user-friendly features such as mapping and visualization could increase the use of open data by community residents. Information available in multiple languages also communicates a message that government is responsive to all its residents. Yet research on 100 cities and counties with high proportions of Spanish speakers shows that many government websites have limited information available in Spanish (McDonald, 2015). Online 311 systems for service requests and social media websites present new opportunities for demonstrating responsiveness to citizens and neighborhoods, especially when responses are open to everyone, as on social media platforms. Though Mergel (2013) suggests that government agencies often miss the opportunity to use social media as a tool for responding to citizen questions or comments, cities that actively use digital platforms to connect with citizens in open dialogue can increase feedback, as discussed in the next section on participation (Bertot. Jaeger, and Grimes, 2010; Bonsón et al., 2012; Chun et al., 2010; Gottschalk 2009). When the City of Chicago invited ideas for how to cut the budget on Twitter, local administrators used relevant departments to respond personally to each comment. Comments posted by officials could also be responsive if they acknowledge the concerns or ideas that citizens express and explain why they were or were not acted upon.

### Openness to Participation

Digital governance "supports democratic decision-making" (Medaglia, 2012, p. 346). Participation in government policy processes is desirable in order to create better, more representative policies because it enables information sharing and potential support and consensus (Nabatchi, 2012). Participation also enables an informed citizenry because it promotes education about government and policy and raises awareness of public issues. This reinforces perceptions of government transparency, legitimacy, equity in policy development, and positive views of government (Lukensmeyer and Torres, 2006, p. 5). The latter is true even if individuals do not choose to actively participate. It is the belief that government is open to citizen participation that matters for trust and confidence in government (Hibbing and Theiss-Morse, 2002).

Government can use technology to promote equitable access to government by enabling communication, dialogue, networking, and collaboration. Social networking sites like Facebook, Twitter, and blogs can be used for these functions (Mergel, 2013). Additionally, governments can host online town hall meetings, crowdsource information about neighborhood problems, sponsor competitions for ideas to improve government, and invite citizens to rank policy ideas or budget proposals. In addition to social media, there are commercially available platforms for hosting online discussions and presenting background resources. The City of Phoenix held both online and offline town hall meetings to develop priorities for redevelopment along a lightrail, reaching residents with different preferences and needs for participation (ReinventPHX, n.d.). The City of Pittsburgh asked its residents for ideas on data they would like to see on its open data portal (City of Pittsburgh, n.d.). Cities such as New York, Chicago, and San Francisco have hosted competitions for ideas, and one winning contribution in Chicago was a Spanish-language platform for neighborhood participation in redesigning a park (Mi Parque – Little Village, n.d.). Technology offers new and varied options for engagement while reinforcing representative democracy. Though technology should not be viewed as a panacea for political and social issues or equality in access to government (Wilhelm, 2002), participation-enabling communication technology may improve convenience and expand access to government, provide timely and relevant information, and facilitate participation in the policy process (OECD, 2003).

In addition, effective digital governance requires citizens who have access to technology and possess the skills and knowledge to use it effectively for civic engagement activities (Mossberger, Tolbert, and McNeal, 2008). Lack of access and digital literacy skills pose challenges for digital governance in communities of color. For off-line engagement, differences in participation may stem from historic racial inequities in access to government and civic engagement knowledge and opportunities (Foster-Bey, 2008). Online, technology disparities magnify existing gaps in participation, especially in low-income communities of color. The dilemma is that while technology has much to offer in the way of fostering greater government responsiveness and accountability, technology inequalities remain persistent challenges.

## Conclusion: What Should Local Governments Do?

For communities of color, various factors matter for whether and how they are able to engage in participatory governance. Historical discrimination, segregation, and political exclusion of communities of color contribute to a lack of trust and confidence in government, leading to feelings of being disconnected from government. While technology expands opportunities for engagement, differences in broadband access and use can mean unequal access to government services, information, and communication. Therefore, addressing issues in technology access and use, alone, is insufficient for involving communities of color in local governance. Instead, it should be viewed as an important component of a larger strategy to engage these individuals and communities.

Given both the potential of digital government and inequalities in technology access and use, local governments must follow a dual strategy of using technology for transparency and engagement, and assisting residents in becoming digital citizens. And, while there are clearly disparities in access and use, governments should not neglect the use of digital platforms, even in low-income cities or neighborhoods. The Black Lives Matters movement, for example, has demonstrated that there is vibrant participation online among people of color, including through social media. While Flint, MI, has one of the lowest rates of home broadband access in the U.S., a study by the Pew Research Center showed that online searches about Flint's water increased long before government alerts or media coverage of the issue. The Internet was still a primary source of information for residents trying to understand what was wrong with their water (Mitchell, Stocking, and Matsa, 2016). Although it is important to recognize inequalities in access and use, two-thirds of Blacks and nearly as many Latinos do, in fact, have broadband at home. For those who rely on smartphones, mobile technologies make a difference for the use of digital government, especially for Latinos in immigrant gateway neighborhoods (Mossberger, Tolbert, and Anderson, 2017).

How should local governments address digital governance in an inclusive way? Local government strategies should include the following:

- *Citizen-centered information.* Information that is oriented toward the needs of all residents and neighborhoods, including multilingual information and data that citizens can use to identify needs in their own communities.
- *Mobile-friendly platforms and mobile apps to connect with residents.* Mobile use is increasingly important in low-income Black and Hispanic communities, including for some who rely on this as their primary form of Internet access.
- *Support for public access.* For those who are either offline or less-connected (relying on smartphones), local governments play an important role in providing public access and assistance in libraries and other community spaces. Blacks and Latinos have traditionally been most likely to use the Internet outside of the home, including at public libraries, and access to government services is one of the most common uses of help in libraries (Becker et al., 2010; Kaplan and Mossberger, 2012; Mossberger and Tolbert, 2009; Mossberger, Tolbert, and Stansbury, 2003). Local governments may consider how collaboration with libraries and community centers can help to introduce residents to other opportunities for interacting with government online, such as participation in community forums, beyond filing taxes or looking up services.
- *Promotion of affordable broadband.* In some communities, this has meant advertising discounted broadband through the private sector or nonprofits (such as Comcast Internet Essentials or Connect2Compete) while in other places, municipal broadband or public-private partnerships have provided affordable options. For example, Minneapolis has a public-private partnership that offers community benefits such as low-cost access and a digital inclusion fund (City of Minneapolis Information Technology Department, 2015), and over time Google Fiber has provided various types of support for digital inclusion in its partner cities (Bergen, 2016). Places such as Chattanooga and Urbana-Champaign have developed their own networks with low-cost options for residents.
- *Programs of outreach to residents and neighborhood organizations are important.* Local governments need to determine what information citizens care about. In terms of data, what do community groups and residents need, and what kinds of visualization or other assistance would help them to use it? How can individual residents and neighborhood groups participate and contribute information, through social media, crowdsourcing, or other means? Working with community organizations and nonprofits can provide linkages so that data are used, and governments are aware of information needs across different neighborhoods and populations.

Local government is uniquely positioned to advance open and inclusive governance through a comprehensive approach that combines digital inclusion with digital government that is transparent, responsive, and open to participation. The City of Seattle, for example, has a digital equity manager who has been working with neighborhood organizations for two decades now (McBeath 2016), and who has described the city's efforts on digital inclusion as being motivated by a desire to promote civic engagement across all neighborhoods (Mossberger, Tolbert, and Franko, 2013). The city has a Digital Equity Initiative that uses funds from the cable franchise to provide digital inclusion grants for neighborhood organizations and to offer free broadband to community groups (www.seattle.gov/tech/initiatives/digital-equity). This reflects a more general orientation toward neighborhood outreach in Seattle, which includes a dedicated Department of Neighborhoods and a Participatory Budgeting initiative (City of Seattle, n.d.).

Seattle is not alone in their efforts. Other cities have local government staff dedicated to digital inclusion efforts (such as Boston and Portland), and digital inclusion plans (e.g., Austin and Louisville, among others).[4] Smart city initiatives provide opportunities to focus on equity and inclusion by taking a bottom-up approach. Particularly at the planning and evaluation stages, cities consider the implications of their initiatives for digital inclusion equity by engaging citizens, particularly communities of color, in key planning and decision-making discussions. Citizens are able to help guide the evolution of the initiative by determining community needs for data and smart technology and the implications of these initiatives after adoption (Horrigan, 2019). In Portland, the Smart City PDX initiative works with the city's Office for Community Technology and broader Digital Inclusion Network in the city and county to ensure that smart city plans consider and include digital inclusion and equity (Horrigan, 2019; Portland, n.d.). In Chicago, the Smart Chicago organization was launched by the city with the MacArthur Foundation and the Chicago Community Trust to promote Civic Tech and Digital Inclusion, involving community organizations and nonprofits in the conversation about open data, among other topics.[5] When planning for the Array of Things, a network of sensors collecting data on air quality in low-income Chicago neighborhoods, the city and its partners at the Argonne National Laboratory and the University of Chicago conducted public meetings through Smart Chicago and engaged affected communities to discuss privacy issues as well as the potential benefits from sensor deployment (Thornton, 2018). These cities and others provide models for addressing the tension between digital government and digital inequality.

Local governments must address the issues of lack of trust and confidence in government among communities of color, understanding their connection with governance. Governance requires government to promote transparency, listen to, and value the contributions of citizens, ensure equity in access to government information and decision-making processes, and provide opportunities for two-way communication between government and citizens and among citizens. Technology is one mechanism for achieving these aims, but local governments must also consider how its use reflects disparities in society including income, education, race, and ethnicity, which are persistent factors in the "digital divide." Therefore, strategies that incorporate technology as a key mechanism for governance should seek to overcome these challenges in order to create an inclusive government for communities of color and create policies that reflect their needs and values.

## Discussion Questions

1   What is the role of government in building digital capacity (e.g., enabling Internet access, building digital literacy skills)? What programs and activities would you include in a local government technology plan?
2   How can the full representation of communities of color be assured online participation, such as feedback about local governance issues or finding relevant information online? What strategies are needed?
3   What are the implications of generally limited Internet access for communities of color in rural areas? Would local government outreach look different in such an area compared to a poor urban neighborhood?
4   Given a history of strained relationships between government and communities of color, how would you build trust as a government official when using online platforms?
5   How can local governments measure the effects of engaging communities of color online? How can local governments use this information to leverage and justify the investment in technologies?

## Notes

1   According to Pew's 2019 internet/broadband home fact sheet, 73 percent of the population had home broadband (high-speed internet) subscriptions (Pew Research Center, 2019a). Dial-up is negligible in the U.S., so we refer to this as home access, as opposed to mobile access through smartphones.
2   This compares with 70 percent who had broadband at home citywide, and home broadband adoption that was as low as 39 percent in West Garfield Park, and as high as 91 percent in O'Hare (Mossberger, Tolbert, and Anderson, 2015).
3   See also Tolbert and Mossberger (2006).
4   The National Digital Inclusion Alliance, an organization of non-profits, libraries, and governments involved in digital inclusion programs, has a list of local government Trailblazers who meet specified criteria, including government funding for digital inclusion efforts (see www.digitalinclusion.org/digital-inclusion-trailblazers/). In other cities, such as Chicago, local governments have worked with foundations and nonprofits.
5   The collaborative later became City Tech Collaborative, see www.cct.org/about/partnerships_initiatives/smart-chicago-collaborative/

# References

Abrego, Leisy J., and Shannon Gleeson. 2013. "Immigration policies hurt immigrant families more than they help." Houston: James A. Baker III Institute for Public Policy of Rice University.

Andersen, Thomas Barnebeck. 2009. "E-government as an anti-corruption strategy." *Information Economics and Policy* 21(3): 201–210.

Arreola, Javier, and Alberto Altamirano. 2016. "Obstacles and enablers to unlock Hispanic political participation." *Latino USA*. Available at: http://latinousa.org/2016/05/23/obstacles-and-enablers-to-unlock-hispanic-political-participation/ (accessed May 23, 2016).

Becker, Samantha, Michael D. Crandall, Karen E. Fisher, Bo Kinney, et al. 2010. *Opportunity for all: How the American public benefits from internet access at U.S. libraries.* Washington, DC: Institute of Museum and Library Services.

Bergen, Mark. (2016). "Google Fiber is ending a free-Internet offer in its first city." *Recode.* Available at: www.recode.net/2016/4/9/11586006/free-google-fiber-kansas-city (accessed April 9, 2016).

Bertot, John C., Paul T. Jaeger, and Justin M. Grimes. 2010. "Using ICTs to create a culture of transparency: E-government and social media as openness and anti-corruption tools for societies." *Government Information Quarterly* 27(3): 264–271.

Bobo, Lawrence, and Franklin D.Gilliam. 1990. "Race, sociopolitical participation, and black empowerment." *American Political Science Review* 84(02): 377–393.

Bonsón, Enrique, Lourdes Torres, Sonio Royo, and Francisco Flores. 2012. "Local e-government 2.0: Social media and corporate transparency in municipalities." *Government Information Quarterly* 29(2): 123–132.

Bureau of Justice Statistics. 2016. "Prisoners in 2015. U.S." Washington, DC: U.S. Department of Justice. Available at: www.bjs.gov/content/pub/pdf/p15.pdf

Carter, Lemuria, and France Bélanger. 2005. "The utilization of e-government services: Citizen trust, innovation and acceptance factors." *Information Systems Journal* 15(1): 5–25.

Chicago Metropolitan Agency for Planning. 2017. "MetroPulse Community data snapshot: Gage Park." *The Chicago Community Trust and Affiliates*. Available at: www.cmap.illinois.gov/documents/10180/126764/Gage+Park.pdf

Christensen, Tom, and Per Lægreid. 2005. "Trust in government: The relative importance of service satisfaction, political factors, and demography." *Public Performance & Management Review* 28(4): 487–511.

Chun, Soon, Stuart Shulman, Rodrigo Sandoval, and Eduard Hovy. 2010. "Government 2.0: Making connections between citizens, data and government." *Information Polity* 15(1): 1–9.

City of Minneapolis, Information Technology Department. 2015. "Wireless Minneapolis Community Benefits Agreement. Outcomes as of July 2015." Available at: www.ci.minneapolis.mn.us/www/groups/public/@bis/documents/webcontent/wcms1p-144836.pdf

City of Pittsburgh. n.d. "All topics." Available at: http://pittsburghpa.mindmixer.com/topics/all.

City of Seattle. n.d. "Funding opportunities." Available at: www.seattle.gov/neighborhoods/funding-opportunities.

Cooper, M.N., and Shah, D. 2000. *Disconnected, disadvantaged, and disenfranchised: Explorations in the digital divide.* Washington, DC: Consumer Federation of American and Consumers Union.

Craig, Stephen C., Richard G. Niemi, and Glenn E. Silver. (1990). "Political efficacy and trust: A report on the NES pilot study items." *Political Behavior* 12(3): 289–314.

Doherty, Carroll, Jocelyn Kiley, and Bridget Johnson. 2017. "Public trust in government remains near historic lows as partisan attitudes shift." Washington, DC: Pew Research Center. Available at: www.people-press.org/2017/05/03/public-trust-in-governm ent-remains-near-historic-lows-as-partisan-attitudes-shift/ (accessed May 3, 2017).

Donovan, Todd, and Shaun Bowler. 2004. *Reforming the republic: Democratic institutions for the new America.* Upper Saddle River, NJ: Pearson/Prentice Hall.

Dreier, Peter, John H. Mollenkopf, and Todd Swanstrom. 2004. *Place matters: Metropolitics for the 21st century,* 2nd edn. Lawrence, KS: University Press of Kansas.

Florido, Adrian. (2015). "Mass deportation may sound unlikely, but it's happened before." *NPR.* Available at: www.npr.org/sections/codeswitch/2015/09/08/ 437579834/mass-deportation-may-sound-unlikely-but-its-happened-before

Foster-Bey, J. (2008). "Do race, ethnicity, citizenship, and socio-economic status determine civic engagement?" CIRCLE Working Paper #62. Center for Information and Research on Civic Learning and Engagement (CIRCLE).

Gallup. 2016. "In depth: Topics A to Z, Trust in government." Available at: www. gallup.com/poll/5392/trust-government.aspx.

Gauld, Robin, Andrew Gray, and Sasha McComb. 2009. "How responsive is e-govern-ment? Evidence from Australia and New Zealand." *Government Information Quarterly* 26 (1): 69–74.

Gottschalk, Petter. 2009. "Maturity levels for interoperability in digital government." *Government Information Quarterly* 26(1): 75–81.

Grimmelikhuijsen, Stephen G., and Albert J. Meijer. 2012. "The effects of transparency on the perceived trustworthiness of a government organization: Evidence from an online experiment." *Journal of Public Administration Research and Theory* 24(1): 137–157.

Grimmelikhuijsen, Stephen G., Gregory Porumbescu, Boram Hong, and Tobin Im. 2013. "The effect of transparency on trust in government: A cross-national comparative experiment." *Public Administration Review* 73(4): 575–586.

Hendrick, Rebecca M. 2012. *Managing the fiscal metropolis: Financial policies, practices and health of Chicago suburban municipalities.* Washington, DC: Georgetown University Press.

Hibbing, John R., and Elizabeth Theiss-Morse. 2002. *Stealth democracy: Americans' beliefs about how government should work.* New York, NY: Cambridge University Press.

Horrigan, J. 2019. *Smart cities and digital equity.* Columbus, OH: National Digital Inclusion Alliance. Available at: www.digitalinclusion.org/smart-cities-and-digital-equity/

Hung, Shin-Yuan, King-Zoo Tang, Chia-Ming Chang, and Ching-De Ke. 2009. "User acceptance of intergovernmental services: An example of electronic document management system." *Government Information Quarterly* 26(2): 387–397.

Iceland, John, and Rima Wilkes. 2006. "Does socioeconomic status matter? Race, class, and residential segregation." *Social Problems* 53(2): 248–273.

Kang, C. 2011. "As smartphones proliferate, some users are cutting the computer cord." *Washington Post.* July 11, 2011. Available at: www.washingtonpost.com/ business/economy/as-smartphones-proliferate-some-users-are-cutting-the-comp utercord/2011/07/11/gIQA6ASi9H_story.html (accessed February 5, 2012).

Kaplan, David, and Karen Mossberger. 2012. "Prospects for poor neighborhoods in the broadband era: Neighborhood-level influences on technology use at work." *Economic Development Quarterly* 26(1): 95–105.

Kellar, Elizabeth K 2014. "The hard work of restoring trust in government: Countering the public's cynicism and mistrust starts with honest, open communication." *Governing*. Available at: www.governing.com/columns/smart-mgmt/col-hard-work-res toring-trust-government-honest-open-communication.html (accessed November 5, 2014).

Kim, Soonhee, and Jooho Lee. 2012. "E-participation, transparency, and trust in local government." *Public Administration Review* 72(6): 819–828.

Kneebone, Elizabeth, and Natalie Holmes. 2016. "U.S. concentrated poverty in the wake of the Great Recession." Washington, DC: The Brookings Institution. Available at: www.brookings.edu/research/reports2/2016/03/31-concentrated-poverty-recession-kneebone-holmes

Kraut, R., Brynin, M., and Kiesler, S. (Eds.). 2006. *Computers, phones, and the Internet: Domesticating information technology*, vol. 2. Oxford : Oxford University Press.

Levi, Margaret, and Laura Stoker. 2000. "Political trust and trustworthiness." *Annual Review of Political Science* 3: 475–507.

Lewis, James H., and David K. Hamilton. 2011. "Race and regionalism: The structure of local government and racial disparity." *Urban Affairs Review* 47(3): 349–384.

Logan, John R., and Brian J. Stults. 2011. *The persistence of segregation in the metropolis: New findings from the 2010 Census*. Providence, RI: Brown University.

Lukensmeyer, Carolyn J., and Lars Hasselblad Torres. 2006. *Public deliberation: A manager's guide to citizen participation*. Washington, DC: IBM Center for the Business of Government.

Mitchell, Amy, Katerina Eva Matsa, and Galen Stocking. 2017. "Searching for news: The Flint water crisis." Washington, DC: Pew Research Center. Available at: www.journalism.org/essay/searching-for-news/

McBeath, R. 2016. "The keys to digital inclusion: An interview with David Keyes, Digital Equity Manager, City of Seattle." *Benton Foundation blog*, June 3, 2016. Available at: www.benton.org/blog/keyes-digital-inclusion-interview-david-keyes-digital-equity-manager-city-seattle

McDonald, J.S. 2015. "Language as a barrier to local government access: Spanish language access to local government websites." Tempe, AZ: Center for Policy Informatics, Arizona State University.

McNeal, Ramona, Kathleen Hale, and Lisa Dotterweich. 2008. "Citizen–government interaction and the Internet: Expectations and accomplishments in contact, quality, and trust." *Journal of Information Technology & Politics* 5(2): 213–229.

Medaglia, Rony. 2012. "eParticipation research: Moving characterization forward (2006–2011)." *Government Information Quarterly* 29(3): 346–360.

Mergel, Ines. 2013. "Social media adoption and resulting tactics in the US federal government." *Government Information Quarterly* 30(2): 123–130.

Mi Parque – Little Village. n.d. Available at: https://miparquelv.wordpress.com/

Mitchell, Amy, Galen Stocking, and Katerina Eva Matsa. 2016. "Long-form reading shows signs of life in our mobile news world." Available at: www.journalism.org/2016/05/05/long-form-reading-shows-signs-of-life-in-our-mobile-news-world/

Mossberger, Karen, and Benedict Jimenez. 2009. "Can e-government promote civic engagement? A study of local government websites in Illinois and the U.S." Chicago: Institute for Policy and Civic Engagement, University of Illinois at Chicago. Available at: https://ipce.uic.edu/interior/egovtfinalreport2009.pdf

Mossberger, Karen, and Caroline J. Tolbert. 2010. "Digital democracy: How politics online is changing electoral participation." In *The Oxford handbook of American elections and political behaviour*, edited by Jan E. Leighley (pp. 200–218). Oxford: Oxford University Press.

Mossberger, Karen, Caroline J. Tolbert, and Christopher Anderson. 2015. "Digital excellence in Chicago: Tracking trends in Internet use 2008–2013." Available at: www.chicago.gov/content/dam/city/depts/doit/general/DEI/digital_excellence_in_chicago_2008-2013.pdf

Mossberger, Karen, Caroline J. Tolbert, and Christopher Anderson. 2017. "The mobile Internet and digital citizenship in African-American and Latino communities." *Information, Communication and Society* 20(10): 1587–1606.

Mossberger, Karen, Caroline J. Tolbert, Daniel Bowen, and Benedict Jimenez. 2012. "Unraveling different barriers to Internet use: Urban residents and neighborhood effects." *Urban Affairs Review*, 48(6): 771–810.

Mossberger, Karen, Caroline J. Tolbert, and William Franko. 2013. *Digital cities: The Internet and the geography of opportunity*. New York, NY: Oxford University Press.

Mossberger, Karen, Caroline J. Tolbert, and Michele Gilbert. 2006. "Race, place and information technology." *Urban Affairs Review* 41(5): 583–620.

Mossberger, Karen, Caroline J. Tolbert, and Ramona S. McNeal. 2008. *Digital citizenship: The Internet, participation and society*. Cambridge, MA: MIT Press.

Mossberger, Karen, Caroline J. Tolbert, and Mary Stansbury. 2003. *Virtual inequality: Beyond the digital divide*. Washington, DC: Georgetown University Press.

Mossberger, Karen, and Yonghong Wu. 2012. "Civic engagement and local e-government: Social networking comes of age." Chicago: Institute for Policy and Civic Engagement, University of Illinois at Chicago. Available at: https://ipce.uic.edu/interior/CELocalEGovSMFullReport2012.pdf

Nabatchi, Tina. 2012. *A manager's guide to evaluating citizen participation*. Washington, DC: IBM Center for the Business of Government.

New York City Council. 2015. "Council 2.0: A roadmap to digital inclusion and open government." Available at: http://council.nyc.gov/wp-content/uploads/2016/05/techplan.pdf

Noveck, Beth Simone. 2009. *Wiki government: How technology can make government better, democracy stronger, and citizens more powerful*. Washington, DC: Brookings Institution Press.

Nunnally, Shayla C. 2012. *Trust in black America: Race, discrimination, and politics*. New York, NY: New York University Press.

Nye, Joseph S., Philip Zelikow, and David C. King. 1997. *Why people don't trust government*. Cambridge, MA: Harvard University Press.

Oates, Wallace E. 1972. *Fiscal federalism*. New York, NY: Harcourt Brace Jovanovich.

OECD (Organization for Economic Cooperation and Development). 2003. "The case for e-government: Excerpts from the OECD Report 'The e-government imperative'." *OECD Journal on Budgeting* 3(1): 1987–1996.

OECD (Organization for Economic Cooperation and Development). 2019. "Broadband statistics update." Available at: www.oecd.org/sti/broadband/broadband-statistics-update.htm

Pack, Janet Rothenberg, Samara R. Potter, and William G. Gale. 2002. "Problems and prospects for urban areas." Conference Report #13. Washington DC: Brookings Institute. Available at: www.brookings.edu/research/problems-and-prospects-for-urban-areas/

Parent, Michael, Christine A. Vandebeek, and Andrew C. Gemino. 2005. "Building citizen trust through e-government." *Government Information Quarterly* 22(4): 720–736.

Parkhurst, Nicholet Deschine, Traci Morris, Emery Tahy, and Karen Mossberger. 2015. "The digital reality: E-government and access to technology and broadband for American Indian and Alaska Native populations." Paper presented at 16th Annual International Conference on Digital Government Research, Phoenix, AZ, May.

Pew Research Center. 2015. "Beyond distrust: How Americans view their government." Available at: www.people-press.org/2015/11/23/beyond-distrust-how-am ericans-view-their-government/

Pew Research Center. 2018. "Mobile fact sheet." Available at: www.pewInternet. org/fact-sheet/mobile/

Pew Research Center. 2019a. "Internet/broadband fact sheet." Available at: www. pewInternet.org/fact-sheet/Internet-broadband/

Pew Research Center. 2019b. "Smartphones help Blacks and Hispanics bridge some but not all digital gaps with Whites." Available at: www.pewresearch.org/fact-tank/2019/ 08/20/smartphones-help-blacks-hispanics-bridge-some-but-not-all-digital-gaps-with-whites/Portland, Office of Community Technology. Available at: www.portlandore gon.gov/oct/73859

Reddick, Christopher G., and Jeffrey Roy. 2013. "Business perceptions and satisfaction with e-government: Findings from a Canadian survey." *Government Information Quarterly* 30(1): 1–9.

ReinventPHX. n.d. Available at: http://phoenix.mindmixer.com/category/rein vent-phx

Relly, Jeannine E., and Meghna Sabharwal. 2009. "Perceptions of transparency of government policymaking: A cross-national study." *Government Information Quarterly* 26(1): 148–157.

Robles, Barbara J. 2011. "Historical and policy dimensions of inequity in income and wealth." In *Justice for all: Promoting social equity in public administration*, edited by Norman J. Johnson, and James H. Svara (pp. 58–77). Armonk, NY: ME Sharpe.

Roman, Alexandru V., and Hugh T. Miller. 2013. "New questions for e-government: Efficiency but not (yet?) democracy." *International Journal of Electronic Government Research* 9(1): 65.

Shim, Dong Chul, and Tae Ho Eom. 2008. "E-government and anti-corruption: Empirical analysis of international data." *International Journal of Public Administration*, 31(3): 298–316.

Shim, Dong Chul, and Tae Ho Eom. 2009. "Anticorruption effects of information communication and technology (ICT) and social capital." *International Review of Administrative Sciences* 75(1): 99–116.

Smith, Aaron. 2015. "US smartphone use in 2015." Washington, DC: Pew Research Center. Available at: www.pewInternet.org/2015/04/01/chapter-one-a -portrait-of-smartphone-ownership/

Smith, Samantha. 2015. "6 key takeaways about how Americans view their government." Washington, DC: Pew Research Center.

Srinuan, C., Srinuan, P., and Bohlin, E. 2012. "An analysis of mobile Internet access in Thailand: Implications for bridging the digital divide." *Telematics and Informatics* 29(3): 254–262.

Stephanopolous, Nicholas O. 2015. "Political powerlessness. 90 New York University Law Review 1527." University of Chicago, Public Law Working Paper No. 526. Available at: https://papers.ssrn.com/sol3/papers.cfm?abstract_id=2583495

Thomas, Craig W. 1998. "Maintaining and restoring public trust in government agencies and their employees." *Administration & Society* 30(2): 166–193.

Thornton, Sean. 2018. "A guide to Chicago's Array of Things Initiative." Ash Center for Democratic Governance and Innovation, Harvard Kennedy School. Available at: https://datasmart.ash.harvard.edu/news/article/a-guide-to-chicagos-array-of-things-initiative-1190.

Tolbert, Caroline J., and Karen Mossberger. 2006. "The effects of e-government on trust and confidence in government." *Public Administration Review* 66(3): 354–369.

Tolbert, Caroline J., and Karen Mossberger. 2015. "U.S. current population survey & American Community Survey geographic estimates of internet use, 1997–2014." Available at: https://policyinformatics.asu.edu/broadband-data-portal/dataaccess/citydata.

Tucker, Cristina Michele, and Anna Maria Santiago. 2013. "The role of acculturation in the civic engagement of Latino immigrants." *Advances in Social Work* 14(1): 178–205.

United NationsPublic Administration Network, and American Society for Public Administration. 2002. "Benchmarking e-government: A global perspective." Available at: http://unpan1.un.org/intradoc/groups/public/documents/un/unpa n021547.pdf

United States Census Bureau. 2015. "Projections of the size and compositions of the U.S. population: 2014–2060." Washington, DC: U.S. Department of Commerce. Available at: www.census.gov/content/dam/Census/library/publications/2015/demo/p25-1143.pdf

United States Department of Housing and Urban Development. 2012. "Housing discrimination against racial and ethnic minorities 2012." Available at: www.huduser.gov/portal/Publications/pdf/HUD-514_HDS2012.pdf

Verdegem, Pieter, and Gino Verleye. 2009. "User-centered e-government in practice: A comprehensive model for measuring user satisfaction." *Government Information Quarterly* 26(3): 487–497.

Welch, Eric W., Charles C. Hinnant, and M. Jae Moon. 2005. "Linking citizen satisfaction with e-government and trust in government." *Journal of Public Administration Research and Theory* 15(3): 371–391.

West, Darrell M. 2004. "E-government and the transformation of service delivery and citizen attitudes." *Public Administration Review* 64(1): 15–27.

Wilhelm, Anthony G. 2002. *Democracy in the digital age: Challenges to political life in cyberspace.* New York, NY: Routledge.

Wong, W., and Welch, E. 2004. "Does e-government promote accountability? A comparative analysis of website openness and government accountability." *Governance* 17(2): 275–297.

Yang, Kaifeng, and Marc Holzer. 2006. "The performance–trust link: Implications for performance measurement." *Public Administration Review* 66(1): 114–126.

Yang, Kaifeng, and Seung-Yong Rho. 2007. "E-government for better performance: Promises, realities, and challenges." *International Journal of Public Administration* 30(11): 1197–1217.

# 6 Racial Diversity and Organizational Performance in the U.S. Nonprofit Sector

*Kelly LeRoux*

## Practitioner Points

- Nonprofits lacking in diversity are constrained in their ability to access new resource networks, to formulate effective organizational strategies, and to market their services to diverse populations, all of which serve to limit organizational growth.
- Government organizations, foundations, and other institutional sources of funding that make grants or issue contracts to nonprofit organizations should take into account the diversity of nonprofit boards and executive leadership when awarding funds to these organizations. Nonprofits with greater board diversity can have greater sustainability and financial performance.
- Nonprofit leaders should work with board chairs and executive leadership teams to examine their organization's diversity practices. Organizations should prioritize expanding racial diversity at the board level; diversity in leadership can shape policy for the rest of the organization's diversity policies and practices. In places where nonprofits are challenged to recruit for racial diversity based on the demographics of the region, they should strive to achieve other kinds of diversity on their boards.

## Introduction

Nonprofit social service organizations play a critical role in communities across America, filling gaps in the social safety net by providing food, clothing, housing, and other basic needs as well as job training, health care, family planning, mental health, and substance abuse treatment, among other services. Political theories of representation along with evidence from the human services literature suggest institutions providing these services are more likely to be viewed as trustworthy and their services more fully accessed when the staff and the leadership of these organizations are reflective of the communities and clients they serve (McBeath et al., 2014; Meyer & Zane, 2013). Yet, there is evidence that both staffing and leadership in these organizations remain surprisingly under-representative as today's nonprofit workforce is roughly 82 percent White. This lack of diversity is even more pronounced in nonprofit governance where only 14 percent of board members nation-wide are people of color and roughly 30 percent of nonprofit service organizations lack a single board member of color (Schwartz et al, 2013).

With the demographic composition of the American population rapidly changing, nonprofit organizations are facing increased demands to diversify their boards. Many major foundations now require grant applicants to submit data on the racial composition of their boards, conveying a normative, institutional belief about the value of diversity. However, there is no clear articulation from foundation executives or program officers of why diversity matters or whether their interest in racial representation among grantee organizations is motivated by social equity and justice concerns or relates more to performance and investment concerns.

At the same time that nonprofits face increased demands to diversify their boards, they have also encountered increased pressures for performance in recent years both from their funding entities such as government and foundations, as well as the general public. While government funding agencies and major foundations have expressed concern with the racial composition of their nonprofit contractors or grantees, they are arguably even more concerned with ensuring that their investment of public money or philanthropic dollars will yield satisfactory returns. As the nonprofit sector has grown and more organizations are vying for limited government and foundation funds, the expectations for fund recipients to demonstrate strong performance outcomes has increased dramatically.

Clearly, diversity is not limited to race and ethnicity, and indicators of organizational performance are not limited to the financial and perceptual measures used to operationalize performance in this analysis. That said, this chapter takes an important step toward understanding the link between diversity and nonprofit organizational performance, measured here through two key financial metrics as well as self-reports of performance by agency administrators. Drawing on theories of representation and requisite variety, this chapter investigates whether increased racial diversity on nonprofit boards enhances organizational performance. If so, how? In other words, what are the underlying mechanisms at work that may cause diversity to influence performance?

These questions are answered in this chapter using a mixed-methods design that includes two phases of research and data collection. Phase I draws on survey data from a random sample of nonprofit social service organizations across the U.S. Multivariate regression is used to examine the effects of racial diversity on three measures of organizational performance: (1) the percentage change in revenue over a five-year period; (2) the percentage change in organizational assets over a five-year period; and (3) a seven-item index capturing administrators' perceptions of organizational performance. Results suggest that racial diversity on the board positively predicts not only self-reported measures of organizational effectiveness but also financial measures of performance. Phase II involved collection of qualitative data through an examination of nine organizational cases representing categories of no racial diversity, some racial diversity, and high racial diversity boards. The case analysis confirms the quantitative results but, more importantly, helps to answer the *how* and *why* questions about the diversity-performance link within nonprofits.

The next section describes some of the theory that grounds the logic of this study and reviews relevant literature. An overview of the data and methods is presented next, followed by a description of the results from the data analysis. The chapter concludes with a discussion of what these research findings mean for nonprofit practitioners, the philanthropic field, government organizations, and others engaged in work within human services policy fields.

## Impacts of Diversity on Organizational Outcomes: A Literature Review

People of color remain underrepresented on boards of all types, including within the for-profit sector (Alliance for Board Diversity, 2008), local government citizen advisory boards, school boards (National School Boards Association, 2008), and state boards and commissions (Norman-Eady, 2002). Perhaps it is most surprising, however, that the nonprofit sector, comprised of so many organizations working for social justice and social change, has invested so little effort and attention in addressing the diversity gap within its own agencies. While there has been more discussion about the problem among nonprofit industry groups in recent years (Suarez, 2017), there have been very few empirical studies examining the effects of racial diversity in nonprofits, which could be helpful in building a case for nonprofit leaders to take action.

Studying United Way-funded agencies in Arizona, Daley and Marsiglia (2001) found that board diversity contributed to effective community problem-solving and improved the effectiveness of program/intervention design and implementation, although their definition of diversity was not linked to racial characteristics of clients served by the organization. Similarly, Brown (2002a) found that nonprofit board diversity contributes to enhanced organizational performance, especially in the area of political orientation, concluding that "racially diverse boards will be more sensitive to the interests and concerns of stakeholders" (p. 17). Nonprofit board diversity is considered to be an important goal of many nonprofit directors but rests on organizational efforts to embrace inclusive governance practices and be proactive in efforts to attain greater diversity (Brown 2002b).

There is a robust body of literature in the field of business management that provides insight on the "value in diversity" argument. Among for-profit businesses, greater racial diversity on boards has been associated with increased sales revenue, more customers, greater market share, and greater relative profits (Herring, 2009). In the banking industry, racial diversity on boards of directors has been linked to improved firm performance as measured by productivity, return on equity, and market performance (Richard, 2001). Similarly, team diversity has been found to be linked to performance of sales groups in the private sector (Jackson and Joshi, 2004). On the other hand, a meta-analysis by Kochan et al. (2003) found no direct effects of diversity on performance and suggested that aspects of organizational context and group processes may account for diversity-performance relationships.

## Theories of Diversity and Representation

The theory of complex adaptive systems and its related assumption of requisite variety provide important lenses through which to view the positive effects of racial diversity on nonprofit performance. Complex adaptive systems (whether biological species, psychological systems, sociocultural systems, or organizations) are open to energy or information, and they are open internally as well as externally, such that the interchanges among their component parts may result in significant changes in the nature of the components themselves and have important consequences for the system as a whole (Weick, 1979; 1987). Complex adaptive systems require system variety in order to evolve. When limitations in systems occur, it is because the individuals who operate and manage complex systems are themselves (as a group) not sufficiently complex to sense and anticipate the problems generated by those systems. This creates a problematic lack of requisite variety, because the variety that exists in the system to be managed exceeds the variety in the people who must regulate it (Ashby, 1956). When people have less variety than is requisite to cope with the system, they miss important information, produce incomplete diagnoses, and generate remedies that are short-sighted and can magnify rather than alleviate a problem.

Drawing from these lines of theory, nonprofit organizations can be viewed as complex adaptive systems in which the variety that often exists in the system to be managed (at the organizational or community level) exceeds the variety in the people who must regulate it (generally the governing board). Diversifying an organization at the board level can increase the inherent variety in the system and thus increase overall intergroup and interpersonal contact. As variety grows, this increased contact allows the organization to buffer against both internal and external complexities, decreases conflict, and promotes creative synthesis such that the structuring and re-structuring of an organization (whether knowingly or unknowingly) can aid in survival and evolutionary potential.

As part of the policy-making and oversight body of nonprofit organizations, board members often have substantial influence in setting organizational goals and priorities and in determining how resources will be allocated to meet those goals. However, board members bring different values, functional expertise, and social connections to their board role, and there are likely to be differences of opinion when it comes to setting organizational priorities. Thus, the composition of the board may be critical in determining nonprofit organizational performance. Theories of representation also offer some insight into the positive benefits that racial representation may have for nonprofit organizational performance. Most of this research has been concerned with how representation influences the accrual of benefits to the represented group, but a growing body of literature demonstrates that representation benefits organizational performance (Andrews, Ashworth, and Meier, 2014; Hong, 2016a; 2016b; Pitts, 2005). This research further underscores the reality that representation matters. A compelling body of evidence linking passive to active representation in public organizations demonstrates that demographic representation makes a clear difference in the enactment of policies designed to benefit specific groups (Wilkins and Keiser, 2006). For example, when organizational structures permit higher levels of administrative discretion to those directly carrying out the work of the agency, policy outcomes favoring minority interests are more likely to result (Meier and Bohte, 2001; Sowa and Selden, 2003).

Racial representation among nonprofit boards may also have tangible consequences, yet there has been far less research on issues in the nonprofit sector. One study directly examined the impact of racial representation of the Black community on nonprofit boards and found that it led to higher levels of political advocacy and political effort on behalf of client groups by the organization, including registering and mobilizing clients to vote (LeRoux, 2009). However, the decisive evidence from political science, and public management research demonstrating the link between active and passive representation (Meier, 1993; Meier and Bohte, 2001; Sowa and Selden, 2003; Welch and Bledsoe; 1988) suggests that representation may bring broader organizational benefits as well. Thus, while there has been a general shortage of representation research in the nonprofit field, the large body of research on representation suggests that racial representation may result in similar kinds of benefits for nonprofit social service organizations and the clients they serve.

Given previous findings related to the impacts of diversity on organizational performance and the logics of the requisite variety theory and representation theories, it is hypothesized here that nonprofits with greater racial diversity on their boards will fare better over time, as measured through both objective and subjective performance measures. A discussion of the methodological approach used to investigate the question of whether and how diversity matters for nonprofit performance is provided below.

## The Study: Methodological Approach

This study used a mixed-method explanatory sequential design, which is an appropriate methodological choice when one data source may be insufficient to explain certain phenomena or a need exists to explain initial results (Creswell and Plano Clark, 2011). The analysis was conducted in two phases. Phase I involved the collection and analysis of quantitative data to answer the question of whether and to what extent racial diversity is linked to nonprofit performance. Phase II involved the collection of qualitative data driven by the results of the first stage to answer the questions of how and why diversity affects organizational performance. As the research took place in two distinct phases, the discussion of the data, measures, and analytic procedures will be organized in two sections.

### Phase 1 Study Details

The first phase of the study relied on a subset of data from the National Non-profit Organizational Studies Project. The National Nonprofit Organizational Studies Project is a multi-module, web-based survey administered to Executive Directors of 501(c)(3) human service organizations. The final response rate to the 2012–2013 survey was 37 percent (n = 241).[1] Nonprofit organizations are the units of analysis in this study, and information about the organizations are obtained through responses from Executive Directors.

### Method of Analysis

This study uses multivariate regression analysis to examine the influence of racial board diversity on nonprofit performance. Multivariate regression is a predictive tool that allows for estimating the effects of one factor (such as board diversity) on another (such as growth in organizational revenues) while also accounting for other factors that could influence the outcome factor. In this case, the outcomes of interests are the percentage change in nonprofit organizational revenues, the percentage change in organizational assets, and nonprofit chief executives' (Executive Director (ED) or CEO) self-reported organizational performance. While knowing how board diversity influences these outcomes is the main focus of this chapter, other characteristics such as the organization's age and capacity, the education level of the ED/CEO, the level of wealth in the community where the nonprofit is located, and more may also influence revenues, assets, and performance. A list of these variables can be found in Table 6.1, which also provides some basic descriptive information about the data.

The basic hypothesis is that racial diversity on nonprofit boards will improve nonprofit performance. Three outcome measures are used to examine nonprofit organizational performance: (1) the percentage change in total revenues over the five-year period leading up to the collection of the survey data (2006–2011); (2) the percentage change in total assets over the five-year period (2006–2011); and (3) an index comprised of seven items measuring the ED/CEO's perceptions of organizational effectiveness. The seven perceptual items include ratings of achieving core mission, making strategic decisions, increasing the organization's funding, meeting funders' performance expectations, raising public awareness of a cause, using social media to communicate with stakeholders, and influencing policy or government decisions (local, state, or national) that pertain to the organization's mission. Each question asked respondents to rate the effectiveness of their organization for each item on a scale of 1 to 5 (1 = not at all effective, 5 = completely effective).[2]

*Table 6.1* Descriptive statistics

| Variable | Observa-tions | Mean | Standard deviation | Mini-mum | Max-imum |
|---|---|---|---|---|---|
| % change in revenue | 198 | 26.54 | 59.58 | -144.26 | 373.60 |
| % change in assets | 222 | 55.27 | 128.97 | -97.18 | 963.15 |
| ED perceived performance (index) | 229 | 24.19 | 3.59 | 7.00 | 35.00 |
| Board diversity index | 221 | 0.24 | 0.22 | 0.00 | 1.00 |
| ED education level | 201 | 3.74 | 0.48 | 2.00 | 4.00 |
| Founder | 219 | 0.26 | 0.44 | 0.00 | 1.00 |
| Organizational age | 241 | 32.81 | 17.21 | 1.00 | 94.00 |
| Number of full-time employees | 241 | 94.98 | 183.41 | 0.00 | 1500.00 |
| NP Association Member | 239 | 0.49 | 0.50 | 0.00 | 1.00 |
| Per capita income of county | 241 | 27646.79 | 11172.64 | 9568.00 | 84236.00 |

It is important to note that these measures of organizational performance are imperfect. The financial measures capture change in revenue that happened over the five years prior to the point at which the board's diversity composition was recorded. Since data on the board composition at the start of this five-year time period are not available, it is possible that other factors could have influenced financial growth over this time period. As such, we can conclude only whether there is a positive or negative association between nonprofit board diversity and financial growth. Self-reported measures of organizational effectiveness also have limitations, as Executive Directors/CEOs of the organization might be susceptible to social desirability bias such that they overstate how well their organization is performing. Yet, given the wide-ranging methods for measuring organizational performance across the nonprofit literature, many scholars have emphasized the fact that performance is multidimensional and they encourage the combining of both objective and perceptual measures (Brown, 2000a; Herman and Renz, 2004; Sowa, Selden, and Sandfort, 2004). The measures used in this analysis not only adhere to this advice, but they go beyond previous studies of nonprofit organizational performance that have relied almost exclusively on perceptual measures.

The key independent variable of interest in this study is racial diversity of nonprofit boards. Racial diversity on the board was captured through a survey question answered by the Executive Director (ED) asking for the number of people serving on the board in each of five racial groups: Black/African American, Hispanic, White, Asian/Pacific Islander, and Other/Mixed Race. From this information, percentages of each group's racial composition on the board can be calculated and used to create an inverse Hirschman-Herfindahl index (HHI).[3] The index ranges from 0 to 1 where 0 equals no diversity and 1 indicates equal representation of each of the five racial groups. After the proportions of each racial group were squared and summed, the scale was reversed by subtracting the HHI from 1.0, so that values closer to zero reflect greater racial concentration and values closer to 1 reflect greater diversity.

In addition to racial diversity on the board, other factors may help to explain nonprofit financial performance; some of these factors can be accounted for with control variables. One such factor is the education level of the ED/CEO.[4] Four additional control variables tap organizational attributes that may all positively influence performance: age of the organization, which can be considered a measure of stability; whether the ED/CEO founded the organization, which is sometimes linked with organizational growth (Block and Rosenberg, 2002); number of full-time equivalent employees, which is a common indicator of overall resources and capacity; and whether or not the organization is a member of its state nonprofit association (NP Association). Nonprofit associations exist as important institutional influences on their members, as they function as vehicles for the dissemination of important policy and regulatory information and help to diffuse best practices throughout the sector. A final control variable is per capita income of the county in which the nonprofit is located; this measure attempts to capture the quality of the resource environment. Presumably, nonprofits located in regions with higher incomes will have a higher probability of growing their budgets over time, particularly the portion of income that comes from public support.

### Does Diversity Matter for Nonprofit Performance Outcomes?

The results displayed in Table 6.2 confirm that racial diversity of nonprofit boards does indeed advantage nonprofit performance in a number of ways.

The results presented in the first column of Table 6.2 show the impact of racial diversity on total revenue growth (percentage change in organizational revenues over the five-year period). Racial diversity on the board has a positive, statistically significant effect ($p < .05$) on organizational revenues. For a one-unit increase in the nonprofit diversity index (moving from not diverse at all to very diverse), organizational revenues increased by 49.3 percent over the five-year period, holding all other variables constant at their means. The current ED being a founder of the organization is also a factor that helps to explain nonprofits' increase in revenues over time. When the ED is the founder of the organization, revenues increase by roughly 6.5 percent over the five-year period. Executive Directors who are founders are typically powerful personalities who invest considerable time and energy in resource acquisition for the organization, both on and off the clock.

The results displayed in the second column of Table 6.2 reveal a similar effect of racial diversity on financial performance when performance is measured as a percentage increase in organizational assets over the five-year

*Table 6.2* Effects of racial diversity on nonprofit organizational performance

| | % change in revenues, 2006–2011 | % change in assets, 2006–2011 | ED/CEO perceptions of performance, 2006–2011 |
|---|---|---|---|
| Diversity index | 49.378★★ | 95.244★ | 2.368★★ |
| | (25.091) | (56.209) | (1.128) |
| ED educational level | 6.546 | 44.942 ★★★ | -.841★ |
| | (15.536) | (10.124) | (.472) |
| ED is founder | 41.882★★★ | 9.046 | .127 |
| | (15.264) | (22.241) | (.614) |
| Age of organization | .313 | -1.290★ | -.021★ |
| | (.355) | (.782) | (.013) |
| Number of FTEs | .033 | -.032 | .003★★★ |
| | (.030) | (.027) | (.001) |
| Member of state NP Association | 1.006 | 40.410★★ | .731 |
| | (11.388) | (20.058) | (.489) |
| Per capita income | -.000 | -.000 | -.000 |
| | (.001) | (.001) | (.000) |
| Constant | -52.871 | -107.552★★ | 27.327★★★ |
| | (71.305) | (44.481) | (2.012) |
| Adjusted $R^2$ | .167 | .109 | .090 |
| Root MSE | 54.429 | 120.4 | 3.293 |
| F | 1.59★ | 3.89★★★ | 3.09★★★ |
| N of cases | 159 | 176 | 184 |

Given that all three dependent variables are continuous, all models are estimated using ordinary least squares regression (OLS). Robust standard errors are used to correct for heteroskedasticity common in cross-sectional analyses.

period. For each unit increase in the nonprofit diversity index, organizational assets increase by 95.2 percent over five years, holding all other variables constant at their means. When organizations hold a membership in their state nonprofit association, assets increase by 40.4 percent over the five-year period. Nonprofit associations are important institutions for professional networking, capacity-building, peer learning, and disseminating and promoting best practices, and nonprofits that belong to these associations have significant growth advantages. The education level of the ED also accounts for some of the explanation of asset growth; for each unit increase on the ordinal-ranked education scale, organizational assets increase

44.9 percent. Somewhat unexpectedly, organizational age is negatively associated with asset growth, with each year of age associated with a decline in assets of 1.2 percent.

Finally, the results also show racial diversity to be a key factor in explaining administrative perceptions of organizational effectiveness. The results in column 3 of Table 6.2 show that for a one-unit increase in the board diversity measure, the ED's perception of organizational effectiveness increases, meaning that nonprofit executives view their organizations as more effective regarding mission fulfillment, resource acquisition, and more when their boards are more diverse. Organizational size is also a positive predictor of administrative perceptions of effectiveness, with each additional full-time equivalent employee linked to an .003 increase in the effectiveness index. Two additional variables achieve statistical significance but have opposite effects than predicted. First, education level is negatively related to ED perceptions of performance, suggesting that leaders with lower educational attainment tend to view their organization's performance more favorably than those with more education. Similarly, organizational age is negatively associated with ED perceptions, meaning that EDs of older organizations are likely to rate their performance more critically than those of younger organizations. While the explanation for these counterintuitive findings is not entirely clear, one possibility is that the education and organizational age measures are tapping into professional experience, with newer, or less well-established organizations being directed by EDs who have not (or not yet) achieved higher levels of educational attainment. Taken together, these factors account for 9 percent of the total variance in the model predicting ED perceptions of organizational effectiveness.

The statistical significance of the racial diversity variable across all three models provides consistent evidence of a positive link between board diversity and nonprofit organizational performance. It should be noted that the R-squared values in each of the models are somewhat low, meaning that the variables in the model account for a somewhat small share of the total explanation for nonprofit performance. Many other factors might help to explain nonprofit performance, including other measures of capacity, board characteristics and functional expertise, and competition in the nonprofit's resource environment. Although data are not available to account for these factors here, these variables should be included in future studies of nonprofit performance.

Having established a statistical link between racial diversity on the board and organizational performance, we now turn to the second question, which is *why* and *how* does diversity impact these outcomes? The next section answers these questions after a brief description of the qualitative data collection approach.

### Phase II Study Details

The second phase of the study involved an in-depth examination of multiple cases. Nine nonprofit organizations were purposely selected for analysis with three organizations in categories of (1) no racial diversity; (2) some racial diversity; and (3) high levels of racial diversity. No diversity is defined as having an all-White board of directors. Some diversity is defined as having a board with at least some representation by racial minorities (greater than zero but less than 20 percent), and high diversity is defined as having a board in which racial minorities are represented at levels of greater than 20 percent of the board. Cases were selected from within the large central cities of Chicago and Detroit as well as two rural counties in Illinois and Michigan in an attempt to ensure geographic diversity and account for variations in diversity levels within the local population. All organizations are 501(c)(3) human service providers with missions similar to those studied in Phase I.

The analysis of these nine cases relied on multiple data sources including publicly available financial statements, annual reports, websites, and personal interviews with Executive Directors and/or board members. A total of 14 interviews were conducted across the nine cases, with at least one interview from each organizational case (for five cases, two interviews were obtained). Among those interviewed, five were men and nine were women; interviewees also included one Black, one Latino, one Asian, and nine Caucasians.

Interviews followed a semi-structured format with questions pertaining to board recruitment strategies, priorities, and challenges as well as perceptions of the effects of diversity. Interviews lasted anywhere from 30–90 minutes, and each interview was recorded and transcribed. The interview data were analyzed using the process of open coding prescribed by Glaser (1992), adhering to the procedure of coding for relevance with respect to conditions, interactions among the actors, strategies and tactics, and consequences (Strauss, 1987). Two individuals independently analyzed each interview transcript and identified concepts within various conditions, with the charge of searching for consistency of concepts among respondents' reports. Independent analysis of the transcripts and intensive analysis resulted in the emergence of three broad explanations relating to the question of why and how diversity affects performance.

### How Does Diversity Affect Performance?

Before turning to the discussion of the mechanisms underlying the diversity-performance link, it is important to note how well the nine organizational cases confirm the findings of the statistical analysis. The performance of the nine cases is generally consistent with the patterns that emerged from Phase I of the study with some important caveats and qualifiers. Analysis of 990 forms and annual reports (years 2012–2015) reveal that two of the three "high diversity" organizational cases experienced the greatest revenue growth of all nine cases, while the third had minimal growth. When the interview subjects at these high growth cases were asked about the causes, responses tended to focus on specific grants they were awarded or other resource opportunities that arose. When asked about the role of the board in the organization's financial success, respondents emphasized specific skills or connections or status held by board members rather than race or any other type of diversity.

Among the "some diversity" cases, one had impressive growth and two essentially remained stable, neither gaining nor losing a significant amount of income over the period of study. Among the "no diversity" cases, one had reported a loss of revenue on form 990 over two of three years, one remained no-growth/budget-stable, and one demonstrated significant financial growth. Worthy of note is that two of the three "no diversity" cases were situated in more rural locales with very small non-White populations. The "no diversity" organization with high revenue growth is situated in a county that is 95 percent White and thus faces a very narrow prospect of having persons of color represented on the board. However, what is interesting about this case is that before any questions about board diversity were asked, the ED spoke with pride of her efforts to achieve gender balance on her board, commenting that ten years ago the board had been made up entirely of men but she had succeeded in reshaping the board to now reflect 40 percent women. She also discussed recent efforts to add younger people (mid-thirties) to the board in an attempt to capture some new skills and different generational perspectives. This perhaps suggests that diversity in general is key and that nonprofits situated in regions with low levels of racial diversity should strive to attain diversity of other kinds on their boards (e.g., gender, age, sexual orientation, functional diversity).

Interview subjects representing all three categories of "high diversity" to "no diversity" organizations consistently reported that recruiting specific skills to the board was their first priority and that demographic diversity was a secondary consideration. A respondent from one of the "no diversity" organizations made a comment that was reflected by many others: "We look for different professional backgrounds, for us, that's the most important thing." Another respondent from one of the "some diversity" organizations stated,

> We're a small board, a working board, so a lot of times for us, it comes down to replacing someone with a specific skill, like, we lost our accountant so we need an accountant, and we need someone who can commit 20 hours a month, so while we'd like to get more diverse, we're driven by, "Can I get two of the three things we really need?," so it's not that diversity is less important, sometimes it's just less urgent.

Finally, many interview subjects, particularly those situated in regions with less racially diverse populations, expressed thoughts that suggested a sensitivity to the notion of tokenism. As one respondent representing a youth service organization stated, "I can only think of one [non-White] person that I know fairly well in this town, he's a really good guy but I wouldn't ask him to be on my board, without a particular role in mind." A respondent from one of the 'some diversity' organizations stated, "We're [board members] all close enough we have the discussions like, 'Hey, do we really need another White male on this board?' but at the same time we wouldn't nominate someone without a clear idea of how we wanted them to contribute."

These comments suggest that nonprofit leaders are relatively tuned in to issues of inclusion and generally do not seek out racial diversity simply for the sake of diversity; instead, racially diverse board members are sought under conditions when nonprofit leaders have a plan for new members to be engaged and full participants in the governance process.

The critical question of *how* racial diversity on nonprofit boards might create the conditions for growth and enhanced organizational performance remains. The answer to this complex question can be distilled into three explanations: (1) expansion of resource networks; (2) enhanced problem-solving and strategic capability; and (3) increased consumer demand/expanded market share.

### Expansion of Resource Networks

The most common theme that arose among interview subjects was that of networks, and, specifically, the mention of personal networks and ways they might expand the pool of potential donors or connections to people in the community in a position to provide financial support to the organization. This simple quote from one of the "some diversity" cases summarizes the sentiments of several interviews: "It all comes down to networks. More diversity means access to more networks." Another interview subject representing one of the "high diversity cases" stated:

> We work actively to make sure our board is diverse—we have board members that are African American, Hispanic, Middle Eastern, and we think that's important, to get those groups sort of represented so you can tap into some of those different networks in the community.

A respondent from one of the "no diversity" cases (that had no-growth/budget stable but is embedded in a region with a high degree of racial diversity) offered,

> I think on some level we know we're missing out, there's this whole other part of the community we're not reaching [as supporters] that we should. I think diversity helps with getting into these networks, but whenever board spots need filled a lot of times, it's easier to go back to our same circles of people.

A board member for one of the "high diversity" cases, who is Black and financially supports the organization for which she is a board member, as well as other organizations in the community, made a comment that suggests people of color are paying attention to diversity and representation and are unwilling to leverage their own personal networks when they perceive that diversity has not been prioritized by an organization. This respondent described a three-part test she relies on when determining whether or not to make a charitable contribution to an organization (and whether to make an appeal to others):

> I don't care how much good you're doing in the community ... in order for me to write you a check and go to my friends and ask for support, you have to pass three tests: 1. Are there people of color on your leadership team? 2. Are there people of color on your board? and 3. Can I see that you're making an effort to buy from the minority-owned businesses? [Buy meaning purchase of services agreements related to organizational needs.]

Moreover, diversity appears to help leverage other types of connections that may financially benefit an organization beyond donor networks. One respondent described how they were able to "get on the radar" of a local foundation that ultimately paved the way for an invitation to submit a proposal based on a contact facilitated by one of the organization's board members of color. In short, personal networks of board members appear to play an important role in predicting organizational performance. When nonprofits have highly diverse boards, they have access to a wider range of networks that can be accessed in serving the organization's financial and overall well-being.

### Enhanced Problem-Solving and Strategic Capability

Many of the participants expressed ideas that align with the "requisite variety" principle that diversity is necessary for organizational evolution. A nonprofit lacking in board diversity (all one race or nearly so) can be representative of its community, but the lack of diversity may ultimately constrain its field of information, cause it to miss important cues from the environment, and lead to incomplete diagnoses of problems and incomplete strategies for action. A comment from one of the "some diversity" cases, exemplifies this point: "With a more diverse group you get alternative ways to think and plan that might let you break out of your conventional way." Another respondent from one of the "no diversity" no-growth/budget stable cases situated in a low diversity region lamented the lack of opportunity to have diversity on her board and observed ways she thought it could be helpful in deliberating organizational business: "I think any time you get people in a room or around a table together who have different lived experiences you're going to get a richer conversation, you're probably going to learn something." A comment from a White board member at one of the "some diversity" cases also illustrates how lack of diversity can limit an organization's field of information and can constrain the ability to effectively problem-solve:

> I think it's important whenever you're talking, or reaching out, or seeking opinions about certain things, that you're doing so with an eye towards how each of those groups [served by the organization] will

understand what your organization is doing, or how it may potentially impact those groups, and you may not be able to, from your own perspective, be sensitive to some of those things, so I think when you're able to get all those opinions, and let a lot of different people inform what you're doing, you're going to be more effective.

As these comments suggest, organizations that are lacking in diversity may have a diminished capacity to absorb and process information from their environment. This point aligns directly with the perspective of organizations as open systems that require variety (diversity) in order for organizational evolution and growth to occur.

### Expanded Market Share

A final explanation for the role of board diversity in nonprofit performance relates to competitive advantages in the marketplace. More diverse nonprofits appear better positioned to attract the largest shares of customers or clients from within a regional service market. While this theme was somewhat unexpected, it aligns with the reality that nonprofits today behave increasingly like for-profit firms in their efforts to grow and sustain themselves. Given that earned income is the largest and fastest-growing source of revenue in the nonprofit sector (McKeever and Pettijohn, 2014), it is perhaps unsurprising that some nonprofits view diversity as essential to their ability to effectively market their services and to attract "customers." Most of the comments related to this theme emerged from the "high diversity" and, to a lesser extent, "some diversity" cases. One board member of a "high diversity" high-performing organization who also worked in the for-profit sector (tech industry) conveyed a distinct business orientation in her perspective on diversity: "No question, diversity helps the bottom line. We figured this out in the corporate world a long time ago. It's [diversity] beneficial because you have people on board and you're connecting to more segments of the market." A respondent at another high-diversity case conveyed a similar point in stating, "We're always thinking about our programming and thinking how do we offer things more people will want to come to, and to be successful with that, you need to make it appealing to as many different groups as possible. I don't know [if] we could do that without our [diverse] board."

Another Executive Director highlighted the point about nonprofits' ability to capture market share, especially in competitive markets where clients have choices. In this case, the Executive Director is referring to diversity on the front lines of service but still conveying how clients of color may help to shape a market by consciously or unconsciously using representation as a factor in provider choice:

> In a place like [name of city] where people have a lot of choices, I think people rely a lot on word-of-mouth, and on some level people will want the places where they know there's more staff who look like them.

Overall, the theme of increased market share aligns with the "value in diversity" and "business case for diversity" arguments so prevalent in the business management literature. As nonprofits become more competitive with one another and increasingly compete against for-profit firms (Salamon, Sokolowski, and Geller, 2012), this tendency is perhaps natural. However, this fact, combined with the growing number of MBAs hired to lead nonprofits, presents a risk in which diversity is viewed by nonprofit leaders and board members primarily from an instrumental perspective rather than as a fundamental matter of social equity and inclusion.

## Conclusion

Achieving equitable levels of racial representation in public service delivery, particularly in the managerial and leadership ranks, is an issue of enduring concern for the field of public administration and management. As partners in public service, providing essential health and human services through contracts and grants, nonprofits occupy an important place in the system of government service delivery. Given their service to racially diverse populations, nonprofit human service organizations are well positioned to help further public sector goals of greater social equity. While current nonprofit norms of leadership recruitment are not yet fully aligned with this public sector priority, there is a growing concern in the nonprofit practitioner community and among institutional funders about the diversity gap in nonprofits.

At the same time, nonprofits face increased pressures to demonstrate their effectiveness so as to merit continued funding and to maintain their trust and legitimacy in the eyes of the public. This study confronts both of these issues. The aim of this chapter was to empirically examine the effects of racial diversity on nonprofit boards on various measures of nonprofit organizational performance. It offers evidence that racial diversity at the board level is valuable for nonprofits, with greater diversity being linked to annual revenue growth, asset growth, and higher perceptions of performance by agency administrators. This study further found that racial diversity works to advantage organizational growth through expanding resource networks, enhanced problem-solving and strategic capability generated by diverse life experiences, and by helping expand market share.

Clearly, diversity is not limited to race and ethnicity, and some nonprofit organizations may have diversity goals that aim to expand inclusivity not only of underrepresented racial and ethnic minorities, but also members of the LGBT community, persons with disabilities, generational diversity, religious diversity, and so on. The findings of this study support the requisite variety theory, and it is possible that *diversity in general* (not just racial diversity) is what drives organizational processing of information and productive transaction with the resource environment in ways that aid organizational growth and evolution. As one case in this study demonstrated, organizational performance can be enhanced through efforts to achieve other types of diversity when local population demographics make the achievement of racial diversity more challenging. While most of the discussion about diversity (and lack thereof) in the nonprofit practice community relates to race and calls for greater attention to increasing racial diversity on boards, future studies of nonprofit board diversity would benefit from capturing a wider range of diversity variables that account for factors such as gender, sexual orientation, and functional expertise.

As is the case in any social science analysis, this study has its limitations. The data used here capture board diversity at a single point in time. In reality, nonprofit boards are dynamic, and membership is not stable over time. An ideal study would capture how changes in board diversity correspond to changes in financial performance (or other objective measures of performance) over time. Unfortunately, there is no ready source of data on nonprofit board demographics and representative samples must be captured through surveys which ask administrators to provide detailed numerical information on board members. This type of data collection poses challenges in terms of resources and time, as well as decreased response rates when subjects are asked to provide information as opposed to simply checking boxes.

While finance data are publicly available, it is time-consuming to seek these data on a set of nonprofits that has been surveyed, especially for multiple years. It has also been observed that there is a great deal of volatility in nonprofit finances from year to year, so future studies may consider using a moving average over three or five years. There are also a variety of other financial metrics that could be used, including a viability ratio (ratio of net assets to long-term debt), operating reserves, fundraising efficiency, or year-to-year donor growth and retention.

Measures of organizational performance are not limited to how well the organization is doing financially or how well administrators perceive their organization to be performing. Other indicators of performance can include clients' and other stakeholders' satisfaction with services, diversity of funding over time, or how well the organization meets pre-specified performance targets or treatment goals (whether clients of nonprofit job training programs are able to find competitive employment or keep their job as measured at some time point after program participation, for example). This line of research could also be expanded by looking at diversity of the nonprofit workforce at various levels (street-level, supervisory, managerial) and its impact on performance, as the analysis discussed in this chapter is limited to capturing diversity and representation at the highest level (the governing body). In sum, it will be important for future research to replicate and build upon these findings, but it will involve an intensive commitment of time and resources.

The results of the studies reported here have direct implications for nonprofit administrators and board chairs tasked with the responsibility of board recruitment and development. Nonprofits lacking in diversity are constrained in their ability to access new resource networks, formulate effective organizational strategies, and market their services to diverse populations, all of which serve to limit organizational growth. Nonprofit leaders should work with their board chairs and executive leadership teams to examine the organization's diversity practices. Organizations should make it a priority to recruit for racial diversity at the board level, which can help to shape policy for the rest of the organization's diversity policies and practices. In places where nonprofits are challenged to recruit for racial diversity based on demographics of the region, nonprofits should strive to achieve other kinds of diversity on their boards, as diversity of all types can benefit organizational performance.

The findings also have implications for government agencies that fund nonprofit social service organizations, and the philanthropic/foundation community that also funds the work of these organizations. Institutional funders have become extremely preoccupied with finding solutions to enhance the effectiveness of nonprofit service providers. The results reported in this chapter point to the positive return-on-investment that could be expected from directing more resources (both public and philanthropic) into nonprofit service organizations that are making diversity a priority. Government organizations, foundations, and other institutional sources of funding that award grants or issue contracts to nonprofit organizations may wish to consider taking into account the diversity of nonprofit boards and executive leadership when awarding funds to these organizations.

This study provides an important step in establishing a link between racial diversity on nonprofit boards and organizational performance. The study also demonstrates some of the specific ways in which racial diversity aids in nonprofits' growth potential. Taken together, the findings point to some important benefits and advantages of diversity in nonprofit governance. Ultimately, this study contributes to public debate on the value of diversity and representation in charitable institutions and offers some direction for others interested in studying these issues.

## Discussion Questions

1   Consider nonprofit organizations in your community or those with which you are familiar. How diverse are the governing boards and positions of leadership of these organizations? Are the governing boards racially representative of the clients served and communities where they are located?

2   What are some of the short- and long-term strategies you would recommend to increase diversity on a governing board and among agency leadership? In thinking through these strategies, remember that many nonprofits lack the resources to hire a consultant or a diversity officer.

3   Would your recommendations to increase diversity in a nonprofit organization vary for those organizations situated in urban or rural environments? Would your recommendations change for increasing diversity among members of the governing board compared to front-line employees?

4   Why has the lack of racial diversity in nonprofit governance and leadership persisted? What might be some of the root causes of this problem within a sector otherwise known for creating social good?

5   As nonprofits become more like private firms, how will their diversity practices change (if at all)? Does having an entrepreneurial leader or business-like culture within a nonprofit help or harm organizational diversity efforts?

## Acknowledgments

I wish to thank the RGK Center for Philanthropy and Community Service for their support of this project, as well as Julie Langer-McCarthy for excellent research assistance.

## Notes

1   The survey spanned several weeks of late 2012 and early 2013. The sampling frame was constructed using National Taxonomy of Exempt Entities (NTEE) codes, with a common core of questions administered to all participants and varying question modules administered to different groups across the full sample. This study analyzes the subset of respondents who were administered the governance question module. Respondents are all Executive Directors or CEOs of 501c(3) nonprofit organizations with a primary mission of mental health, housing, workforce development, and family planning. The method of administering the survey conformed to standard research procedures for internet surveys (Dillman, 2008). Each respondent in the study sample received an initial letter through U.S. mail which introduced the study and provided details about how to participate. Each potential respondent was then sent an e-mail approximately one week later with a unique link to access and complete the survey. Multiple e-mail reminders were sent to non-respondents over an eight-week period.

2   The data used to create the first two outcome variables were obtained independently from the organizations using the 990 reports publicly available in Guidestar. The third variable was created from a series of survey questions asking respondents to rate the effectiveness of their organization on a scale of 1 to 5 (1 = not at all effective, 5 = completely effective) on seven different items. These seven items were combined to create an index capturing the ED's perception of organizational effectiveness ($\alpha$ =.708).

3   A Hirschman-Herfindahl index is commonly used to measure revenue concentration in nonprofit studies (Fischer, Wilsker, and Young, 2011), and is calculated by summing and squaring the proportion of each different revenue source reported by nonprofits (sources include the government, private contributions, commercial/earned income, and more). Using this measure, values closer to zero signal greater revenue diversity and values closer to 1 reflect greater revenue concentration. The same method was used to calculate racial diversity, but the index was reversed to make the interpretation more straightforward.

4   ED/CEO education is measured as 1 = high school diploma/GED, 2 = some college, 3 = bachelor's degree, 4 = master's degree, 5 = doctorate/JD.

## References

Alliance for Board Diversity. 2008. *Women and minorities on Fortune 100 boards.* Washington, DC: Catalyst, Prout Group, The Executive Leadership Council, and the Hispanic Association on Corporate Responsibility.

Andrews, Rhys, Rachel Ashworth, and Kenneth J. Meier. 2014. "Representative bureaucracy and fire service performance." *International Public Management Journal* 17(1): 1–24.

Ashby, Ross. 1956. *An introduction to cybernetics*. London: Chapman & Hall.

Block, Stephen R., and Steven Rosenberg. 2002. "Toward an understanding of founder's syndrome: An assessment of power and privilege among founders of nonprofit organizations." *Nonprofit Management and Leadership* 12(4): 353–368.

Brown, William A. 2002a. "Racial diversity and performance of nonprofit boards of directors." *Journal of Applied Management and Entrepreneurship* 7(4): 43–57.

Brown, William A. 2002b. "Inclusive governance practices in nonprofit organizations and implications for performance." *Nonprofit Management & Leadership* 12(4): 369–385.

Creswell, John W., and Vicki L. Plano Clark. 2011. *Designing and conducting mixed methods research,* 2nd edn. Thousand Oaks, CA: Sage.

Daley, John Michael, and Flavio Francisco Marsiglia. 2001. "Social diversity within nonprofit boards: Members' view on status and issues." *Journal of the Community Development Society* 32(2): 290–309.

Dillman, Don A., Jolene D. Smyth, and Leah Milani Christian. 2008. *Internet, mail, and mixed-mode surveys: The tailored design method*. Hoboken, NJ: John Wiley & Sons.

Eisinger, Peter K. 1982. "Black employment in municipal jobs: The impact of black political power." *American Political Science Review* 76(2): 380–392.

Fischer, Robert, Amanda Wilsker, and Dennis Young, 2011. "Exploring the revenue mix of nonprofit organizations: Does it relate to publicness?" *Nonprofit and Voluntary Sector Quarterly* 40(4): 662–681.

Glaser, Barney G. 1992. *Basics of grounded theory analysis*. Mill Valley, CA: Sociology Press.

Herman, Robert D. and David O. Renz. 2004. "Doing things right: Effectiveness in local nonprofit organizations, a panel study." *Public Administration Review* 64(6): 694–704.

Herring, Cedric. 2009. "Does diversity pay? Race, gender, and the business case for diversity." *American Sociological Review* 74(2): 208–224.

Hong, Sounman. 2016a. "Representative bureaucracy, organizational integrity, and citizen coproduction: Does an increase in police ethnic representativeness reduce crime?" *Journal of Policy Analysis and Management* 35(1): 11–33.

Hong, Sounman. 2016b. "Does increasing ethnic representativeness reduce police misconduct? Evidence from police reform in England and Wales." *Public Administration Review* 77(2): 195–205.

Jackson, Susan and Aparna Joshi. 2004. "Diversity in social context: A multi-attribute, multilevel analysis of team diversity and sales performance." *Journal of Organizational Behavior* 25(6): 675–702.

Kochan, Thomas, Katerina Bezrukova, Robin Ely, Susan Jackson, Aparna Joshi, et al. 2003. "The effects of diversity on business performance: Report of the diversity research network." *Human Resources Management,* 42(1): 3–21.

LeRoux, Kelly. 2009. "The effects of descriptive representation on nonprofits' civic intermediary roles: Testing the racial mismatch hypothesis in the social services sector." *Nonprofit and Voluntary Sector Quarterly* 38(5): 741–760.

McBeath, Bowen, Emmeline Chuang, Alicia Bunger, and Jennifer Blakeslee. 2014. "Under what conditions does caseworker-caregiver racial/ethnic similarity matter for housing service provision? An application of representative bureaucracy theory." *Social Service Review* 88(1): 135–165.

McKeever, Brice, and Sarah L. Pettijohn. 2014. *The nonprofit sector in brief 2014. Public charities, giving and volunteering.* Washington, DC: Urban Institute.

Meier, Kenneth J. 1993. "Latinos and representative bureaucracy: Testing the Thompson and Henderson Hypotheses." *Journal of Public Administration Research Theory* 3(4): 393–414.

Meier, Kenneth J. and John Bohte. 2001. "Structure and discretion: Missing links in representative bureaucracy." *Journal of Public Administration Research Theory* 11(4): 455–470.

Meyer, Oanh, and Nolan Zane. 2013. "The influence of race and ethnicity in clients' experiences of mental health treatment." *Journal of Community Psychology* 41(7): 884–901.

Mosher, Frederick C. 1982. *Democracy and the public service,* 2nd edn. New York, NY: Oxford University Press.

National School Boards Association. 2008. "A question of representation: Diversity and 21st century school boards." Available at: www.nsba.org

Norman-Eady, Sandra. 2002. "Diversity on state boards and commissions." Hartford, CT: Office of Legislative Research, July 23.

Pitts, David. W. 2005. "Diversity, representation, and performance: Evidence about race and ethnicity in public organizations." *Journal of Public Administration Research & Theory* 15(4): 615–631.

Richard, Orlando C. 2001. "Racial diversity, business strategy, and firm performance: A resource-based view." *Academy of Management Journal* 43(2): 164–177.

Salamon, Lester M., S. Wojciech Sokolowski, and Stephanie L. Geller. 2012. "Holding the fort: Nonprofit employment in a decade of turmoil." *Nonprofit Employment Bulletin* 39: 1–17.

Schwartz, Robert, James Weinberg, Dana Hagenbuch, and Allison Scott. 2013. "The voice of nonprofit talent: Perceptions of diversity in the workplace." Common Good Careers & Level Playing Field Institute. Available at: www.commongoodca reers.org/diversityreport.pdf.

Sowa, Jessica E., and Sally Coleman Selden. 2003. "Administrative discretion and active representation: An expansion of the theory of representative bureaucracy." *Public Administration Review* 63(6): 700–710.

Sowa, Jessica, Sally Coleman Selden, and Jodi Sandfort. 2004. "No longer unmeasurable? A multidimensional integrated model of nonprofit organizational effectiveness." *Nonprofit and Voluntary Sector Quarterly* 33(4): 711–728.

Strauss, Anselm. 1987. *Qualitative analysis for social scientists.* New York, NY: Cambridge University Press.

Suarez, Cynthia. 2017. "The nonprofit racial leadership gap: Flipping the lens." *The Nonprofit Quarterly,* June 8. Available at: https://nonprofitquarterly.org/nonprofit-ra cial-leadership-gap-flipping-lens/

Weick, Karl E. 1979. *The social psychology of organizing.* Reading, MA: Addison-Wesley.

Weick, Karl E. 1987. "Organizational culture as a source of high reliability." *California Management Review* 29(2): 112–127.

Welch, Susan, and Timothy Bledsoe. 1988. *Urban reform and its consequences: A study in representation.* Chicago: University of Chicago Press.

Wilkins, Vicky M., and Lael R. Keiser. 2006. "Linking passive and active representation for gender: The case of child support agencies." *Journal of Public Administration Research Theory* 16(1): 87–102.

# 7 A Janus-faced Public Administration and Race

## International Experiences

*Alketa Peci, Andre Dantas Cabral, Eunji Lee, and Vanessa Brulon Soares*

## Practitioner points

- The concept of race and how it is understood by public administration practitioners and scholars vary greatly across countries. Some countries explicitly acknowledge racial tensions and inequities while others do not.
- Race is defined through social constructions. As such, racial issues need to be viewed within a country's broader historical and social context. Minority groups are not likely to be viewed in the same way across jurisdictional boundaries.
- Public administration matters for racial equity in terms of policies that contain structural racism as well as individual-level racism and inherent bias. Public institutions and policies may contribute to or detract from racial equity in the surrounding environment in multiple forms of governance structures around the world.

## Introduction

Exclusion is pervasive in society. Race, despite being a contested biological construct, is one of the most visible facets of social exclusion. As such, an individual's race can influence access to goods and services, literacy, workplace promotion, policing strategies, crime sentences, and even life expectancy (Taylor, 2006). In other words, race has consequences for the general welfare of a society, and public administrators must respond to these consequences.

Within a causal and intimate relationship of race and the hundreds of forces moving in society are immersed the specific links between public administration (e.g., the bureaucracy) and race. In order to cover this complex relationship, we rely on a "most different" systems research design in which contrasting cases are compared by choosing three countries where the politics of race are vastly different (Skocpol and Somers, 1980). The first case focuses on racial relations between minority groups and police in the United Kingdom, a prominent case of a Western perspective related to public administration and race. The second case presents the difficulties of guaranteeing access to university education for Blacks and mixed minorities in Brazil, a country where a history of miscegenation and a myth of racial democracy have created challenges for the implementation of compensatory policies. Finally, we present the case of South Korea, where society is considered homogeneous, race and nationality are almost the same, and "multiculturalism" appears as an approach for working with foreign ethnic groups. We expand our analysis not just geographically but also longitudinally by historically analyzing each policy in their respective contexts (Lijphart, 1971).

Focusing on country-level comparisons presents some limitations when analyzing how states and public administrators interact with the concept of race. In fact, our analysis overlooks the fact that racial and ethnic discrimination may not always occur within national boundaries and jurisdictions. Indeed, racial and ethnic communities often exceed national borders. For example, 25–35 million Kurds make up the fourth-largest ethnic group in the Middle East but they do not have their own nation state; instead Kurds inhabit a region straddling the borders of Turkey, Iraq, Syria, Iran, and Armenia (BBC, 2018). This lack of jurisdiction appears to justify their state persecution by various countries. At a minimum, it influences the "invisibility" of Kurds within the development and implementation of public policy by national governments. This is also the case for Roma (gypsies). According to Barany (1998), reliable estimates put the world's Roma population at about 10 million, of which almost three-fourths reside in Eastern Europe, while one million live in the United States. Roma have historically faced persecution and genocide both under the Nazis and under communist regimes, and they continue to be invisible, situated at the bottom rung of the socioeconomic scale in the countries where they live. The sparse research regarding Roma and public administration indicates a historical relation marked by confusion, ambiguity, harsh persecution, and qualified tolerance (e.g., Mayall, 1995).

The contrasting cases considered here enable us to formulate statements that are valid regardless of the system within which the formulations are made (Meckstroth, 1975; Teune and Przeworski, 1970). Themes in the three cases support the idea of a "Janus-faced" relationship between public administration and race, synthetized in two opposing dimensions: public administration's role in racial formation and exploitation versus public administration's role in promoting social equity. The complexity of the public administration-race relationship demands further examples, as we also provide throughout the chapter.

Scholars generally agree that the notion of race is socially constructed, and state actors have played a part in both constructing and sustaining racial categories. The role of government in racial categorization strategies is different from one context to another and from one historical moment to another. In some countries, like the U.S. or the Netherlands, the government has played a central role in racial formation. Race (e.g., Black, Native American) has often been defined by law, and the bureaucracy was active in elaborating a process that certified members of specific racial categorizations. Other countries, like Brazil, rely on the self-declaration of race, counting on a broad range of racial self-classifications that have helped to sustain the myth of a "racial democracy."

Yet public administration not only constructs but relies on racial categories to design and implement public policies targeting racial equity. Tabulating, generating, and reporting data related to race are preconditions for promoting affirmative action strategies at a later stage.

History also indicates cases in which public administration has been permeated by racial prejudice or has even induced racial inequality. The illustrative case of policing in the United Kingdom indicates a bureaucracy that, at specific moments of its history, was saturated with racial prejudice toward immigrants. The Korean case illustrates how the governmental apparatus that relied on immigrants to build a unifying national project neglects the inclusion of exploited foreign groups in welfare policies. More international examples also provide cases where the state deliberately has suppressed or systematically eliminated members of distinct racial, ethnic, and religious groups.

On the other hand, public administration can be perceived as a key actor responsible for repairing racial injustice and promoting racial equity. Affirmative action and representative bureaucracy are seen as reflections of these approaches, and they emerge when political and social movements create pressure for a more inclusive bureaucracy. Below, we discuss examples of affirmative action and representative bureaucracy that highlight resistance coming from established social groups. We also discuss the opportunities that a proactive public administration workforce may have in promoting racial equity.

## Public Administration's Role in Race Formation and Exploitation

The modern state plays an important role in race formation and categorization by defining race, categorizing citizens, and producing statistics to classify the population (Taylor, 2006; Yanow, 2015; Yanow, van der Haar, and Völke, 2016). During the era of slavery and after the Emancipation Proclamation of 1863, the government played an important role in U.S. racial categorization. The designation as "American Indian" through a federal acknowledgment process was based on the assumption that the U.S. government declared someone to be an American Indian, and it was translated through bureaucratic processes, forms, and documents (Taylor, 2006). Similar procedures were adopted in the Netherlands in 1999 in standardizing two categories used to differentiate "foreign" from "native" with assumptions that reinforced racial divides (Yanow, van der Haar, and Völke, 2016).

On the opposite end of the spectrum are examples of states rejecting the concept of race. An emblematic example is France, where the government almost completely ignores the notion of race in the name of universalism. Yet protests by young immigrants in France from 2005 to 2007 are a vivid example of how race and ethnicity are present in French society, even without the incorporation of these concepts by the state (Meier and Hawes, 2009).

A conciliatory trend is based on the idea of race as self-declared, exemplified in recent Latin American experiences with Blacks and indigenous people. The self-declaration strategy was a reflection of the historical homogenizing role-model of the Latin American state. Dominant White/*criollo* elites in the region adopted the emancipatory discourse of liberalism in the nineteenth century, intending to erase racial/ethnic differences in the name of a homogenizing nation (Garfield, 2000; Sieder, 2002). Despite the unifying discourse of national identity and equal citizenship, society remained divided by deep racial, ethnic, social, and class discrimination. Public administration played an important role in materializing the myth of "racial democracy" in countries like Brazil or *mestizo* states in the Latin American region. In Brazil, the "Indian National Day" was proclaimed as a cultural icon in 1934, and museum exhibitions, radio programs, and movies, all receiving financial support from the Department of Indigenous Protection (a public bureaucracy), highlighted the indigenous contribution to the "national character." Mexico established the "Indian National Day" in 1940 and created the Interamerican Indigenous Institute (Garfield, 2000). This homogenizing discourse, however, was not reflected in the social inclusion of Blacks and indigenous populations in the region. The critique of this racial/ethnic homogenizing model began to grow in the late 1990s, mainly due to developing international jurisprudence, indigenous political movements supported by international nongovernmental organizations (NGOs), and constitutional processes recognizing the multicultural and multi-ethnic nature of Latin American populations. The critique advocated a multicultural, pluralist, and ethnically heterogeneous state (Sieder, 2002), and advanced in indigenous territorial recognition in countries like Bolivia, Brazil, and Ecuador.

Last, but not least, the powers of the modern state have not always supported racial inclusion and have often been deliberately used to suppress or systematically eliminate members of distinct racial, ethnic, religious, national or political groups. History refers to many genocide cases (e.g., aborigines in Tanzania or the current conflict in Myanmar) when the state has been either directly involved or indirectly complicit through negligence (Harff and Gurr, 1988).

## Public Administration's Role in Promoting Racial Equity

Properly diagnosed, racial inequality demands state intervention and a role for public administration. Affirmative action and bureaucratic representation have been two traditional strategies that reflect a proactive role of public institutions and bureaucracies in dealing with racial inequality.

Affirmative action programs are adopted when universal public policies are not able to resolve persistent inequality problems regarding historically excluded groups (Feres and Toste Daflon, 2015). They seek to create opportunities for underprivileged groups by facilitating their access to higher social stratum (ibid.; Kellough, 1992). Affirmative action can be controversial, however, because many hold a strong belief in individual rights and argue that it is not correct to make distinctions along lines of race, ethnicity, or gender (Kellough, 1992). In many contexts, the government may endorse the opposition to quotas; in the United Kingdom, for example, quotas or other forms of fixed recruitment are condemned by the Race Relations Act of 1976 as positive prejudice. Other European countries follow the same trend.

Public bureaucracies play a crucial role in designing and implementing affirmative action policies. The first affirmative action policy was implemented in India in the 1950s (Feres and Toste Daflon, 2015) when the government criminalized the caste system and created "reservation policies" with the aim of helping the promotion of historically underprivileged groups through quotas for political representation in legislatures, in the public service, and in institutions of higher education (ibid.).

Affirmative action policies also exist in an increasing number of Brazilian public institutions aiming to address long-standing racial inequalities. Conventional wisdom regarding "racial democracy" was challenged by growing evidence of deep socioeconomic inequalities that Afro-Brazilians—who make up more than 50 percent of the Brazilian population—face in terms of public health, education, labor markets, and politics (Smith, 2010). After gradual legal steps toward affirmative action at the state level, a 2012 federal law set aside 50 percent of the places in federal higher educational institutions for Black, mixed race, and indigenous students (Feres and Toste Daflon, 2015).

A more proactive public administration role toward race is reflected in bureaucratic representativeness, which can be understood as the capacity of the bureaucracy to represent the general public (Meier and Capers, 2012). A representative bureaucracy is seen as the means to promote racial equity because it can represent the diversity of the population (Bradbury and Kellough, 2007; Meier and Capers, 2012). A bureaucratic agency would be passively representative if the demographics of its agents were similar to those of the general population. Studies show that passive representation serves as a measure of enfranchisement for diverse groups (S. Hong, 2017; Kellough, 1992; Meier, 1993; Riccucci and Saidel, 1997; Selden, 1997). In contrast, a bureaucratic agency would be actively representative if bureaucrats replied to, pushed, and put forward the needs of their demographic counterparts (Mosher, 1968). More recently, a series of studies have demonstrated that representation is also important symbolically by representing groups in cognitive processes and changing the attitudes of those who are represented toward the bureaucracy (Theobald and Haider-Markel, 2009). For example, representation has a positive effect on the perceived legitimacy of the police among Blacks (ibid.), women (Meier and Nicholson-Crotty, 2006), and even the general public (Riccucci, Van Ryzin, and Lavena, 2015). The transposition of bureaucratic representativeness in other international contexts, however, faces resistance, particularly in the context of countries that juxtapose the nascent idea of multiculturalism with the tradition of a homogenizing state, as is the case in Latin American and many European countries. Many fear that in acknowledging the concept of race, racial divisions will actually be reinforced.

## Racial Relations, Violence, and Police Targets in the United Kingdom

Conflicts between the police and minority groups have a long history in Britain. Solomos (1991) traces the crucial point for the introduction of diverse minority groups in the United Kingdom to the period between 1945 and 1950. This was a time of increasing immigration, with populations from various parts of the Commonwealth moving to the United Kingdom after the end of World War II as part of a migration of labor from less developed countries to industrialized western European nations (Castles, Booth, and Wallace, 1984). The influx of minority immigrants influenced developments in British racial discourse, such as linking race and immigration as an issue. Although various reactions by civil society occurred during this period, there was a delay between growing concerns related to race by the public and the implementation of official policies by government. As such, between 1945 and 1962 (when the Commonwealth Immigration Act created a series of restrictions on the movement of immigrants), there were no limitations placed on the entrance of colonial labor.

The lack of previous official restrictions to immigration did not mean that the government did not make an attempt to restrict it. Carter, Harris, and Joshi (1987) argue that "Labour and Conservative governments had by 1952 instituted a number of covert, and sometimes illegal, administrative measures designed to discourage Black immigration." By the time restrictions on immigration were introduced, a large number of minority immigrants had already settled in the United Kingdom, and the country faced racial gaps as a native issue as well as an immigration issue.

Devoid of any clear policy designed to prevent misconduct on racial matters, the police response to racial crimes during this period was non-existent in the best of cases and clearly hostile in the worst. A good example is provided by Fryer (1984): by 1948, the National Union of Seaman (NUS) in Liverpool was trying to keep Black sailors off of the ships. When conflicts sparked, police retaliated against Black sailors with brutal force. Similar events occurred over the next decade; these included violent riots in Notting Hill and Nottingham when hundreds of Whites attacked Blacks on the streets and in their homes over a period of days (Gordon, 1993). The lack of action by police during those riots raised questions about the commitment by the government to solve racially motivated crimes (Bowling, 1999; Rawlings, 2012).

The issue of racial bias among police gained awareness in the public arena during the 1960s and 1970s (Gordon, 1993) as cases of systemic racism by police authorities began to appear in independent and official reports and allegations of differences in treatment experienced by Whites and other minorities began to be more common in public discourse. In the words of Gordon (ibid.):

> The literature from this period showed a remarkable degree of consensus about the failings of the police, generally highlighting inactivity in the face

of racist violence, a slowness to respond to incidents, a refusal or failure to recognize or accept a racial motivation (or the possibility of one) and hostility to those complaining.

A report by the Institute of Race Relations (1979) highlighted the plight of the British Black community in its interactions with the police. The report showed numerous cases of police refusing to take action against criminals who targeted the Black community, even in the presence of witnesses, refusing to recognize racist incidents, and failing to protect Black communities from racial crimes. The report also highlighted poor relations between the Black community and the police. Black parents were reported to express concerns when their children went outside since they were more likely to be targeted by the police on their way to work or school and could be held at a police station for hours. Other studies also highlighted the discrepancies in the interactions of Blacks and Whites with the police. Willis (1983) showed that Black males had a higher probability of being stopped and searched by the police, even with prosecution rates being similar for both groups after stops. Smith and Gray (1983) documented the same kind of abuse by the London police to stop and search minorities, which in turn led to the disintegration of the relationship between minorities and the police. These concerning trends are still present, as evidence suggests that Blacks are at least six times more likely than Whites to be stopped and searched by the English and Welsh police (Equality and Human Rights Commission, 2010).

In face of growing evidence, the government implemented policies aimed at reducing the racial tension between both groups. According to Her Majesty's Inspectorate of Constabulary (2003), while U.S. police began training on race and diversity in the 1940s, similar actions only began to appear in England and Wales in the 1960s. The Metropolitan Police introduced elements of "social and humanitarian" skills in probationer training in the early 1970s, and "race and community relations" became a specific part of the curriculum in 1973. Yet, much of this early training lacked focus and was poorly conceived (Webster, 2003). Riots occurred in numerous cities and towns throughout the country in 1981, many of them related to tensions between the Black community (especially young Black males) and the police that were sparked by instances of racist policing (Keith, 1993; Kettle and Hodges, 1982). Such incidents led to the recognition of the problem by the government in a report by the Home Office in the same year though racist incidents would plague the United Kingdom for the next few decades.

In 1993, the murder of a Black 19-year-old student, Stephen Lawrence, in London reignited the discussion on the institutional racism inside the British police. Although police arrested five suspects, no one was convicted. Eventually, a judicial inquiry led by Sir Willian Macpherson was formed to investigate the case. The inquiry produced a report highlighting critical failures by the police as well as recommending actions to reduce institutional racism in the force (Macpherson, 1999). The Macpherson Report highlighted the huge discrepancy between the proportion of minorities in society and the proportion of minorities on the police force; different from other sectors such as the National Health Service and the London Transport where minority representation was more prominent, the police force was still predominantly male and White.

Findings from the report contributed to the passage of the Race Relations Act of 2000 designed to increase the fight against institutional racism and promote good relations between minorities and the police. The act established a 10-year target for each police unit to increase its proportion of ethnic minority officers to be comparable to that of the community it served. All 43 police forces in England and Wales were required to meet targets set by the government to increase the number of recruits from minority ethnic communities. These targets varied from region to region according to the make-up of the ethnic population in each region (Bhugowandeen, 2013). A national target was set by the government in 1999 to have the share of ethnic minority officers reflect the national average of 7 percent of ethnic minorities in England and Wales by 2009. In 2012, the proportion of police officers who considered themselves to be from a minority ethnic background had risen from under 2 percent in 1997 to 5 percent.

Recruitment targets may have helped to increase minority representation, but such policies have also resulted in advantages and disadvantages that extended beyond the initial intent of the policy. Bhugowandeen (ibid.) notes that the progress of racial relations between police and the general population became more evident, particularly as the process was closely monitored by examining bodies that were part of the bureaucracy. One requirement of the Macpherson Report was that the progress of each police unit was to be published and inspected annually. This influx of data facilitated research that could attempt to understand the effect of racial representativeness on police performance and additional outcomes (S. Hong 2015; 2016; 2017). Further, as Bhugowandeen (2013) points out, establishing recruitment goals acted as incentives in persuading Blacks and other ethnic minorities to consider a career in the police force.

In comparison to other public agencies (e.g., the National Health Service or London Transport) that have high percentages of ethnic minorities and female employees, the police service remained predominantly White and male. Among factors contributing to the lack of minority applicants, Bhugowandeen (ibid.) points to the dearth of role models as a barrier to entry for Black and minority groups and to the poor reputation of the police as a male, sexist institution. Currently, growing diversity among the population as a result of Polish, Romanian, or Bulgarian immigrants settling in the United Kingdom following the entry of their countries into the European Union continues to make it difficult for the police to be representative. The post-Brexit context not only reflects the challenges of racial and ethnic diversity in the United Kingdom but also will further test the role of public administration institutions in promoting racial equity.

Because some police units had already achieved their targets before the institution of the Race Relations Act while others still had to recruit a large number of minority officers (Brain, 2010), the implementation of the policy reflected a quasi-experimental approach that allowed researchers to observe the effects of an increase in minority representation on the performance of the police in general. S. Hong (2015; 2016; 2017) tested the effects of the new recruitment policy and showed that an increase in the percentage of minority officers on the force was linked to both a decrease in crime in the affected regions as well as a decrease in racial profiling during police searches. Such findings support the notion that more representative police forces generate positive results and do not discriminate against the minority community.

## Access to University Education in a "Racial Democracy": The Brazilian Case

Brazil is often seen as a successful case in terms of racial issues. There is a perception that the country maintains a racial democracy with conviviality between different racial and ethnic groups. The lack of an official public policy of segregation by the government throughout its history, coupled with miscegenation between ethnicities (or the mixing of groups), has led to a narrative where "peaceful" coexistence among ethnicities is considered the norm. The myth of racial democracy, however, began to be questioned by scholars in the 1970s. Upon the return to democratic governance in 1989, public policies aimed at combating systemic racism in society started to be discussed and then implemented.

The ethnic origins of Brazilian society are complex and involve waves of European and Asian immigration, African slave movements, and the enslavement and assimilation of indigenous communities. While public administration institutions like the National Institution of Geography and Statistics (Instituto Brasileiro de Geografia, IBGE) track the ethnic composition of the country through census data, racial classifications can be quite murky. In Brazil, central statistical records classify individuals according to a gradation of colors—White, Brown, Black, and Yellow— which is not wholly coincident with the "categories of practice" in everyday social relations (Loveman, 1999). Currently, 7.52 percent of the population considers itself Black while 43.42 percent considers itself Brown (Instituto Brasileiro de Geografia, 2010). Considering that those statistics are based on self-reporting, the racial status of citizens can "flow" from Black to Brown and, in certain places, even to White depending on the subject's (and the appraiser's) social and psychological idiosyncrasies. Such fluidity makes it more difficult to fully understand and address the historical and institutional racism in Brazilian society.

Government policy on miscegenation can be traced to the end of the nineteenth century. After the abolishment of slavery, the demand for cheap labor fueled a strategic response from the state. The government funded

European immigration, forbidding the entry of Africans and Asians. The objective of this policy was not simply to supply labor to the fields but also to make the population less dark (Santos, 2001). The idea behind the policy was that, as White Europeans entered the country and mingled with the "inferior" Black population, a "whitening" would occur in the general population (Schwarcz, 2013). Indeed, being a "mulatto" and rejecting Black heritage was a way to increase one's social status and to gain access to the Brazilian national elite (Skidmore, 1976). Native indigenous populations also were included in this strategy (Garfield, 2000). This process created an intrinsic "fuzziness" to the Brazilian racial composition, blurring the lines between Blacks and Whites and thus creating a scenario very different from the one found in countries such as the United States, where segregation was the norm.

This racial and ethnic miscegenation was not exclusive to Brazil but was a characteristic of Latin America more broadly. Even with the racist tone regarding the whitening of an "inferior" population, different aspects of the same processes were underway in several countries in Latin America during the twentieth century: "raza cósmica" in Mexico, "criolismo moderno" in Peru, "democracia racial" in Brazil, "racialismo afro-latino" racialism in Cuba, and "mestiçagem nacional" in Colombia (Oliveira, 2017). Such ideologies were used as a symbolic part of the nationalistic unification processes aimed at overcoming acute class differences through narratives of racial mixing and *Mestizo* states (Linz and Stepan, 1996; Sieder, 2002).

At its core, racial democracy insisted that miscegenation and the lack of segregation halted the development of racist institutions in Brazil. Thus, the explanation for the predominance of Blacks among the lower classes and their absence from social elites was solely caused by the legacy of slavery and class discrimination (Freyre, 1933). Unlike countries such as the United States where Jim Crow laws created clear segregation based on "hard" racial categories, the "soft" nature of Brazil racial policies engendered in the mind of the Brazilian populace the idea that race was not a salient characteristic and that racial conflicts had been conquered in previous decades, even resulting in the myth of a benign slavery (ibid.). This notion was also accepted by Blacks (Andrews, 1996; Marx, 1998; Telles, 2004) who assumed that systemic racial discrimination was impossible or at least very unlikely because racial intermixing would prevent any form of racism (Andrews, 1996; Freyre, 1933; Twine, 1998). These individuals became less likely to self-identify as Blacks (Bailey and Telles, 2006) and to portray positive stereotypical image of individuals with a darker complexion (Oliveira, 1999).

The historical myth of racial democracy provides a powerful explanation for why Brazil's racial inequalities have gone unchallenged for so long. Since the discussion of race and racism was almost taboo throughout society and government, and since the institutional tools of racial discrimination were absent (or at least hidden), there was no clear target around which a social movement could form, delaying the creation of a politically cohesive equity movement such as occurred in the United States (Marx, 1998).

The national consensus started to disintegrate, however, after the 1970s. Evidence provided by scholars on social movements demonstrated the persistence of racial inequality such that, irrespective of the racial democracy ideology, asymmetries based on ethnic and racial classifications remained (Hasenbalg, 1979; Wood and de Carvalho, 1988). For example, the proportion of Black students attending public colleges was meager compared to White students even though Brazil had the largest contingent of Afro-descendants outside the African continent.

Affirmative action policies were implemented to improve this situation. In Brazil, the best known practice of affirmative action is the quota system, which consists of establishing a certain number or percentage of positions to be dedicated to a defined group (Moehlecke, 2002). The idea of implementing quotas throughout the federal bureaucracy was first discussed during the government of Fernando Henrique Cardoso in the 1990s. Years later, through pressure from social movements and civil society, the debate was reignited; and a quota system was adopted in some state-level universities. By 2001, the reservation of seats had been implemented by the state universities of Bahia, Rio de Janeiro, and Mato Grosso do Sul (Silva, 2008). In 2004, the University of Brasilia became the first federal university to adopt quotas for Blacks and indigenous people. In 2005, one year after the implementation of the quotas policy, the percentage of Black students in Brazilian public universities was approximately 5.5 percent. Ten years after the implementation of the policy, this number had more than doubled to 12.8 percent (Instituto Brasileiro de Geografia, 2016), indicating that quotas have played an important role in providing the Black community access to higher education.

Despite the success of the policy regarding the access of Black students to the higher education system, the implementation of quotas in Brazilian society was extremely controversial as the idea directly challenged some of the tenets of a racial democracy (Maggie, 2005; Smith, 2010). As such, a series of studies were conducted in individual universities comparing the performance of quota students and non-quota students in the various courses offered by universities. The results were inconclusive. Some pointed out that the differences between quota students and non-quota students were minimal, and, in some cases, the quota students even surpassed the performance of non-quota students (dos Santos and Queiroz, 2013; Veloso, 2009). Others, however, found the results of non-quota students were better than those of quota students (Valente and Berry, 2017).

More recent larger analyses using the Enade grades (the Brazilian standardized test used to measure the quality of higher education) have also been performed. Waltenberg and de Carvalho (2012) focused on data from the 2008 Enade and found a decrease in grades from federal and state universities that implemented quotas. Pereira, Bittencourt, and Braga (2015) use a difference-in-differences design and propensity score matching model to calculate the effect of quota students in the same dataset. The authors conclude that the quota students had a negative (and statistically significant) impact on some courses and a positive and statistically significant impact in others (while statistically controlling for social origin to predict most of the differences in performance between quota and non-quota students who enrolled at universities). Finally, Valente and Berry (2017) indicate that affirmative action students admitted at public federal universities perform at similar levels to non-affirmative action students whereas quota students in private universities perform slightly better than students admitted through traditional methods.

From a public policy perspective, even mixed findings of student performance might be considered evidence of a successful policy. Given that the programs were designed to make up for disadvantages affecting a set of students, a finding of no differences between the groups would indicate that the program had achieved what it was intended to accomplish.

Another line of research on quotas deals with the perception of the policy by multiple groups in society and the risks of its implementation. For example, Maggie (2005) discusses concerns that the quota policy may create clear racial boundaries on which students are evaluated (Black or White) and consequently will develop a type of racialization that might not match the Brazilian society. Brandão and De Marins (2007) observed the attitudes of high school students to racial quotas. Students were mostly against racial quotas, and responses highlighted the challenge of racial classification; a binary self-classification scale of Black vs. White inflated the proportion of White students since *pardos* (mulattos) tended to considered themselves more White than Black. Nery and Costa (2009), in working to understand the relationship between quota and non-quota students enrolled at a university, detect a general disregard of racial issues and distinctions between quota students and non-quota students. Lima, Neves, and Silva (2014) found that even though students considered the economic situation of Blacks as unequal and unfair in comparison to Whites in Brazil, they were mostly against social and, even more so, racial quotas.

Perhaps the most controversial aspect of the quota policy is the so-called "Race Tribunals." The University of Brasilia created a tribunal composed of members of the Black movement as well as an anthropologist to evaluate the "blackness" of students who enrolled in the selection process as Blacks (Maggie, 2005; Maio and Santos, 2005). The policy was viewed as highly subjective; "racial evaluators" would often deny or approve entrance in the quota system for candidates with similar appearances. Scandals of racial fraud for high-end courses, such as medicine or diplomacy, often appear in newspapers with White (or almost White) students claiming to be Black in order to pass the entrance exams (*Folha de São Paulo*, 2017). Such discrepancies create a difficult dilemma for the implementation of policy, and discussions of how to solve such challenges continue.

## Racial Policy in a "Uniform" Society: Multiculturalism in South Korea

Along with Iceland and Japan, South Korea is considered one of the most homogeneous countries in terms of race (Kymlicka, 2007). This homogeneity is not only the result of an old demographic profile but is also promoted through strategies to build the Korean identity as a single ethnicity and Korea as a modern nation. The goal of achieving a single ethnicity can be traced to the first half of the twentieth century. The Japanese used "racial superiority" as one of the means for justifying the colonization of Korea, aiming to "civilize" its inferior neighbor (K.I. Kim, 2008). In attempts to push back on this logic, independent Korean activists garnered support for the purity and single ethnicity of Koreans (Han and Han, 2007).

Beyond the creation of a 'single ethnicity' belief, Korea also formulated its first modern ideas about other races, mirroring minority groups in Western culture. Independent activists and scholars described Western countries as role models for an independent Korea and also potential allies that could help Korea escape from its colonial status (Y.H. Kim, 2009). This admiration of Western culture and technology left little room for criticism (Ha, 2012), even of the racist ideas that positioned White Europeans as a successful race (Yoo, 1997). Some scholars assert that this culture of admiring the West (along with its White proponents) was reinforced by Japan's successful adoption of Western systems and technology (Ha, 2012; Shin, 2006).

Colonization ended after World War II. The Korean War took place five years later, dividing the country between South and North Korea. Post-war conditions had another important effect on the development of Korean concepts of ethnicity and race. The difficult economic situation faced by South Korea and attempts by the United States, the primary ally of the country, to send soldiers to distribute care packages to the Korean public (Ha, 2012) further expanded the positive image among Koreans of Western ideals and the White demographic. Additionally, U.S. soldiers who stayed in camp bases in South Korea contributed the first wave of modern miscegenation in South Korea (M. Lee, 2008). Although the government went as far as calling prostitutes patriots and prepared lectures for them on how to treat Americans with appropriate etiquette, it did not consider the arrival of American-Korean children in society. These children suffered from discrimination because of their physical appearance as well as stigmas surrounding the sex worker industry.

As in the Latin American region, the lack of policies regarding race and diversity during this period reflected the strategy of the Korean government to strengthen the identity of a self-reliant Korea, concentrated on economic development. The focus on the Korean identity alone made it difficult to accept policies related to the other races and ethnicities (Ahn, 2013; M. Lee, 2008). The first official public policies related to "other races" were designed for immigrant workers who occupied unskilled professions. Workers originally from Southeast or Northeast Asia (e.g. Vietnam, the Philippines) started immigrating to South Korea in large numbers in the 1980s (Shim, 2007). Predicting a possible lack of domestic workers in unskilled positions, the Korean government launched an "Industrial Trainee Program" in 1991. The policy was criticized as a form of modern slavery because the status of trainees did not guarantee appropriate working conditions or compensation (W. P.

Hong, 2006). As such, the program resulted in the increase in illegal immigrant workers who could be paid more than trainees (W-D. Lee and B.-H. Lee, 2003).

The emergence of NGOs formed by Koreans and immigrant workers' associations against the discrimination of workers led to some of the first debates regarding the defense of racial and ethnic minorities in Korean society (W. P. Hong, 2006). This discourse led to the establishment of the Employment Permit System in 2003 which guaranteed an improvement in working conditions. Additionally, in 2009, basic social welfare benefits for immigrant workers began to be provided through the Act on the Treatment of Foreigners in Korea (Kang and Park, 2014). However, the policy concentrated on working conditions with little attention to protection from discrimination. Besides a reduced focus on fair treatment, workers can rarely gain citizenship because the current immigration policy generally accepts immigration of a foreigner only when s/he marries a Korean citizen.

In term of immigration and racial policy, marriage with immigrants has received greater attention from government, with special attention to cases where a female immigrant is marrying a Korean male (J.-S. Lee, 2014). Significant gender imbalances in rural areas led Korean men to import wives from other countries. Indeed, the sharp increase in female marriage immigrants in the early 2000s along with a rise in the number of multicultural children (*damunhwa janyeo*) led to the introduction of the Multicultural Family Support Act in 2007 (Heo, 2017). While at the beginning of the twenty-first century the majority of female marriage immigrants were *Joseonjok* (Chinese women who are descendants of Koreans who went to China during the Japanese colonization), the number of brides from Southeast and Northeast Asia increased rapidly after 2003, so that the latter group outnumbered the former in 2011 (S. L. Lee, 2012). The considerable increase in numbers of brides from other parts of Asia led to a new wave of miscegenation that was visible in terms of immigrants' skin color and appearance. The children of Korean and Southeast/Northeast Asians, often termed "Kosian" (Korean plus Asian), have suffered discrimination similar to the Korean-Americans born in earlier decades (M. Lee, 2008). However, unlike Korean-Americans, Kosians received more policy support.

The scale of policies created to assist immigrants should also be noted. The Multicultural Family Support Act, for example, is implemented by 11 government ministries and is supervised by a committee within the Prime Minister's office (N.H.J. Kim, 2016). The Minister of Gender Equality and Family oversees the implementation of the Basic Plan for Multicultural Family Policy that is based on three goals set by the Presidential Committee: (1) creating a proper environment for immigrants and their children in Korea; (2) unifying terms and policy goals across government ministries; and (3) enhancing multicultural sensitivity among Korean citizens (ibid.). Plans for each goal have been developed and implemented sequentially. The first period, extending from 2010–2012, focused on the assimilation of married immigrants through education in the Korean language and culture as well as providing services, such as translation and counseling. The second period (2013–2017) also worked to include Korean spouses and other Korean family members. Despite reduced effects of the policy on the participation of other family members in practice (H.S. Kim, 2014), this expansion of the target population can be considered a step forward because it aims to further the appreciation of multiculturalism in Korean society (ibid.).

The policy has its limitations, of course. First, the still small number of policy beneficiaries is likely to impede the achievement of a more ambitious culture of multiculturalism in practice (J. Lee and Baik, 2012). We argue that multicultural policies should be based on political interventions which prevent discrimination of the minority group; mitigate political, social, and economic conflict between minority and majority groups; and enable the minority group to enjoy human rights (Oh, 2007). However, the current Korean policy is likely to exclude male marriage immigrants and other foreigners, including immigrant workers and their families as well as foreign students (J. Lee and Baik, 2012). In particular, the exclusion of male marriage immigrants and biased attention to female marriage immigrants reflect the strong emphasis of Korean society on patriarchy (Hong, Lee, and Hwang, 2014; H.Y. Kim, 2014) and ethnic nationalism (H. Kim, 2007). Unfortunately, the universal benefits given for marriages between a Korean and a foreigner also risk generating anti-immigration attitudes and perceptions of reverse discrimination among the Korean public (J. Lee and Baik, 2012; Park and Park, 2014) which might lead to an increase in hostility toward foreigners.

Second, in spite of efforts to integrate Koreans with minority groups through policy design, the policy and the relevant discourse are still criticized as biased in assimilating foreigners in Korea (H.Y. Kim, 2014; J.-S. Lee, 2014; Park and Park, 2014). According to experts, at the local level, even other family members are not likely to be enthusiastic and willing to learn about the language and culture of an immigrant family member (Kang and Park, 2014). In this regard, greater efforts are required to create a participative culture that values multiculturalism.

Addressing the limitations of this policy will be desirable because of the growing number of foreigners in Korea, but it will also be challenging. First, unlike some Western countries that have attempted to manage multiculturalism for decades, Korea is not a country that was formed by immigrants, and it often valued pure Korean lineage (Y. Lee, 2009). Second, Korea has been divided. More specifically, the nationalism and exclusivity of pure Koreans have played an important role in uniting the population in modern times, but Korea still experiences continuing division (Han and Han, 2007). In this regard, importing experiences from Western cases of multiculturalism must be done with consideration of the context and through considerable communication efforts (J. Lee and Baik, 2012; Yoon, 2008).

## Conclusion

The interaction of public administration and race is difficult to generalize due to the diversity of the racial and ethnic contexts as well as the history of race in a given country. In this chapter, we relied on three highly contrasting cases of the United Kingdom, Brazil, and Korea to abstract public administration patterns in relation to racial diversity. By focusing on highly diverse contexts, we highlight the origins of specific racial contexts and how minority groups can be systematically excluded from society and public policy. The historical perspective helps to identify what the concepts of race and ethnicity mean to a particular nation. Race and ethnicity are intimately related to class, religion, and nationality, and the salience of those factors will influence the kind of challenges a racial majority or minority will suffer as well as the racial policies a government may or may not adopt.

We observed an ambiguous and complex relationship between public administration and race where sometimes public institutions support racial categorization and exploitation while, in other cases, public administration becomes a key force in fostering affirmative action and promoting racial equity within and beyond the public sector. States and the bureaucracies that represent them have intervened in racial inequalities and conflicts throughout history. State intervention was both an aggravating factor in such conflicts, adopting clearly discriminatory policies and strengthening ethnic inequalities in certain societies, as well as a remedial process, with policies aimed at alleviating the historical debt suffered by certain minority groups. Whether due to historical discrepancies and injustices, modern migratory movements, or even contemporary waves of prejudice that still plague nations in much of the world, conflicts or social challenges rooted in race categorization and discrimination can still be observed globally.

Recognition of multiculturalism, as we highlight in three cases here, has deep implications for public administration and democracy. Only legally and politically recognized ethnic/racial groups can push for a voice in the policy and administration processes. These demands cannot merely be answered by electoral democracy, as the post-Brexit context indicates. Affirmative action in education systems or quotas for public administration institutions have to be viewed within the broader challenges of multiculturalism and demands for a proactive bureaucracy. Despite resistance, as we demonstrate in the Brazilian case, sustainable affirmative policies help to change attitudes among lower social-racial classes that need representation (Forum Brasileiro de Segurança Pública, 2017).

More importantly, public administration is essential in achieving racial equity. The Janus-faced relationship between public administration and race may be reflected in the current adoption of inclusion policies to compensate for the application of discriminatory policies in times past, as our cases also demonstrate. Ultimately, strengthening representation within public bureaucracies reflects how public administration is capable of going beyond its role in restricting and limiting citizens' behavior toward strengthening and enabling them.

This examination of race and public administration using a least similar systems approach serves as an international comparison to the U.S. case. The history of slavery followed by an extensive period of segregation that was enforced by law and practice has made the issue both more salient and more difficult to counteract in terms of public policy. Race has been on the national policy agenda (or seeking to get on the national policy agenda) for a long time in the U.S. and could be considered the major political cleavage in contemporary politics. In contrast, racial issues were either submerged by national culture (Brazil) or avoided by initially homogeneous populations (the United Kingdom, Korea) until more recently in other countries. The comparative cases also indicate that no nation is likely exempt from issues of race in public administration. Ethnically homogeneous countries, such as Korea, face issues of race based on immigration and see similar pressures regarding gender, disability, and more. When a country is generally more heterogeneous in terms of race, it means that public administrators sometimes have to face more daunting political obstacles to overcome racial issues. Finally, the international cases also indicate that new issues of race and diversity are likely to be placed on the U.S. public administration agenda. The United States continues to grow more diverse; immigration will continue, and individuals of different races will become part of the clientele of public agencies. The challenges to public administration posed by race will continue and grow in both complexity and nuance.

## References

Ahn, Ji-Hyun. 2013. "Global migration and the racial project in transition: institutionalizing racial difference through the discourse of multiculturalism in South Korea." *Journal of Multicultural Discourses* 8(1): 29–47.

Andrews, George Reid. 1996. "Brazilian racial democracy, 1900–1990: An American counterpoint." *Journal of Contemporary History* 31(3): 483–507.

Bahk, Jinwook, Agnus M. Kim, and Young-Ho Khang. 2017. "Associations of multicultural status with depressive mood and suicidality among Korean adolescents: The roles of parental country of birth and socioeconomic position." *BMC Public Health* 17(1): 116.

Bailey, Stanley R., and Edward E. Telles. 2006. "Multiracial versus collective black categories: Examining census classification debates in Brazil." *Ethnicities* 6(1): 74–101.

Barany, Zoltan D. 1998. "Orphans of transition: Gypsies in Eastern Europe." *Journal of Democracy* 9(3): 142–156.

BBC. 2018. "Who are the Kurds?" Available at: www.bbc.com/news/world-middle-east-29702440 (accessed January 15, 2018).

Bezerra, Teresa Olinda Caminha. 2011. "A política pública de cotas em universidades, desempenho acadêmico e inclusão social." *Sustainable Business International Journal* 9.

Bhugowandeen, Bela. 2013. "Diversity in the British police: Adapting to a multicultural society." *Mémoire(s), identité(s), marginalité(s) dans le monde occidental contemporain. Cahiers du MIMMOC* 10.

Bowling, Benjamin. 1999. *Violent racism: Victimization, policing and social context.* New York, NY: Oxford University Press.

Bradbury, Mark D., and J. Edward Kellough. 2007. "Representative bureaucracy: Exploring the potential for active representation in local government." *Journal of Public Administration Research and Theory* 18(4): 697–714.

Bradbury, Mark D., and J. Edward Kellough. 2011. "Representative bureaucracy: Assessing the evidence on active representation." *The American Review of Public Administration* 41(2): 157–167.

Brain, Timothy. 2010. *A history of policing in England and Wales from 1974: A turbulent journey.* New York, NY: Oxford University Press.

Brandão, Andre Augusto, and Mani Tebet A. de Marins. 2007. "Cotas para negros no Ensino Superior e formas de classificação racial." *Educação e Pesquisa* 33(1): 27–45.

Carter, Bob, Clive Harris, and Shirley Joshi. 1987. "The 1951–1955 Conservative government and the racialization of black immigration." *Immigrants & Minorities* 6 (3): 335–347.

Castles, Stephen, Heather Booth, and Tina Wallace. 1984. *Here for good: Western Europe's new ethnic minorities.* London: Pluto Press.

Collier, David. 1993. "The comparative method." In A.D. Finifter (Ed.) *Political science: The state of the discipline II* (pp. 105–119). Washington DC: American Political Science Association.

dos Santos, Jocelio Telos, and Delcele Mascarenhas Queiroz. 2013. *O impacto das cotas nas universidades brasileiras (2004–2012).* Salvador: CEAO.

Equality and Human Rights Commission. (2010). *Stop and think: A critical review of the use of stop and search powers in England and Wales.* London: EHRC.

FeresJr, João, and Verônica Toste Daflon. 2015. "Ação afirmativa na Índia e no Brasil: Um estudo sobre a retórica acadêmica." *Sociologias* 17(40): 92–123.

*Folha de São Paulo.* 2017. "Brancos usam cota para negros e entram no curso de medicina da UFMG." Available at: www1.folha.uol.com.br/educacao/2017/09/1921245-brancos-usam-cota-para-negros-e-entram-no-curso-de-medicina-da-ufmg.shtml

Forum Brasileiro de Segurança Pública. 2017. *Medo da violencia e o apoio ao autoritarismo no Brasil. Texto para discussão,* 1. São Paulo: FBSP.

Freyre, Gilberto. 1933. *The masters and the slaves.* New York, NY: Knopf.

Freyre, Gilberto. 1992. *Casa grande e senzala.* Madrid, Spain: Marcial Pons Historia.

Fryer, Peter. 1984. *Staying power: The history of black people in Britain.* Sterling, VA: Pluto Press.

Garfield, Seth. 2000. "As raízes de uma planta que hoje é o Brasil: Os índios e o Estado-Nação na era Vargas." *Revista Brasileira de História,* 20(39): 13–36.

Gordon, Paul. 1993. "The police and racist violence in Britain." In *Racist violence in Europe.* London: Palgrave Macmillan.

Ha, Sang-Bok. 2012. "Yellow skin, white masks: A historical consideration of internalized racism and multiculturalism in South Korea." *Studies in Humanities* 33: 525–556.

Han, Geon-Soo, and Kyung-Koo Han. 2007. "Ideal and reality of Korean multicultural society: Beyond discrimination based on pure-bloodism and civilization theory." *Korean Sociological Association Research Report* 07-7: 71-116. Presidential

Committee on Northeast Asian Cooperation Initiative. Available at: www.dbpia.co. kr/journal/articleDetail?nodeId=NODE00913420&language=ko_KR

Harff, Barbara, and Ted Robert Gurr. 1988. "Victims of the state: Genocides, politicides and group repression since 1945." *International Review of Victimology* 1(1): 23–41.

Hasenbalg, Carlos Alfredo. 1979. *Discriminação e desigualdades raciais no Brasil.* Rio de Janeiro: Graal.

Heo, Nayoung. 2017. "'We are not simply 'multicultural': Intersecting ethnic and religious identities of Japanese-Korean young adults in South Korea." *Ethnic and Racial Studies* 41(15): 1–20.

Her Majesty Inspectorate of Constabulary. 2003. *Diversity matters.* London: The Home Office.

Hong, Dal Ah Gi, Sun Woo Lee, and Eun Kyung Hwang. 2014. "A study of immigrant wives' perceived conflicts with their mother-in-laws and coping experiences." *Korean Journal of Human Ecology* 23(5): 789–805.

Hong, Sounman. 2015. "Ethnic diversity in public organizations and public service performance: Empirical investigation." *Academy of Management Proceedings* 1:11334.

Hong, Sounman. 2016. "Representative bureaucracy, organizational integrity, and citizen coproduction: Does an increase in police ethnic representativeness reduce crime?" *Journal of Policy Analysis and Management* 35(1): 11–33.

Hong, Sounman 2017. "Black in blue: Racial profiling and representative bureaucracy in policing revisited." *Journal of Public Administration Research and Theory* 27(4): 547–561.

Hong, W. P. 2006. "Changes in immigrant workforce policy and challenges." *Minjok Yeonku* 28: 87–191.

Institute of Race Relations. 1979. *Policing against Black people: Evidence submitted to the Royal Commission on Criminal Procedure.* London: Institute of Race Relations.

Instituto Brasileiro de Geografia. 2010. "Tabela 2094: População residente por cor ou raça e religião." In *Consultado em 5 de março de 2014.* Rio de Janeiro: IBGE.

Instituto Brasileiro de Geografia. 2016. *Síntese de indicadores sociais.* Rio de Janeiro: IBGE.

Kang, Ki-Jung, and Su-Sun Park. 2014. "A study on expert opinions about multicultural family policy and delivery system on the social integration perspective in the multicultural age: Focused on multicultural family support." *Korean Journal of Family Welfare* 19(4): 669–691.

Keith, Michael. 1993. *Race, riots and policing: Lore and disorder in a multi-racist society.* London: UCL Press.

Kellough, J. Edward. 1992. "Affirmative action in government employment." *The Annals of the American Academy of Political and Social Science* 523(1): 117–130.

Kettle, Martin, and Lucy Hodges. 1982. *Uprising! The police, the people, and the riots in Britain's cities.* London: Pan Books.

Kim, H. 2007. "State-leading multiculturalism in Korea: Theory of multiculturalism and adaptation by Korea." In *Multiculturalism in Korea: A critical review.* Gyeonggido, Republic of Korea: Hanul Academy.

Kim, H. Y. 2014. "Multi-culturalism and multi-cultural family policy: About the gap between theory and policy." *Women's Studies* 87(2): 7–43.

Kim, K.-I. 2008. "Civilization, race, and Asian solidarity: Comparing Yu Gil-jun and Yoon Chi-ho." *Korean Social History Association Journal* 78: 129–167.

Kim, N. H. J. 2016. "Naturalizing Korean ethnicity and making 'ethnic' difference: A comparison of North Korean settlement and foreign bride incorporation policies in South Korea." *Asian Ethnicity* 17(2): 185–198.

Kim, Y. Hee. 2009. "The concept of the oriental and its origin in the Daehan Empire —centering on the process reflected in newspapers." *Concepts and Communication* 4: 97–131. Available at: www.kci.go.kr/kciportal/ci/sereArticleSearch/ciSereArtiView. kci?sereArticleSearchBean.artiId=ART001632119

Kymlicka, Will. 2007. *Multicultural odysseys: Navigating the new international politics of diversity.* Oxford: Oxford University Press.

Lee, J.-S. 2014. "Multicultural policy and nationalism in Korea." *Journal of Korean Association of National Thought* 8(3): 199–231.

Lee, Mary. 2008. "Mixed race peoples in the Korean national imaginary and family." *Korean Studies* 32: 56–85.

Lee, Sang Lim. 2012. "Change of multicultural family and challenge for policy making." *Health and Welfare Issue and Focus* 157: 1–8.

Lee, Jong-doo, and Mi-Youn Baik. 2012. "'Korean specialities' and multicultural policy." *Journal of International Politics* 17(3): 335–361.

Lee, Won-Duck, and Byoung-Hoon Lee. 2003. "Korean industrial relations in the era of globalisation." *Journal of Industrial Relations* 45(4): 505–520.

Lee, Yoonkyung. 2009. "Migration, migrants, and contested ethno-nationalism in Korea." *Critical Asian Studies* 41(3): 363–380.

Lima, Marcus Eugenio Oliveira, Paulo Sergio da Costa Neves, and Paula Bacellar Silva. 2014. "A implantação de cotas na universidade: Paternalismo e ameaça à posição dos grupos dominantes." *Revista Brasileira de Educação* 19(56).

Linz, Juan J., and Alfred Stepan. 1996. *Problems of democratic transition and consolidation: Southern Europe, South America, and post-communist Europe.* Baltimore, MD: Johns Hopkins University Press.

Lijphart, Arend. 1971. "Comparative politics and the comparative method." *American Political Science Review* 65(3): 682–693.

Loveman, Mara. 1999. "Is 'race' essential?" *American Sociological Review* 64(6): 891–898.

Macpherson, William. 1999. *The Stephen Lawrence inquiry.* London: HMSO. CM 4262-I.

Maggie, Yvonne. 2005. "Políticas de cotas e o vestibular da UnB ou a marca que cria sociedades divididas." *Horizontes antropológicos* 11(23): 286–291.

Maio, Marcos Chor, and Ricardo Ventura Santos. 2005. "Política de cotas raciais, os 'olhos da sociedade' e os usos da antropologia: O caso do vestibular da Universidade de Brasília (UnB)." *Horizontes antropológicos* 11(23): 181–214.

Marx, Anthony W. 1998. *Making race and nation: A comparison of South Africa, the United States, and Brazil.* New York, NY: Cambridge University Press.

Mayall, David. 1995. *English gypsies and state policies*, vol. 7. Hatfield: University of Hertfordshire Press.

Meckstroth, Theodore W. 1975. "'Most different systems' and 'most similar systems': A study in the logic of comparative inquiry." *Comparative Political Studies* 8 (2): 132–157.

Meier, Kenneth J. 1993. "Latinos and representative bureaucracy: Testing the Thompson and Henderson hypotheses." *Journal of Public Administration Research and Theory* 3(4): 393–414.

Mendes Jr, Alvaro Alberto Ferreira, and Fabio Waltenberg. 2014. "Políticas de cotas não raciais aumentam a admissão de pretos e pardos na universidade? Simulações para a UERJ." *Planejamento e Políticas Públicas* 44: 229–256.

Meier, Kenneth J., and K. Juree Capers. 2012. "Representative bureaucracy: Four questions." In *The Sage handbook of public administration*, edited by B. Guy Peters and Jon Pierre (pp. 420–430). London: Sage Publications.

Meier, Kenneth J., and Daniel P. Hawes, 2009. "Ethnic conflict in France: A case for representative bureaucracy?" *The American Review of Public Administration* 39(3): 269–285.

Meier, Kenneth J., and Jill Nicholson-Crotty. 2006. "Gender, representative bureaucracy, and law enforcement: The case of sexual assault." *Public Administration Review* 66(6): 850–860.

Moehlecke, Sabrina. 2002. "Ação afirmativa: História e debates no Brasil." *Cadernos de Pesquisa* 117(11): 197–217.

Mosher, Frederick C. 1968. *Democracy and the public service*. New York, NY: Oxford University Press.

Nery, Maria da Penha, and Liana Fortunato Costa. 2009. "Afetividade entre estudantes e sistema de cotas para negros." *Paideia* 19(43): 257–266.

Oh, K. S. 2007. "What is multiculturalism? Critical view regarding discussion for multicultural society." In *Multiculturalism in Korea: A critical review*. Gyeonggido, Republic of Korea: Hanul Academy.

Oliveira, Cloves Luiz Pereira. 1999. "Struggling for a place: Race, gender and class in political elections in Brazil." In *Race in contemporary Brazil: From indifference to inequality*. University Park, PA: The Pennsylvania State University Press.

Oliveira, Nuno. 2017. "Fronteiras colectivas e repertórios etnorraciais no Brasil contemporaneo." *Sociologia, Problemas e Práticas* 85: 47–66.

Park, Jong-Dae, and Ji-Hai Park. 2014. "A study of policy of multi-cultural society in Korea and suggestions for an advanced policy response." *The Journal of Cultural Policy* 28(1): 35–63.

Pereira, Joaquim Israel Ribas, Mauricio Bittencourt, and Bernardo Braga. 2015. "Affirmative action in higher education: Impacts of the national exam in Brazil." Proceedings of the 55th Congress of the European Regional Science Association, Lisbon, Portugal, August 25–28.

Rawlings, Philip. 2012. *Policing: A short history*. London: Willan.

Riccucci, Norma M., and Gregg G. Van Ryzin. 2017. "Representative bureaucracy: A lever to enhance social equity, coproduction, and democracy." *Public Administration Review* 77(1): 21–30.

Riccucci, Norma M., Gregg G. Van Ryzin, and Cecilia F. Lavena. 2015. "Representative bureaucracy in policing: Does it increase perceived legitimacy?" *Journal of Public Administration Research and Theory* 24(3): 537–551.

Santos, Helio. 2001. *A busca de um caminho para o Brasil: A trilha do círculo vicioso*. São Paolo: Senac.

Schwarcz, Lilia Moritz. 2013. *Nem preto nem branco, muito pelo contrário: Cor e raça na sociabilidade brasileira*. São Paolo: Clara Enigma.

Selden, Sally Coleman. 1997. *The promise of representative bureaucracy: Diversity and responsiveness in a government agency*. Armonk, NY: M.E. Sharpe.

Shim, B.S. 2007. "Formation and transformation of migrant worker policy: Analysis of multiculturalist policy in Korea." *Discourse 201* 10(2): 41–76.

Shin, Gi-Wook. 2006. *Ethnic nationalism in Korea: Genealogy, politics and legacy*. Stanford, CA: Stanford University Press.

Sieder, Rachel (Ed.) 2002. *Multiculturalism in Latin America: Indigenous rights, diversity and democracy*. New York, NY: Palgrave Macmillan.

Silva, P. 2008. "Normas sociais e preconceito: O impacto da meritocracia e da igualdade no preconceito implícito e explícito contra os cotistas." PhD dissertation, Universidade Federal da Bahia, Salvador.

Skidmore, Thomas E.. 1976. *Preto no branco: Raça e nacionalidade no pensamento brasileiro*, vol. 9. São Paulo: Paz e Terra.

Skocpol, Theda, and Margaret Somers. 1980. "The uses of comparative history in macrosocial inquiry." *Comparative Studies in Society and History* 22(2): 174–197.

Smith, Amy Erica. 2010. "Who supports affirmative action in Brazil?" *Americas Barometer Insights* 49: 1–8.

Smith, David J., and Jeremy Gray. 1983. *The police in action: Police and people in London*, vol. 4. London: PSI.

Solomos, John. 1991. *Black youth, racism and the state: The politics of ideology and policy*. New York, NY: Cambridge University Press Archive.

Taylor, H.F. (2006). "Defining race." In *Race and ethnicity in society: The changing landscape*, edited by Elizabeth Higginbotham and Margaret L. Andersen (pp. 47–54). Belmont, CA: Thomson Wadsworth.

Telles, Edward Eric. 2004. *O significado da raça na sociedade brasileira*. Princeton, NJ: Princeton University Press.

Teune, Henry, and Adam Przeworski. 1970. *The logic of comparative social inquiry*. New York, NY: Wiley-Interscience.

Theobald, Nick A., and Donald P. Haider-Markel. 2009. "Race, bureaucracy, and symbolic representation: Interactions between citizens and police." *Journal of Public Administration Research and Theory* 19(2), 409–426.

Twine, France Winddance. 1998. *Racism in a racial democracy: The maintenance of white supremacy in Brazil*. New Brunswick, NJ: Rutgers University Press.

Valente, Rubia R., and Brian J. Berry. 2017. "Performance of students admitted through affirmative action in Brazil." *Latin American Research Review* 52 (1): 18–34.

Velloso, Jacques. 2013. "Cotistas e não-cotistas: Rendimento de alunos da Universidade de Brasília." *Cadernos de Pesquisa* 39(137): 621–644.

Veloso, F. 2009. "15 anos de avanços na educação no Brasil: Onde estamos?" [15 years of improving Brazilian education: Where are we?]. In *Educação básica no Brasil: Construindo o país do futuro*, edited by F. Veloso, S. Pessôa, R. Henriques, and F. Giambiagi. Rio de Janeiro: Elsevier.

Waltenberg, Fabio D., and Marcia de Carvalho. 2012. "Cotas aumentam a diversidade dos estudantes sem comprometer o desempenho." *Sinais Sociais* 20(7): 36–77.

Webster, Colin. 2003. "Race, space and fear: Imagined geographies of racism, crime, violence and disorder in Northern England." *Capital & Class* 27(2): 95–122.

Wilkins, Vickie M., and Brian N. Williams. 2008. "Black or blue: Racial profiling and representative bureaucracy." *Public Administration Review* 68(4): 654–664.

Willis, Carole F. 1983. *The use, effectiveness, and impact of police stop and search powers*, vol. 15. London: The Home Office.

Wood, Charles H., and José Alberto De Carvalho. 1988. *The demography of inequality in Brazil*. New York, NY: Cambridge University Press.

Yanow, Dvora. 2015. *Constructing "race" and "ethnicity" in America: Category-making in public policy and administration*. New York, NY: Routledge.

Yanow, Dvora, Marleen van der Haar, and Karlijn Völke. 2016. "Troubled taxonomies and the calculating state: Everyday categorizing and 'race-ethnicity'—The Netherlands case." *Journal of Race, Ethnicity and Politics* 1(2): 187–226.

Yoo, Sun-Young. 1997. "Cultural identity of the yellow colony." *Media & Society* 18: 81–122.

Yoon, In-Jin. 2008. "The development and characteristics of multiculturalism in South Korea: With a focus on the relationship of the state and civil society." *Korean Journal of Sociology* 42(2): 72–103.

# 8 Race and Public Administration

## Current Status and Future Issues

*Kenneth J. Meier and Amanda Rutherford*

## Introduction

Public administration in the United States must confront the issue of race, given that race is one of the most fundamental political cleavages in the nation. Individual chapters on education, criminal justice, health care, and digital government have shown that significant racial disparities exist in the outputs and outcomes of governmental programs. Chapter 7 on comparative race and public administration demonstrates that this problem is not unique to the U.S., and Chapter 6 on nonprofits showed other sectors also face challenges related to race and representation. Still, persistent racial inequities pose a formidable obstacle to a public administration that is designed to serve all people. Further, while the chapters in this text help to illustrate the extent to which race touches many corners of public policy and nonprofit management, they are unfortunately nowhere near exhaustive. Below, we briefly review additional work that has been done on race in the policy areas of employment, housing, the environment, and welfare.

## Employment, Wealth, and Jobs

Even a cursory glance at statistics on employment and income in the United States reveals major racial disparities. According to the 2015 American Community Survey, the median Black household income ($38,555) is only 63 percent of the median White household income; Latino household income ($46,882) is somewhat better but less than 77 percent of White income. Measures of wealth show greater disparities with Whites ($171,000) greatly exceeding Blacks ($17,409) and Latinos ($20,920). The income and wealth gaps reflect both differences in unemployment rates (Whites 3.9 percent, Blacks 7.3 percent, and Latinos 5.4 percent) and differences in education and skill levels (36.2 percent of Whites are college graduates, compared to 22.5 percent of Blacks and 15.5 percent of Latinos). Government tends to be a more favorable employment venue for minorities. Blacks hold 17.1 percent of public sector jobs (18.2 percent of federal government jobs) compared to 12 percent in the overall economy. Latinos, in contrast, hold 17 percent of jobs in the overall economy but only 11.6 percent of public sector jobs and 8.8 percent of federal government jobs.

Title VII of the Civil Rights Act of 1964 prohibits discrimination in employment on the basis of race, color, religion, sex, or national origin. State and local governments supplement national law and may provide more extensive protections. The Civil Rights Act of 1964 also created the federal Equal Employment Opportunity Commission (EEOC) with the authority to collect data, investigate charges of discrimination, and seek to resolve disputes. The basic law of employment discrimination centers on the criteria used to hire, compensate, promote, and fire employees and whether these criteria are what are termed "Bona Fide Occupational Qualifications" (BFOQs). Racial disparities on tests or other job evaluation tools (disparities in outcomes) might be acceptable under the law if the employer can show that performance on the test can be related to job performance, thus establishing it as a BFOQ. The original Supreme Court case related to this issue, *Griggs v. Duke Power* (1970), considered an education requirement for blue-collar workers that eliminated a much larger proportion of Black applicants than White ones (as well as an aptitude test). Because the plaintiffs were able to show clear racial disparities, the burden of proof shifted to the employer to demonstrate that the criteria was a BFOQ. Although the Supreme Court later reversed the Duke Power case in *Ward's Cove v. Antonio* in 1989, the Civil Rights Act of 1991 reinstated, albeit somewhat ambiguously, the principles set in the Duke Power case. The policies on discrimination in employment include not just decisions on hiring but also the creation of a hostile working environment and engaging in retaliation against employees who file complaints that allege discrimination with the EEOC or state agencies.

The purpose of federal and state laws was to level the employment playing field and reduce the level of job discrimination in hiring. Although racial disparities in employment could still exist under the law, they were supposed to be related to objective differences in qualifications rather than overt discrimination (Huffman and Cohen, 2004). Unfortunately, a large number of experimental studies appear to demonstrate that discrimination is still common. Quillian et al. (2017) conducted a meta-analysis of 28 field experiments concerning hiring discrimination against Blacks or Latinos. These experiments involved submitting applications to advertised jobs involving fictitious job candidates who are identical in all respects but race, which is often cued via names or other racial indicators. The analysts then measure the percentage of applicants who get contacted by the employer for further screening for each racial group. Using 55,842 applications submitted for 26,326 positions, Whites received on average 36 percent more call-backs than Blacks and 24 percent more call-backs than Latinos. Controlling for such factors as applicant education, gender, occupational group, and local labor market conditions did not appreciably affect these results. The authors conclude that substantial discrimination exists in the hiring process and that the levels of discrimination have remained largely unchanged over time. One important caveat to these "resume" discrimination studies is that they involve private sector organizations only. Though it is an empirical question regarding whether the same trends would be observed in the public sector, we cannot say we are optimistic about finding a different, more encouraging result.

Other studies find that population distributions and segregation contribute to greater disparities in minority employment and wages. Despite decades of research showing greater Black-White inequality in local areas where the Black population is relatively large, little is known about the mechanisms for this effect. Huffman and Cohen (2004), in a comprehensive study, show that Blacks are more likely to be segregated into Black-dominated jobs—and thus lower-paying ones—when the Black population is larger. At the same time, the authors do not find that the wage penalty for working in a Black-dominated job (the devaluation effect) increases as a function of Black population size. They conclude that discrimination against workers—especially exclusion from better-paying jobs—is an important mechanism on the impact of Black population size on the racial wage gap.

Western and Pettit's (2005) examination of wage inequality finds that 58 percent of the racial wage gap for men between the ages of 22–30 can be attributed to criminal records. With the dramatic increase in Black incarceration rates during the late twentieth-century war on drugs (Meier, 1994), employers could point to criminal records as the reason for differences in hiring patterns. This has led to some proposals to "ban the box," that is, prohibit employers from asking about applicants' criminal histories on job applications. Agan and Starr (2017) examined whether banning the box might result in more discrimination against Black applications because employers would assume a criminal record when one did not exist. They sent some 15,000 online job applications on behalf of fictitious young, male applicants to employers in New Jersey and New York City before and after the adoption of ban the box policies. These applications randomly varied whether the applicant had a distinctly Black or distinctly White name and the felony conviction status of the applicant. They found the obvious first—that employers who asked about criminal records were 63 percent more likely to call applicants with no record; that is, a criminal record was a major factor in limiting employment. At the same time, however, ban the box policies themselves appeared to encourage racial discrimination. The gap between Black and White call-backs grew dramatically at companies that removed the box after the policy went into effect. Before the ban the box policy, White applicants to employers with the box received 7 percent more call-backs than similar Black applicants, but the ban increased the gap to 43 percent. The authors attribute this increase to using racial stereotypes to assume differences in felony conviction rates.

## Housing

Government programs have long played a role in both exacerbating and seeking to ameliorate racial disparities in housing. The federal Fair Housing

Act of 1968 and its amendments prohibit discrimination in housing on the basis of race or color, religion, national origin, familial status, or age. Discrimination in housing can result from both systemic barriers created by public and private institutions (e.g., redlining) and from the actions of individual landlords and homeowners selling their home. In the latter case, public laws that prohibit discrimination in housing are difficult to enforce. In home sales, no seller can be compelled to sell a home to another person, making any claims of discrimination difficult to prove. Landlords are also probably sensitive to antidiscrimination laws and thus are unlikely to overtly refer to race when declining to rent to an individual. At the same time, systematic audit studies indicate extensive discrimination on the basis of race in rental housing (Ondrich, Stricker, and Yinger, 1998).

With the creation of the Federal Housing Authority in 1934 and the subsequent establishment of secondary mortgage markets, the federal government has had a commitment to increase low-income home ownership via loan programs and accompanying standards for quality housing. The requirement that federal home loan programs be financially sound, however, led to redlining practices where FHA loans were not available in poor and minority neighborhoods. The result was an increase in the cost of quality housing for minority applicants at the same time as creating greater incentives for housing in White suburban areas (Bradford, 1979). Pressures from the civil rights movement in the 1960s led to a change in policy that pushed federal agencies to prohibit redlining and seek to house the nation's poor through mortgages and rental assistance. Unfortunately, these programs were poorly run, subject to substantial fraud on the part of developers and realtors, and generally did little initially to improve the housing status of minorities in the United States (ibid.). The Federal Housing Enterprises Financial Safety and Soundness Act of 1992 recognized the racial problems in the mortgage programs and set aside a portion of loans for underserved groups (Moulton, 2014). By 2012, Blacks were twice as likely to use FHA mortgage guarantees as Whites (Schwartz, 2014).

The second front in the quest to improve low-income housing is rental assistance programs. At the present time, the federal government subsidizes about 20 percent of rental housing, including public housing for about 1.3 million tenants (DiPasquale, 2011), and minorities are the recipients of a significant portion of this effort. The tenants in Chicago's public housing programs, for example, are virtually all Black (Chaskin, Khare, and Joseph, 2012). Rental assistance programs can operate via the creation of public housing, privately owned units of public housing, subsidized rental programs, and voucher systems that permit individuals to seek their own housing (Newman, 2008; Pardee, 2006).

Large-scale public housing developments began in the 1930s and, in some situations, housed thousands of people (Pardee, 2006). Beginning in the 1960s, the Department of Housing and Urban Development (HUD) took over public housing developments and also established partnerships with the private sector to provide subsidized housing. Public housing, however, has never been politically popular (MacDonald, 2000), and many of the subsidized housing cooperatives have been phased out. HUD currently stresses voucher programs which allow individual families to locate their own housing (Pardee, 2006). Given that 57 percent of rental properties are outside of central cities, vouchers were initially perceived as opening up additional housing to minority families in a wider range of communities (DiPasquale, 2011). In practice, however, rental assistance programs are significantly underfunded and have long waiting lists for qualified families. With the move to voucher systems, housing discrimination is less likely to be institutional and more likely to be individual, with the result being that it is difficult to observe and counter.

Numerous studies document racial disparities in access to quality housing (Roscigno, Karafin, and Tester, 2009). Myers (2004) finds that Black families pay approximately 10 percent more for comparable housing compared to Whites. Myers and Chan (1995) document a racial gap in access to home mortgages in New Jersey and estimate that 70 percent of this gap can be attributed to racial discrimination. Rugh and Massey (2010) provide evidence that the subprime mortgage crisis disproportionately affected minority home-owners and that these impacts were linked to residential segregation (see also Hyra and Rugh, 2016). Housing discrimination can have impacts that span beyond housing as well. Nelson (2010), for example, has shown that credit discrimination in mortgages sorts Black households into neighborhoods with lower quality schools. Johnson, Meier, and Carroll (2017) find that federal mortgage and rental assistance programs are correlated with greater political participation on the part of recipients.

## Welfare Policy

Race has always been intertwined with welfare policy, often as the result of political compromises in the creation of public policy. Lieberman (2001) demonstrates how the basic U.S. welfare policies either specifically designed in racial disparities or permitted local governments to do so in the implementation process. For nationally implemented programs, such as social security, job categories with large numbers of Blacks, such as domestic and farm workers, were initially excluded from coverage. For other programs, such as unemployment insurance and social assistance programs, the federal government used local governments to administer policies and allowed individual states the freedom to discriminate in the implementation process (see also Katznelson, 2005).

Racial disparities in welfare policy, primarily focused on supporting dependent children, can occur either through state-to-state policy variation or via discretion in the implementation process. Within broad limits states were allowed to set benefit levels and the conditions for receiving benefits (Piven and Cloward, 2012). The result was that states with large minority populations set low benefit levels with highly stringent regulations. The issue was nationalized by political campaigns and rhetoric that used welfare as a synonym for race for electoral purposes (Gilens, 2009). The 1996 Personal Responsibility and Work Opportunity Reconciliation Act replaced the New Deal Aid to Families with Dependent Children Act with the Temporary Assistance for Needy Families (TANF) program that included time limits on welfare recipients, work requirements, and the elimination of welfare as an entitlement program.

Extensive studies of the implementation of the TANF program show that variation in local administration allows for the discretion to limit participation by Blacks in even these scaled down programs (Soss, Fording, and Schram, 2011). Detailed assessments of program implementation in Florida demonstrate that racial disparities in implementation are correlated with local partisan control (ibid.), reflecting the national partisanship divide on the issue.

Racial disparities can be found in a wide variety of welfare programs. Studies on child protective services find that children of racial minorities are far more likely to be subject to action by child protective services agencies (U.S. Government Accountability Office, 2007) and subsequently placed in foster care. Becker, Jordan, and Larsen (2007) conclude that race is the most consistent predictor of unsuccessful foster care (defined as a successful permanent placement) with advantages favoring Caucasian children (see also Putnam-Hornstein et al., 2013). Using individual level data, Mumpower (2010) shows that the predictive models that are used to determine action predict outcomes for White children much more accurately than for minority children. That means there are proportionately more false negatives (children who need action taken but do not get it) and more false positives (children who are unnecessarily taken from their families) among Black children. Disparities in this case are partially determined by the decision rules which, while not biased, generate more errors for minority children.

Racial disparities can even arise in federally funded and mandated programs. The Special Supplemental Nutrition Program for Women, Infants, and Children (WIC) is a federal grant program that provides supplemental food, health care referrals, and nutritional information to low-income pregnant and postpartum women and children up to the age of 5 who are found to be at nutritional risk. The creation of the program had a major impact on health outcomes such as infant mortality rates, but these effects were only observed for Whites (Copeland and Meier, 1987). The racial disparities in impact occurred as the result of the federal funding formula that rewarded states that were able to fully spend their allotment in the initial years; those states were states with good outreach programs and fewer minority residents.

## Environmental Justice

The issue of environmental justice concerns the maldistribution of pollution in the United States relative to both race and social class. More specifically, the location of pollution is often coterminous with greater concentrations of racial minorities and low-income individuals. Initially, this area of research focused on racial discrimination in the location of harmful pollutants, but determining whether racial discrimination underlies the correlation between minority communities and pollution is difficult simply because low-income individuals, including minorities, often can only afford housing in areas that are not pristine. Which came first, the minority neighborhood or the location of the pollution source, is often difficult to determine and, in the view of the environmental justice movement (Ringquist, 2005), simply the wrong policy question. Rather than placing blame for the problem, the movement seeks to document the problem and determine ways that it can be remediated. At the federal level, the Office of Environmental Justice in the Environmental Protection Agency is a symbolic statement of such concerns although virtually all environmental protection programs—air pollution, water pollution, pesticides, noise pollution, or toxic substance remediation—touch on issues of environmental justice.

An extensive meta-analysis of 49 environmental equity studies found a consistent correlation between environmental problems and the racial composition of neighborhoods nearby but less evidence of correlation with social class (Ringquist, 2005). This conclusion held whether the environmental concern was noxious facilities, superfund sites, or measured pollution levels. The proximity to pollution sources in turn is associated with significant health problems. Hipp and Lakon's (2010) study in Southern California, for example, showed that neighborhoods with 15 percent or more Latinos were exposed to 84.3 percent more toxic waste. Morello-Frosch and Shenassa (2006) report strong relationships between exposure to environment problems and maternal and child health disparities (see also Payne-Sturges and Gee, 2006). Adverse health effects can result from exposure to lead (Navas-Acien et al., 2007), exposure to airborne fine particulate matter or cigarette smoke (Pope et al., 2009), or unsafe drinking water (Switzer and Teodoro, 2017). All of these health-related environmental hazards are more likely to be present in minority neighborhoods than in White neighborhoods.

A more recent issue in environment justice is whether or not bureaucratic enforcement of pollution laws eases the problem or makes it worse. Because much of environmental enforcement is triggered by complaints or the ability of residents to mobilize politically, one concern is that enforcement efforts designed to limit pollution will be directed away from minority communities. A systematic assessment by Konisky (2009) finds that state governments engage in fewer enforcement actions in poor neighborhoods but did not uncover any racial correlates. Konisky's work does not demonstrate that enforcement efforts made the situation better in minority areas, but it does show that it did not make the situation worse.

## Energy Justice

The link between race and energy policy or what has become termed "energy justice" has two parts. The first is very similar to the issues of environmental justice, and the second is a distinct focus on energy affordability (Heffron and McCauley, 2017; Jenkins et al., 2016; Reames, 2016). Environmentally linked questions of race and energy concern the location of energy generation plants and transmission lines as well as resulting externalities. Because the production of energy generates traditional pollution in the burning of fuels to produce energy, health risks present in residential areas near plants are similar to those in the environmental justice realm (Jenkins et al., 2016). Even renewable forms of energy raise some concerns with the location of windfarms or solar farms near minority communities. Similar to environmental justice concerns, whether energy-related environmental concerns are driven by race or class remains in dispute. The strong correlations between race and class, however, do indicate these energy burdens tend to be concentrated in minority communities.

The second concern is the cost of energy which is likely to place a greater burden on poor consumers than on wealthy consumers, which often results in racial divides (see Reames, 2016). Although many energy pricing schemes now have lifeline rates and prohibitions against cutting off energy supplies during wintertime, processes that permit energy companies to pass along costs for planned construction or for investments in conservation continue to adversely affect minority communities. Racial disparities in costs can also occur as the result of what are termed "energy deserts." Reames (ibid.) documents that minority residents are less likely to have access to even simple things like energy-efficient light bulbs and that these residents have to pay substantially more for them at convenient stores rather than at discount retailers.

## Themes in the Study of Race and Public Administration

While there are unique aspects to each of the policy areas reviewed in this book, there are also common themes that cut across policy areas and illustrate more systematic determinants of racial disparities. Some of these themes focus on what public administration can do to address questions of equity, but many others deal with larger problems of governance that relate to political structures or societal factors. The remaining section of this chapter will discuss four themes: (1) the importance of institutions; (2) the need to recognize that bureaucratic procedures are not neutral; (3) the role that representative bureaucracies play in ameliorating racial disparities; and (4) the need to recognize that the various racial disparities are all interrelated.

### Institutions Matter

Questions of race and public administration are invariably tied to institutional structures – bureaucracies, markets, not-for-profit organizations, private organizations, political parties, educational institutions, health providers, and more. Institutions establish the rules of the game and create regularized processes that determine who gets what, when, and how from the political and public administration process (Lasswell, 1936). Institutions are created to manage the large-scale complexities of governing in modern society, yet one needs to be aware that all institutions are designed and those who design institutions have choices (Knight, 1992). Separate from the creation of implementation bureaucracies, the subject of the next section, governing institutions play a major role in creating racial inequities and in limiting the access of minorities to corrective action.

The governance of public programs in the United States is a complex mixture of governments, markets, and the nonprofit sector set within a fragmented political system that decentralizes power and thus program control. The national U.S. government is characterized by a separation of powers among the president, Congress, and the judiciary. Federal responsible for policy implementation might superficially be considered part of the executive branch under the president, but that position is contested both in legal theory and in practice (Rosenbloom, 2002). Each of the three major branches of government is willing to intervene in administrative matters for its own purposes. The fragmentation of power at the national level was designed not to generate uniform policies but rather to create a series of checks and balances that serve more to perpetuate conflict rather than resolve it. This fragmentation, according to Long (1949), means that government bureaucracies rarely are delegated sufficient power to accomplish their tasks and, as a result, need to develop their own power bases among interest groups and other clientele.

The political fragmentation is further exacerbated by the U.S. federal system that vests significant policy-making powers in state and local governments as well as policy implementation powers with substantial discretion. Policy design has increased the fragmentation substantially more with a general preference to implement public policy in networks that combine different levels of government as well as private sector organizations and nonprofit organizations (O'Toole, 1997).

The political fragmentation of U.S. policy has both direct and indirect consequences for racial minorities and public administration. By forcing government bureaucracies to develop their own bases of political support from interest groups, the pressures on most government bureaucracies are heavily skewed toward politically powerful interests and generally underrepresent those who are less well-off, including racial minorities (Schattschneider, 1960). In addition to this direct impact, fragmentation also creates structures and facilitates interests and processes that can be used to redistribute government benefits away from disadvantaged groups. The federal system allows local majorities to resist national pressures for equity by allowing them to fund alternative policies or permitting them to implement federal laws as in the current cases of welfare policy and employment policy (Katznelson 2005; Soss, Fording, and Schram, 2011). State and local governments also often have the authority to add additional administrative burdens to citizens seeking government benefits (Herd et al., 2013), thus discouraging individuals from participating in government programs in which they are legally entitled to participate. The use of networks for policy implementation purposes sets up a similar structure where a wide variety of interests can exercise veto over policy actions. O'Toole and Meier (2004) show in a study of Texas school districts how the networked relationships of local school districts frequently benefits White students at the expense of racial minorities and low-income students.

In addition to the institutional fragmentation of political power, the United States has generally institutionalized the market system as the primary method of addressing social problems. Unlike many European countries where health care and similar issues are considered government functions, the U.S. prefers first that the market system address people's needs and then when it does intervene, it frequently uses private or nonprofit organizations to actually implement these policies. As an illustration, the predominant source of funding for long-term care for the elderly is the federal government, but the over-whelming majority of Medicare and Medicaid funds are actually spent by private firms (65 percent) or nonprofit organizations (28 percent) (Amirkhanyan et al., 2018). The institutional preference for using the private sector reflects the basic biases of markets that focus on questions of efficiency and show less concern for questions of equity (Donahue and Zeckhauser, 2011). All other things being equal, delegation to market-driven systems is likely to downplay equity and generate fewer benefits for racial minorities.

### The Bureaucratic Playing Field is Not Equal

The connection between race and public administration is a widely ignored topic perhaps because the discussion of race and racial inequalities comes into conflict with the reform tradition of American public administration which sought to eliminate the political contamination of the bureaucracy that occurred in the spoils system. Reformers stressed a politically neutral, technocratic bureaucracy that mimicked the American democratic ideal of equity by treating all citizens equally. This American ideal is not so different from the European tradition of Max Weber. Weberian bureaucracy holds up the notion of a merit-based bureaucracy that neutrally applies rules and procedures in an even-handed manner to policy created by politically established procedures (rule of law). In such systems, race, either of the bureaucrat or the citizen, should be irrelevant; it should not affect outcomes in either a positive or negative way.

This book encourages readers to think about this view of bureaucracy and bureaucratic reform in a critical manner. Weberian bureaucracy was originally presented as an ideal-type, not a bureaucracy that actually exists in the world. Here, let us consider such a bureaucracy and why it might reflect or even increase racial inequalities in policy outcomes. First, a Weberian bureaucracy, with its reliance on merit and established procedures, is likely to simply reproduce any inequalities found in society. In other words, it treats all citizens as equals when in fact not all citizens are equal. Some of this inequality might be in the skills needed to interact with bureaucracy, complete forms, or comply with procedures. Soss (1999) documents the skill levels needed to navigate the American welfare system before TANF and the process that ends up denying individuals services they are eligible to receive. A growing literature has since flourished under the concept of "administrative burden," or the procedures established by bureaucracy to limit access to program benefits (Moynihan, Herd, and Harvey, 2015). Administrative burden can often explain why programs designed to ameliorate inequality often fail to do so (Heinrich, 2015; Herd et al., 2013).

Second, bureaucratic procedures are frequently not neutral, even when they are justified in terms of merit principles. Gillborn and Mirza (2000) provide extensive documentation that standardized tests, for example, have strong racial and class biases. When such criteria are used to limit access to quality education (gifted classes, competitive universities), they add to inequalities rather than remove them. Discrimination in employment (see above) has focused on whether job requirements are actually Bona Fide Occupational Qualifications (BFOQs) (e.g., that the requirement—be it a level of education, a test, or some other screening criteria—is related to the ability to perform the job in question). Bureaucracies that cannot demonstrate that their hiring criteria are BFOQs are likely increasing inequity not decreasing it.

Chapter 5 on the digital divide illustrates how the increasing use of internet and social media in local service delivery—seemingly neutral developments—can simply reflect existing differences in services. The lack of access to various forms of media, be it the internet in general or perhaps only accessing information via smartphones, limits communication to and feedback from some segments of society. The result is access that correlates with both race and socioeconomic status. In such cases, public policy needs to recognize this disparity and seek to design systems that minimize the disparate impact. Even without such effort, a standing question that should be incorporated into any program evaluation is whether greater reliance on digital communication by government bodies increases or decreases access across different segments of the population.

Third, readers should ask how and why public bureaucracies are created in the first place. Weber succinctly noted that bureaucracy is a power instrument of the first order ... for those who control the bureaucracy. Public bureaucracies exist for a reason. They are created via a political process to achieve some objective. Students of bureaucratic politics (Meier and Bohte, 2007; Seidman, 1975) have found that it takes substantial political skills and power to create a new bureaucracy. Logic suggests that political forces with sufficient power to create a bureaucracy are likely to also shape that bureaucracy so that it produces what the creating forces desire (Knight, 1992; McCubbins, Noll, and Weingast, 1987). In short, many bureaucracies are designed to be biased. To the extent that the political forces at play during the creation of a bureaucracy reflect inequities that might be linked to race (such as access to political positions), then it should not be surprising if bureaucracies further exacerbate these same inequalities. Katznelson (2005) provides several examples of New Deal programs that appeared neutral in design but either set up racially biased criteria (exempting farm workers and domestic workers from Social Security) or were given to racially biased bureaucracies in the South to implement (e.g., the GI Bill).

One objective of this book is to move away from theoretical arguments based on ideal-types and focus on real-world data and the actual outcomes that result from the bureaucracy. It becomes imperative to ask how the public bureaucracy might design and implement programs in a manner that reduces the level of racial inequality in society. To our Weberian-inspired critics' claim that advocates of representative bureaucracy are creating bureaucratic bias, our response is that evidence via data is needed. Extensive studies show racial disparities in public policy. Many of the proposals in this book and the arguments in this chapter are designed to lessen these inequalities, not replace them with new inequalities. If the contentions of the neo-Weberians are correct, then we should see large numbers of bureaucracies that produce disproportionate benefits to racial minorities. If that is the case, it is fair to ask, where are these bureaucracies?

### The Importance of Bureaucratic Representation

One factor frequently proposed to generate greater racial equity in bureaucratic outcomes is to recruit and maintain bureaucracies that adequately represent minority populations. In Chapter 2, Grissom and Jones summarize extensive work in education that demonstrates that minority students perform better in schools on a wide range of dimensions when there are more minority teachers. In Chapter 4, Zhu and Wright investigate similar cases in the delivery of health care when minorities benefit from being served by bureaucracies that are representative. In Chapter 3, Nicholson-Crotty and Nicholson-Crotty demonstrate similar results for police, an area where race has frequently been the focus of major media efforts. All three of these bureaucracies are viewed as street-level bureaucracies, organizations that vest a great deal of discretion in front-line personnel who deal with highly varied programs not suitable for rigid rules and who must make decisions under time constraints. Other areas that have demonstrated a relationship between bureaucratic representation and outcomes include rural loan programs (Selden, 1997), equal employment agencies (Hindera, 1993), and fire safety (Andrews, Ashworth, and Meier, 2014).

How bureaucratic representation works in practice is still somewhat uncertain because, as discussed by Grissom and Jones, the results could occur because of something the bureaucrat did (active representation) or something the student (or client) did (identified a role model, increased effort). These two paths that link a representative bureaucracy to more equal outcomes suggest that some precise definitions are needed. Passive representation should be defined as a bureaucracy that looks like the clientele it serves in terms of important demographic characteristics (in our case, race). Passively representative bureaucracies might generate more equitable outcomes either because of active representation or symbolic representation. Active representation means that the bureaucrat takes some specific action to improve that status of minority clientele. Symbolic representation means that the client sees the bureaucrat as a symbol and adapts his or her behavior in such a way to improve the outcomes. Each form of representation has multiple avenues.

To illustrate the options for active representation, let us use the example of teachers. A minority teacher interested in improving the educational outcomes of minority students can do so in a variety of ways that would constitute active representation. First, the teacher might teach the student differently, spend more time with the student, or encourage the student in other ways. Second, the teacher might advocate that the school change how it teaches minority students by adopting a different curriculum or changing some other policies. A non-teaching option might be to convince the school to move from punitive disciplinary policies to ameliorative ones that show less bias in racial outcomes (Roch, Pitts, and Navarro, 2010). Third, the teacher might influence other teachers to change their approach to teaching minority students and thus indirectly influence outcomes of other teachers. These options for active representation should underscore that representation is a process; it is an attempt by the bureaucrat to do something to benefit the minority clientele. It should be noted, of course, that the process might not be successful, that is, the outcomes might not change despite the efforts of the bureaucrat perhaps because the problem was not tractable, the client did not respond, or other bureaucrats were unwilling to change.

Symbolic representation also has multiple avenues in a school setting. First, the student might view the teacher as a role model or make extra effort to perform well simply because the teacher looks like the student. A Black male student, for example, rarely sees a Black male teacher, particularly in the elementary grades. Second, just the presence of a minority teacher might result in other teachers and administrators being more sensitive to questions of racial equity and, as a result, then changing their behavior (Atkins and Wilkins, 2013). Such a process actually occurs in appellate court systems where the presence of one minority judge on a multi-member panel appears to change the decisions of the other panel members (Kastellec, 2013). Third, parents of the child might be more likely to participate in the child's education, what we term coproduction, if the teacher shares racial characteristics with the student (Vinopal, 2018). Many public policies rely on the coproduction of policy benefits including education, health care, job training, sanitation, and others.

## The Limits of Symbolic Representation

Symbolic representation is attractive to many organizations because it implies that the bureaucracy need not change anything but that the target populations will change their behavior. Gade and Wilkins' (2012) work on the Veterans Administration, for example, shows that while veterans perceive they are treated better when they interact with bureaucrats who are veterans, in actuality they are less likely to receive the benefit they requested. Symbolic representation holds out the promise of positive results without the organization doing anything different other than becoming more representative (a process that is not as easy as it sounds, given the efforts to recruit more diverse police forces and the discussion found in Chapter 2 by Grissom and Jones on recruiting more Black teachers).

At the same time, logic suggests that symbolic representation has its limits. Symbolic representation is based on the client's perception that he or she will be treated more fairly by a bureaucrat who resembles them. In short, descriptive representation is often expected to act as an indicator of fair treatment. In such a situation—a traffic stop or an application for TANF—the client might take a more conciliatory approach to the bureaucracy and thus generate a more polite response. One way to view this interaction is that clients have a prior perception of how well they will be treated by a bureaucracy. Seeing a bureaucrat that looks like them might contribute to a positive perception. The limit to symbolic representation, however, is how the bureaucrat acts. If the bureaucrat treats the client negatively, quite clearly the client will readjust this prior perception in a negative direction. Essentially, behavior will influence and even determine perceptions.

Cabral and Peci (2017), for example, show that abusive and violent police who are descriptively representative of residents of the Rio favelas do not change the perceptions of residents to be more favorable. The Rio case is merely an extreme case of the U.S. response by some Blacks that descriptively representative police officers are "blue not black" (Wilkins and Williams, 2008). Perhaps the best analogy are the examples of invading countries who set up a puppet government of local residents to rule for them; the examples of Vichy, France, or Quisling in Norway, come to mind. In short, a bureaucracy seeking to enjoy the benefits of symbolic representation needs to make a credible commitment that the perceived inequitable treatment will decline. Without that commitment, symbolic representation will likely have little meaning.

*The Conditions of Active Representation*

Scholars working to understand applications and limits of representative bureaucracy commonly agree on two preconditions for active representation: (1) the bureaucrat must have discretion to act; and (2) the discretion needs to involve a situation where the represented characteristic or identity (e.g., race, gender) is salient (Keiser et al., 2002). When these two conditions hold, substantial empirical work finds a correlation between passive representation and bureaucratic outputs or outcomes that are more equitable (Hong, 2017; Meier, 2018; Selden, 1997). Discretion clearly matters. Watkins-Hayes (2011) demonstrates that the imposition of highly restrictive performance criteria along with the reduction in the skill levels of bureaucrats greatly limited bureaucratic representation in U.S. welfare agencies after the Personal Responsibility and Work Opportunity Act of 1996. Salience also matters. Studies in the U.S. have found numerous cases of representative bureaucracy for race and gender but none for socioeconomic status (but see Vinopal, 2019). The lack of political salience regarding socio-economic status in some policy arenas in the U.S. offers an explanation for this, and the comparative literature on representative bureaucracy (Meier and Morton, 2015) illustrates how the salience of various demographic characteristics varies from country to country. They are also likely to vary from location to location in the United States as well as for the same location at different points in time. Highly visible events like those in Ferguson, Missouri, that Nicholson-Crotty and Nicholson-Crotty discuss in Chapter 3, clearly changed the salience of race for the local police force.

The practical implications of these preconditions for representative bureaucracy to work mean that public and nonprofit organizations do not have full control over the process of active representation. The salience of race is determined by a variety of factors, many of which occur outside the organization. As an illustration, race is generally salient in law enforcement, but the highly visible cases of police shootings in the media in 2016 dramatically increased this salience for both police officers and the general public. In such cases, organizations can do little after the fact to manage that salience; instead, they are placed in a position where they have to respond to the events.

All organizations seek to structure discretion and provide guidelines for its use. Public bureaucracies, however, simply cannot anticipate all possible contingencies and have to rely on the judgments and actions of individual street-level bureaucrats. The result is discretion at the point where bureaucrats interact with citizens. Established protocols (when should police pursue a suspect fleeing in a car; when should force be used, etc.) and training seek to minimize adverse interactions, but at some point all interactions rely on the judgment of the bureaucrat.

The current U.S. welfare-to-work policy regime provides a good illustration of the problems of limiting bureaucratic discretion. The general policy has been to discourage use of welfare with time limits and sanctions (Soss, Fording, and Schram, 2011). States have contracted out the implementation of policies to private firms to cut costs (Watkins-Hayes, 2011). Caseworker positions have been downgraded from being professional social workers to often being former welfare recipients who are put on production quotas and have little job security (ibid.). These changes have greatly limited the impact of representative bureaucracy, and they have also increased racial inequities; such inequities can be linked to partisan control of local governments (Soss, Fording, and Schram, 2011).

*Instrumental Representation*

Within the academic literature there is a modest debate about the merits of active representation by bureaucrats. Pushed primarily by those with traditional Weberian views of bureaucracy (see above), these scholars argue that active representation brings bias into a neutral and technical process (Lim, 2006). Setting aside the empirical claim of bias (discussed above), this section will discuss why a bureaucracy should be interested in furthering active representation in many circumstances. The basic argument is that creating a more representative bureaucracy and further encouraging active representation can enhance the overall performance of the organization; this process might be termed "instrumental representation." The discussion of instrumental representation will address symbolic representation, the advantages of diversity per se, and active representation.

First, the symbolic representation that emanates from a passively representative bureaucracy can contribute to greater trust by and cooperation from clientele and other citizens. In general, bureaucracies should be supportive of symbolic representation as the result of this linkage. Greater trust and a greater willingness to cooperate or even coproduce public goods provide a positive environment for agency programs. Symbolic representation in this way can contribute to organizational effectiveness.

Second, the argument for bureaucratic representation is based on the diversity of values that come to the organization; increasing the diversity of values when making decisions or designing public policy means that more options are considered and more consequences are examined. The result should be better decisions overall (Herring, 2009) although the actual process and the various complicating factors are still fairly large (Roberson, Holmes, and Perry, 2017). At the same time, a diversity of values creates some transaction costs in that it takes longer to consider a set of diverse values and proposals, and one of the benefits—greater deliberation—is likely to make decision-making less efficient but perhaps more effective. An extensive literature on diversity management in both the private sector and the public sector argues that diversity can be managed such that the benefits exceed the costs (Ashikali and Groeneveld, 2015). The diversity of values thus becomes a second way that passive representation benefits an organization.

Third, greater diversity in organizations can bring in new skills and network ties that are not currently present in the organization. Many police forces aggressively recruit Latino officers because they serve populations where the primary language is Spanish. Calderon's (2018) study of immigration enforcement in the U.S. showed that policies to increase language diversity in law enforcement were associated with fewer overall stops and arrests but more arrests of individuals with serious criminal records. In short, the implementation became both more effective and at the same time imposed fewer costs on others. It is widely recognized in the law enforcement community that trust by citizens and a willingness to engage with police officers are a key element in solving crimes (see Chapter 3 by Nicholson-Crotty and Nicholson-Crotty). Representation facilitates the initial contact and perhaps the ability to communicate which improves overall organizational performance.

Fourth, the delivery of public services is often done not by single agencies alone but by a network of providers that includes public, nonprofit, and private organizations; elected officials; local community groups; and the plethora of others (O'Toole, 1997). Effectively operating in these networks requires contact with others and a series of exchanges that are mutually beneficial to the parties involved. Minority employees can bring their own personal and professional networks to public and nonprofit organizations and thus allow the organization to gather better information, acquire additional resources, and provide better services. To the extent that organizations face diversity among their clientele, the network skills of minority employees can enhance overall organizational performance.

Overall, this section suggests that bureaucratic representation might have instrumental value for organizations that are seeking to improve performance. Rather than viewing representation as possibly biasing an organization's actions, an equally plausible scenario is that representation contributes positively to the ability of organizations to implement public programs. Public administrators need to assess the specific benefits and costs of representation for the programs that they administer.

### Policies Are Interlinked

Four chapters have examined individual policy areas, and this chapter added discussions of four more which clearly does not exhaust all the arenas where race and public administration interact. The discussion treated the policy areas separately, and this can misrepresent the extensive inter-relationships of all the policy areas. The disparities created in each of the policy areas contributes to additional disparities in the other policy areas, such that the effects multiply. In many cases, this means that fairly objective procedures in one area simply reflect previous inequities. A few cases will provide some illustrations of this cascading effect.

Access to quality health care, particularly for children, has major influences on the extent and the quality of education children receive (Case, Fertig, and Paxson, 2005). This influence starts from differences in basic levels of health care. Inadequate prenatal care is associated with low birth weights among other health consequences (Kotelchuck, 1994). An extensive UK study documented the detrimental long-term impact of low birth weights on cognitive development and thus future educational attainment (Jefferis, Power, and Hertzman, 2002).

Next, one of the strongest correlates of income is a person's level of education. This relationship means that lack of health care for minorities in the United States will subsequently translate into lower levels of education and then lower levels of employment and lower incomes (Jamison, Jamison, and Hanushek, 2007). Further consequences should be obvious; income and employment disparities will correlate with access to quality housing and contact with the criminal justice system. The process creates an interwoven cycle where disparities in each policy area spill into other policy areas. Lack of income and education, in turn, are correlated with poor health outcomes for children which resets the policy cycle. Virtually all policy areas both reflect inequalities from other policy areas and then further perpetuate these racial gaps.

## Conclusion: Implications for Public Administrators

This chapter has covered a wide range of issues to cover gaps left from the previous chapters and raised some issues that affect all areas of public policy. At times the discussion has moved to the abstract level to trace out why problems of race are endemic to public administration; at other times philosophical issues were addressed. This conclusion will serve to bring the discussion back to practice and the day-to-day concerns of public administrators by focusing on a set of practical guidelines.

First, issues of race and racial disparities exist in virtually all areas of public administration. This text has provided in-depth examples of race and public administration in education, law enforcement, health care, and internet access as well as brief discussions of employment policy, housing, welfare, energy, and the environment. The importance of race in the political process of the U.S. means that racial issues are never far from either the design of public policy or its implementation by various bureaucracies. Although this does not mean that every decision an administrator makes has a racial element to it, it does mean that administrators and street-level bureaucrats need to be aware that race and perceptions of race will affect many decisions.

Second, despite the best intentions of policy designs, it is a mistake to assume that programs and processes are race-neutral. Criteria that are neutral on their face will generate racial disparities when applied to cases where there are existing racial differences in education, income, health status, and other factors. This might mean that many individuals who are targets of public and nonprofit programs might not be reached by normal means. Differences in trust likely arise out of past experience with government programs and thus many clients might be skeptical about their ability to access the services they need.

Third, people matter, particularly in terms of representativeness but also in terms of awareness of existing racial disparities. Discretion exists in all public programs. Being aware of the racial disparities is the first step in making decisions that could address the disparities. The experiences that bureaucrats share with clients as the result of commonalities of race, gender, and other demographic characteristics affect the decisions they make and the effectiveness of public programs. A more representative bureaucracy is likely to bring instrumental benefits to the organization in terms of improved deliberation and performance.

Fourth, the benefits of a representative bureaucracy can come in myriad ways including that: (1) the minority bureaucrat has a better understanding of client problems and uses a different approach or makes a different decision (active representation); (2) the minority bureaucrat participates in policy discussions and the organization, as a result, adopts a more effective policy (active representation); (3) other bureaucrats see how effective the minority bureaucrat is with certain clients and change their own behavior (contagion effects); (4) other bureaucrats modify their behavior that generated racial disparities simply because the minority bureaucrat is present (contagion effect); and/or (5) the client is more likely to trust a bureaucrat who looks like him or her and is either more cooperative or more likely to engage in coproduction (symbolic representation).

Fifth, institutions, organizations and structures all matter. All policies are designed to accomplish some end and those ends reflect the priorities of the individuals who designed the policy. At times policies are intended to be biased; at other times they are inadvertently biased. Public administrators need to be aware of these institutionalized biases and how they affect outcomes.

Sixth, no policy and therefore no public or nonprofit organization exists in isolation. Policies are interrelated and racial disparities in one area will bleed over into other areas and generate disparities in those areas. Institutional procedures by other organizations, including those in networked situations with the bureaucrat's organization, will generate outcomes that create greater disparities for the organization's clients. Many policies are designed to be implemented in policy networks for this very reason; most programs are narrowly tailored to address a specific problem. Problems, however, often overlap the jurisdictions of various agencies, nonprofits, different units of government, and private organizations. Public administrators need to be aware of these inter-dependencies.

# References

Agan, Amanda, and Sonja Starr. 2017. "Ban the box, criminal records, and racial discrimination: A field experiment." *The Quarterly Journal of Economics* 133(1): 191–235.

Amirkhanyan, Anna A., Kenneth J. Meier, Laurence J. O'Toole Jr, Mueen A. Dakhwe, and Shawn Janzen. 2018. "Management and performance in US nursing homes." *Journal of Public Administration Research and Theory* 28(1): 33–49.

Andrews, Rhys, Rachel Ashworth, and Kenneth J. Meier. 2014. "Representative bureaucracy and fire service performance." *International Public Management Journal* 17(1): 1–24.

Ashikali, Tanachia, and Sandra Groeneveld. 2015. "Diversity management for all? An empirical analysis of diversity management outcomes across groups." *Personnel Review* 44(5): 757–780.

Atkins, Danielle N., and Vicky M. Wilkins. 2013. "Going beyond reading, writing, and arithmetic: The effects of teacher representation on teen pregnancy rates." *Journal of Public Administration Research and Theory* 23(4): 771–790.

Becker, Marion A., Neil Jordan, and Rebecca Larsen. 2007. "Predictors of successful permanency planning and length of stay in foster care: The role of race, diagnosis and place of residence." *Children and Youth Services Review* 29(8): 1102–1113.

Bradford, Calvin. 1979. "Financing home ownership: The federal role in neighborhood decline." *Urban Affairs Quarterly* 14(3): 313–335.

Cabral, André Dantas and Alketa Peci. 2017. "Symbolic representation on 'occupied land': differences between targets and outsiders in security policy." Paper presented at the conference on Race, Ethnicity and Public Administration, Texas A&M University, May 19–20, 2017.

Calderon, M. Apolonia. 2018. "¿Hablas español? The role of language congruence as representative bureaucracy." PhD dissertation, Texas A&M University.

Case, Anne, Angela Fertig, and Christina Paxson. 2005. "The lasting impact of childhood health and circumstance." *Journal of Health Economics* 24(2): 365–389.

Chaskin, Robert, Amy Khare, and Mark Joseph. 2012. "Participation, deliberation, and decision making: The dynamics of inclusion and exclusion in mixed-income developments." *Urban Affairs Review* 48(6): 863–906.

Copeland, Gary W., and Kenneth J. Meier. 1987. "Gaining ground: The impact of Medicaid and WIC on infant mortality." *American Politics Quarterly* 15(2): 254–273.

DiPasquale, Denise. 2011. "Rental housing: Current market conditions and the role of federal policy." *Cityscape* 13(2): 57–70.

Donahue, John D., and Richard J. Zeckhauser. 2011. *Collaborative governance: Private roles for public goals in turbulent times.* Princeton, NJ: Princeton University Press.

Gade, Daniel M., and Vicky M. Wilkins. 2012. "Where did you serve? Veteran identity, representative bureaucracy, and vocational rehabilitation." *Journal of Public Administration Research and Theory* 23(2): 267–288.

Gilens, Martin. 2009. *Why Americans hate welfare: Race, media, and the politics of antipoverty policy.* Chicago: University of Chicago Press.

Gillborn, David, and Heidi Safia Mirza. 2000. *Educational inequality: Mapping race, class and gender. A synthesis of research evidence.* London: Office of Standards in Education. Available at: https://eric.ed.gov/?id=ED457311

Heffron, Raphael J., and Darren McCauley. 2017. "The concept of energy justice across the disciplines." *Energy Policy* 105: 658–667.

Heinrich, Carolyn J. 2015. "The bite of administrative burden: A theoretical and empirical investigation." *Journal of Public Administration Research and Theory* 26(3): 403–420.

Herd, Pamela, Thomas DeLeire, Hope Harvey, and Donald P.Moynihan. 2013. "Shifting administrative burden to the state: The case of Medicaid take-up." *Public Administration Review* 73(s1): S69–S81.

Herring, Cedric. 2009. "Does diversity pay? Race, gender, and the business case for diversity." *American Sociological Review* 74(2): 208–224.

Hindera, John J. 1993. "Representative bureaucracy: Further evidence of active representation in the EEOC district offices." *Journal of Public Administration Research and Theory* 3(4): 415–429.

Hipp, John R., and Cynthia M. Lakon. 2010. "Social disparities in health: Disproportionate toxicity proximity in minority communities over a decade." *Health & Place* 16 (4): 674–683.

Hong, Sounman. 2017. "Black in blue: Racial profiling and representative bureaucracy in policing revisited." *Journal of Public Administration Research and Theory* 27(4): 547–561.

Huffman, Matt L., and Philip N. Cohen. 2004. "Racial wage inequality: Job segregation and devaluation across US labor markets." *American Journal of Sociology* 109(4): 902–936.

Hyra, Derek, and Jacob S. Rugh. 2016. "The US great recession: Exploring its association with black neighborhood rise, decline and recovery." *Urban Geography* 37(5): 700–726.

Jamison, Eliot A., Dean T. Jamison, and Eric A. Hanushek. 2007. "The effects of education quality on income growth and mortality decline." *Economics of Education Review* 26(6): 771–788.

Jefferis, Barbara J.M.H., Chris Power, and Clyde Hertzman. 2002. "Birth weight, childhood socioeconomic environment, and cognitive development in the 1958 British birth cohort study." *British Medical Journal* 325(7359): 305–308.

Jenkins, Kirsten, Darren McCauley, Raphael Heffron, Hannes Stephan, and Robert Rehner. 2016. "Energy justice: A conceptual review." *Energy Research & Social Science* 11(1): 174–182.

Johnson, Austin P., Kenneth J. Meier, and Kristen M. Carroll. 2017. "Forty acres and a mule: Housing programs and policy feedback for African-Americans." *Politics, Groups, and Identities* 6(4): 612–630. doi:10.1080/21565503.2016.1234962.

Kastellec, Jonathan P. 2013. "Racial diversity and judicial influence on appellate courts." *American Journal of Political Science* 57(1): 167–183.

Katznelson, Ira. 2005. *When affirmative action was white: An untold history of racial inequality in twentieth-century America.* New York, NY: WW Norton & Company.

Keiser, Lael R., Vicky M. Wilkins, Kenneth J. Meier, and Catherine A. Holland. 2002. "Lipstick and logarithms: Gender, institutional context, and representative bureaucracy." *American Political Science Review* 96(3): 553–564.

Knight, Jack. 1992. *Institutions and social conflict.* New York, NY: Cambridge University Press.

Konisky, David M. 2009. "Inequities in enforcement? Environmental justice and government performance." *Journal of Policy Analysis and Management* 28(1): 102–121.

Kotelchuck, Milton. 1994. "The adequacy of prenatal care utilization index: Its US distribution and association with low birthweight." *American Journal of Public Health* 84(9): 1486–1489.

Lasswell, Harold. 1936. *Who gets what, when, how.* New York, NY: Whittlesey House.

Lieberman, Robert C. 2001. *Shifting the color line: Race and the American welfare state.* New York, NY: John Wiley & Sons.

Lim, Hong-Hai. 2006. "Representative bureaucracy: Rethinking substantive effects and active representation." *Public Administration Review* 66(2): 193–204.

Long, Norton E. 1949. "Power and administration." *Public Administration Review* 9 (4): 257–264.

MacDonald, Heather I. 2000. "Renegotiating the public-private partnership: Efforts to reform Section 8 assisted housing." *Journal of Urban Affairs* 22(3): 279–299.

McCubbins, Mathew D., Roger G. Noll, and Barry R. Weingast. 1987. "Administrative procedures as instruments of political control." *Journal of Law, Economics, & Organization* 3(2): 243–277.

Meier, Kenneth J. 1994. *The politics of sin: Drugs, alcohol and public policy.* Armonk, NY: M.E. Sharpe.

Meier, Kenneth J. 2019. "Theoretical frontiers in representative bureaucracy: New directions for research." *Perspectives on Public Management and Governance* 2(1): 39–56. doi:10.1093/ppmgov/gvy004/5037752.

Meier, Kenneth J., and John Bohte. 2007. *Politics and the bureaucracy: Policymaking in the fourth branch of government.* Belmont, CA: Thomson-Wadsworth.

Meier, Kenneth J., and Tabitha S.M. Morton. 2015. "Representative bureaucracy in a cross-national context: Politics, identity, structure and discretion." In *The politics of representative bureaucracy: Power, legitimacy, performance,* edited by Eckhard Schröter, Patrick von Maravic and B. Guy Peters (pp. 94–112). Cheltenham: Edward Elgar.

Morello-Frosch, Rachel, and Edmond D.Shenassa. 2006. "The environmental 'riskscape' and social inequality: Implications for explaining maternal and child health disparities." *Environmental Health Perspectives* 114(8): 1150–1153.

Moulton, Stephanie. 2014. "Did affordable housing mandates cause the subprime mortgage crisis?" *Journal of Housing Economics* 24(1): 21–38.

Moynihan, Donald, Pamela Herd, and Hope Harvey. 2015. "Administrative burden: Learning, psychological, and compliance costs in citizen-state interactions." *Journal of Public Administration Research and Theory* 25(1): 43–69.

Mumpower, Jeryl L. 2010. "Disproportionality at the 'front end' of the child welfare services system: An analysis of rates of referrals, 'hits,' misses,' and 'false alarms.'" *Journal of Health and Human Services Administration* 33(3): 364–405.

Myers, Caitlin Knowles. 2004. "Discrimination and neighborhood effects: Understanding racial differentials in US housing prices." *Journal of Urban Economics* 56(2): 279–302.

Myers Jr., Samuel L., and Tsze Chan. 1995. "Racial discrimination in housing markets: Accounting for credit risk." *Social Science Quarterly* 76(3): 543–561.

Navas-Acien, Ana, Eliseo Guallar, Ellen K. Silbergeld, and Stephen J. Rothenberg. 2007. "Lead exposure and cardiovascular disease: A systematic review." *Environmental Health Perspectives* 115(3): 472–482.

Nelson, Ashlyn Aiko. 2010. "Credit scores, race, and residential sorting." *Journal of Policy Analysis and Management* 29(1): 39–68.

Newman, Sandra J. 2008. "Does housing matter for poor families? A critical summary of research and issues still to be resolved." *Journal of Policy Analysis and Management* 27 (4): 895–925.

Ondrich, Jan, Alex Stricker, and John Yinger. 1998. "Do real estate brokers choose to discriminate? Evidence from the 1989 housing discrimination study." *Southern Economic Journal* 64(4): 880–901.

O'Toole, Laurence J. 1997. "Treating networks seriously: Practical and research-based agendas in public administration." *Public Administration Review* 57(1): 45–52.

O'Toole, Laurence J., and Kenneth J. Meier. 2004. "Desperately seeking Selznick: Cooptation and the dark side of public management in networks." *Public Administration Review* 64(6): 681–693.

Pardee, Jessica W. 2006. "Welfare reform and housing retrenchment: What happens when two policies collide?" In K.M. Kilty and E.A. Segal (Eds.) *The promise of welfare reform: Political rhetoric and the reality of poverty in the twenty-first century* (pp. 133–141). London: Routledge.

Payne-Sturges, Devon, and Gilbert C. Gee. 2006. "National environmental health measures for minority and low-income populations: Tracking social disparities in environmental health." *Environmental Research* 102(2): 154–171.

Piven, Frances Fox, and Richard Cloward. 2012. *Regulating the poor: The functions of public welfare.* New York, NY: Vintage Books.

Pope, C. Arden, Richard T. Burnett, Daniel Krewski, et al. 2009. "Cardiovascular mortality and exposure to airborne fine particulate matter and cigarette smoke: Shape of the exposure-response relationship." *Circulation* 120(11): 941–948.

Putnam-Hornstein, Emily, Barbara Needell, Bryn King, and Michelle Johnson-Motoyama. 2013. "Racial and ethnic disparities: A population-based examination of risk factors for involvement with child protective services." *Child Abuse & Neglect* 37(1): 33–46.

Quillian, Lincoln, Devah Pager, Ole Hexel, and Arnfinn H. Midtbøen. 2017. "Meta-analysis of field experiments shows no change in racial discrimination in hiring over time." *Proceedings of the National Academy of Sciences* 114(41): 10870–10875.

Reames, Tony Gerard. 2016. "Targeting energy justice: Exploring spatial, racial/ethnic and socioeconomic disparities in urban residential heating energy efficiency." *Energy Policy* 97(4): 549–558.

Ringquist, Evan J. 2005. "Assessing evidence of environmental inequities: A meta-analysis." *Journal of Policy Analysis and Management* 24(2): 223–247.

Roberson, Quinetta, Oscar Holmes IV, and Jamie L. Perry. 2017. "Transforming research on diversity and firm performance: A dynamic capabilities perspective." *Academy of Management Annals* 11(1): 189–216.

Roch, Christine H., David W. Pitts, and Ignacio Navarro. 2010. "Representative bureaucracy and policy tools: Ethnicity, student discipline, and representation in public schools." *Administration & Society* 42(1): 38–65.

Roscigno, Vincent J., Diana L. Karafin, and Griff Tester. 2009. "The complexities and processes of racial housing discrimination." *Social Problems* 56(1): 49–69.

Rosenbloom, David. 2002. *Building a legislative-centered public administration: Congress and the administrative state, 1946–1999*. Tuscaloosa, AL: University of Alabama Press.

Rugh, Jacob S., and Douglas S. Massey. 2010. "Racial segregation and the American foreclosure crisis." *American Sociological Review* 75(5): 629–651.

Schattschneider, E. E. 1960. *The semisovereign people. A realist's view of democracy in America*. Hinsdale, IL: Dryden Press.

Schwartz, Alex. 2014. "The essential if problematic role of FHA mortgage insurance." *Housing Policy Debate* 24(3): 666–669.

Seidman, Harold. 1975. *Politics, position, and power: The dynamics of federal organization*. New York, NY: Oxford University Press.

Selden, Sally Coleman. 1997. *The promise of representative bureaucracy: Diversity and responsiveness in a government agency*. Armonk, NY: M.E. Sharpe.

Soss, Joe. 1999. "Lessons of welfare: Policy design, political learning, and political action." *American Political Science Review* 93(2): 363–380.

Soss, Joe, Richard C. Fording, and Sanford Schram. 2011. *Disciplining the poor: Neoliberal paternalism and the persistent power of race*. Chicago: University of Chicago Press.

Sovacool, Benjamin K., and Michael H. Dworkin. 2014. *Global energy justice*. New York, NY: Cambridge University Press.

Switzer, David, and Manuel P. Teodoro. 2017. "Class, race, ethnicity, and justice in safe drinking water compliance." *Social Science Quarterly* 99(2): 524–535.

U.S. Government Accountability Office. 2007. "African American children in foster care: Additional HHS assistance needed to help states reduce the proportion in care." Washington, DC: U.S. Government.

Vinopal, Katie. 2018. "Understanding individual and organizational level representation: the case of parental involvement in schools." *Journal of Public Administration Research and Theory* 28(1): 1–15.

Vinopal, Katie. 2019. "Socioeconomic representation: Expanding the theory of representative bureaucracy." *Journal of Public Administration Research and Theory*. Available at: https://doi.org/10.1093/jopart/muz024

Watkins-Hayes, Celeste. 2011. "Race, respect, and red tape: Inside the black box of racially representative bureaucracies." *Journal of Public Administration Research and Theory* 21(suppl. 2): i233–i251.

Western, Bruce, and Becky Pettit. 2005. "Black-white wage inequality, employment rates, and incarceration." *American Journal of Sociology* 111(2): 553–578.

Wilkins, Vicky M., and Brian N. Williams. 2008. "Black or blue: Racial profiling and representative bureaucracy." *Public Administration Review* 68(4): 654–664.

# Index

Entries in **bold** denote tables.